# An Eye for Injustice

D1569667

# An Eye for Injustice
## Robert C. Sims and Minidoka

Susan M. Stacy, Editor

WSU
PRESS

Washington State University Press
Pullman, Washington

Washington State University Press
PO Box 645910
Pullman, Washington 99164-5910
Phone: 800-354-7360
Email: wsupress@wsu.edu
Website: wsupress.wsu.edu

*Library of Congress Cataloging-in-Publication Data*

Names: Sims, Robert C. Works. Selections. | Stacy, Susan M., 1943- editor.
Title: An eye for injustice : Robert C. Sims and Minidoka / Susan M. Stacy, editor.
Other titles: Robert C. Sims and Minidoka
Description: Pullman, Washington : Washington State University Press, [2020] | Includes bibliographical references and index.
Identifiers: LCCN 2019038433 | ISBN 9780874223767 (paperback)
Subjects: LCSH: Minidoka Relocation Center--History. | Japanese Americans--Evacuation and relocation, 1942-1945. | World War, 1939-1945--Japanese Americans. | World War, 1939-1945--Concentration camps--Idaho. | Concentration camps--Idaho--History--20th Century. | Japan--Emigration and immigration. | Sims, Robert C. | Robert C. Sims Collection on Minidoka and Japanese Americans, 1891-2014 (Albertsons Library) | Idaho--Race relations. | Minidoka National Historic Site (Idaho and Wash.)--History.
Classification: LCC D769.8.A6 E94 2020 | DDC 940.53/1779635--dc23
LC record available at https://lccn.loc.gov/2019038433

The following publishers have generously given permission to reprint articles: *Idaho Yesterdays*, "The Japanese American Experience in Idaho" and "You Don't Need to Wait Any Longer to Get Out"; *Pacific Northwest Quarterly*, "A Fearless, Clean-Cut, and Patriotic Stand"; *The Advocate*, "Loyalty Questionnaires and Japanese Americans in World War II"; University of Washington Press, "The 'Free Zone' Nikkei: Japanese Americans in Idaho and Eastern Oregon in World War II" in *Nikkei in the Pacific Northwest: Japanese and Japanese Americans and Japanese Canadians in the Twentieth Century*; University of Utah Press and Roger Daniels, "Japanese Americans in Idaho," in *Japanese Americans from Relocation to Redress*. Excerpt from "In the Afterlife" from *Almost Invisible: Poems* by Mark Strand, copyright © 2012 by Mark Strand, is used by permission of Alfred A. Knopf, an imprint of the Knopf Doubleday Publishing Group, a division of Penguin Random House LLC. All rights reserved.

**Publication of this book was made possible with the generous support of Friends of Minidoka and the Japanese American Citizens League, Boise Valley Chapter. Royalties will be donated to Friends of Minidoka.**

*On the cover:* Ayleen Ito (Lee) and Ken Yamaguchi of Block 44, Minidoka. *National Archives and Records Administration, 210-CMB-12-1489.*

# Contents

PREFACE       xi
  *Susan M. Stacy*

AN INTRODUCTION TO BOB SIMS       xv
  *Betty Sims*

PART ONE: ROBERT C. SIMS ON JAPANESE AMERICANS AND MINIDOKA

1  The Japanese American Experience in Idaho       3

2  Idaho's Governor Chase Clark and Japanese
   American Relocation in World War II       23

3  Japanese American Evacuees as Farm Laborers
   During World War II       39

4  The "Free Zone" Nikkei       53

5  Loyalty Questionnaires and Japanese Americans
   in World War II       77

6  "Good Schools are Essential"       85

7  Minidoka: An American Story       103

8  Idaho and Minidoka       113

9  Japanese American Soldiers as Part of
   "The Greatest Generation"       133

10  The Japanese American Return to the
   Pacific Northwest       143

11  The Other Concentration Camps       153

PART TWO: THE PATH TO THE NATIONAL HISTORIC SITE

  12  An Eye to Justice: Minidoka National Historic Site  163
      *Susan M. Stacy*

  13  Creating the Minidoka National Historic Site  179
      *Daniel Sakura*

PART THREE: THE LEGACY OF ROBERT C. SIMS

  14  *Okage Sama De*  187
      *Hanako Wakatsuki*

  15  The Story of Ise Inuzuka  191
      *Jim Azumano*

  16  The Robert C. Sims Collection on
      Minidoka and Japanese Americans, 1891–2014  193
      *Cheryl Oestreicher*

ACKNOWLEDGMENTS  195

APPENDIXES

  A  Ronald Reagan Remarks on Signing the
      Civil Liberties Act of 1988  199

  B  General References  202

  C  War Relocation Authority Population Numbers  204

  D  Glossary  205

BIBLIOGRAPHY  209

CONTRIBUTORS  217

INDEX  219

# Maps and Illustrations

MAPS

Minidoka plat map by Iwao Matsushita     x

Exclusion zone     54

Vicinity map for Minidoka National Historic Site     183

ILLUSTRATIONS

Robert C. Sims     xiv

Child awaiting relocation train     xviii

Japanese Association, circa 1915     2

Japanese family on Idaho farm     5

Japanese float in Boise parade     7

Celebration of Issei naturalization, 1955     19

Governor Clark with President Roosevelt     24

Utah-Idaho Sugar Company advertisement     40

Women harvesting potatoes     45

Nyssa, Oregon, labor camp work call     47

Japanese railroad workers     56

Michi Suyehira and son Henry     58

Nisei baseball team in the 1930s     59

JACL meeting and Governor Clark in 1941     65

Sugar company ad thanks Japanese field workers     69

Mobile labor camp tent at Nyssa, Oregon     70

Sakura family     79

Nisei kindergarten class     84

Hunt High School students at Minidoka     88

Promoting the resettlement policy                          97

Young girl carrying buckets                              102

Wartime propaganda poster by Theodor Geisel            106

Yamaguchi family in barracks                            109

Constructing camp barracks                              119

Transferring from train to bus                          122

Mass Choir rehearsal                                    125

Post-war veteran's lottery house                        128

Minidoka World War II Honor Roll                        134

Gold Star mothers                                        137

Roy Matsumoto                                            138

Seattle "welcome home" sign                             145

Awaiting news of departure                              155

Remains of the waiting room                             162

National Register historic plaque                       166

Bob Sims at Idaho Centennial dedication                 167

Audience member at Idaho Centennial dedication          168

Guard tower                                              184

Minidoka Pilgrimage, 2010                               188

Ise Inuzuka                                              191

President Reagan signs Civil Liberties Act              200

TABLE

Building block structure of U.S. Army, World War II     135

To the memory of Robert C. Sims

More than 40 years ago, shortly after the bombing of Pearl Harbor, 120,000 persons of Japanese ancestry living in the United States were forcibly removed from their homes and placed in makeshift internment camps. This action was taken without trial, without jury. It was based solely on race, for these 120,000 were Americans of Japanese descent.

[It's] not for us today to pass judgment upon those who may have made mistakes... Yet we must recognize that the internment of Japanese Americans was...a mistake....we admit a wrong; here, we reaffirm our commitment as a nation to equal justice under the law.

President Ronald Reagan
The White House
August 1988

We marry activism with the knowledge of history because justice is not self-executing. It is not a gift, it's a challenge. And we cannot rely just on our institutions to protect us.... We should understand that dissent is not the enemy of patriotism.

Dale Minami
Densho 20th Anniversary Gala
Seattle, Washington
September 2016

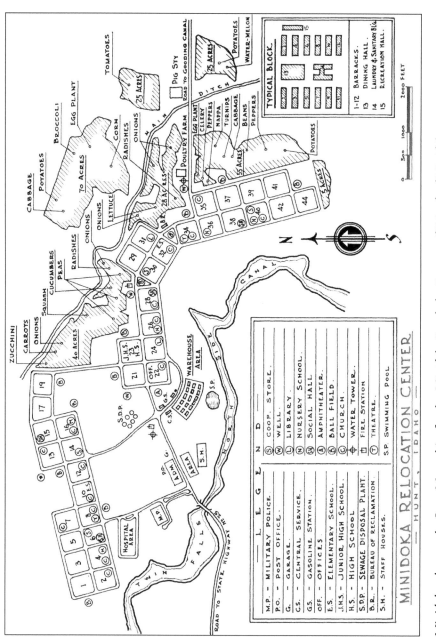

Minidoka plat map by Iwao Matsushita for the *Minidoka Interlude. Courtesy of Friends of Minidoka.*

# Preface

## Susan M. Stacy

The two main characters in this book are Minidoka—the World War II Relocation Center in Idaho—and Robert C. Sims, historian of Minidoka. Bob Sims taught at Boise State University from 1970 to 1999, serving for a time as dean of the College of Social Sciences and Public Affairs. Throughout his career he wrote and spoke passionately and prolifically about the experience of Japanese Americans during World War II, with articles published in *Pacific Northwest Quarterly*, *Idaho Yesterdays*, and others. Co-founder of the annual Minidoka Civil Liberties Symposium, his work and reputation played an important role in the establishment of the Minidoka National Historic Site, a place now preserved and protected by the National Park Service. All of these activities were informed by a deep commitment to social justice.

After Bob Sims died in 2015, his family gave Boise State University his archive of research and writings on Minidoka and the people who were forced to endure life in this camp. Gathered over forty years, his accumulated notes, files, thumb drives, books, images, and other records reflect his continuous inquiry about Japanese Americans incarcerated at this place. Bob Sims felt strongly, and said so frequently, that the scope of history should not be limited to the political activities and conflicts among the groups and institutions who made decisions, but also supply evidence from the people who experienced the impacts of the decisions. His written works certainly reflect this.

Most of his articles appeared in scholarly journals, places intended to be noticed by other historians in his field, not necessarily by general readers. In 2015 Betty Sims, Bob's wife, asked me to look into the archive and consider whether his writings might be made more easily available to such readers. We decided they could be, and that we should proceed to gather them together along with a few of his speeches. We saw it as an introduction for students of all ages—from Idaho and elsewhere—to the history, politics, and people of Minidoka. We included the voices of people who knew Bob Sims and could speak to his character and contributions. And we included archival and other resources to encourage further study and exploration.

The archive contains much of the man. He was driven by the insult to the U.S. Constitution that Minidoka represented—injustice arising largely out of racism. An educator to his core, Sims found many ways to educate people. He directed much of his energy to preserving the site of Minidoka as a place where Americans and Idahoans could learn about this injustice and never forget it. His effort was well rewarded when President Bill Clinton designated Minidoka as a National Internment Monument and again when Congress declared it a National Historic Site. Bob Sims would want it to be known that he did not do it alone, but allied himself with many others working for the same goals. I felt that our book should contain at least some indication of this history he himself contributed to making—and some insight as to the nature of his leadership.

Before I knew Robert C. Sims as a historian, I knew him as the chairman of the Planning and Zoning Commission of Boise City (for whom I then worked). He was a staff favorite because he always did his homework: reading inches-thick staff reports ahead of public hearings, making site visits on his own, and readying his positions. Unlike most other commissioners, he explained his votes, never more eloquently than when his was the lone "yes" or "no" vote. Yet his remarks were so even—in their rationale, in their diplomacy, in their absence of ire or judgment—that he aroused considerable admiration from his peers. In fact, his fellow commissioners chose him to be their leader, the chairman. In reading his papers, I encountered similar moderation in his historical writing, particularly his treatment of Idaho governor Chase Clark.

Betty Sims will say more about what motivated Bob's life of scholarship-with-action. Part one gathers the Minidoka works of Robert C. Sims. After publishing his first overview article, Sims focused on topics such as the role of Governor Chase Clark in the forced-relocation decision, farm labor, the loyalty oath crisis, and others.

Part two looks at how thirty-five years of efforts to memorialize the Minidoka site transformed it from "neglected" to "forever remembered," a property of our National Park System and a splendid educational instrument for highlighting not only a national tragedy but also the resilience of a people dealt with so unjustly. In part three, contributors, each in a position to understand his legacy personally, share their memories. The appendixes include a glossary of terms used throughout the book.

Bob had faith in the power of education to change people. He recognized that he himself had changed because of it. "I became enlightened," he once remarked, and reasoned that so could others. He connected the Minidoka experience to the much broader issue of what it means to be an American citizen. "The experience is more than an injustice to Japanese Americans, for, in a real sense, it threatens everyone. The denial of the civil rights of Americans is something no one should take lightly. Furthermore, there is good reason for Idahoans to recall it, because Idaho played an important role in relocation."

Most books published in recent years about Minidoka or the incarceration of Japanese Americans during World War II discuss the topic of terminology. Before historians uncovered the fact that the word "internment" was a deliberately chosen government-designed euphemism for "incarceration of American citizens without charge or trial," the general public became accustomed to using the World War II language. Bob Sims addressed this and other euphemistic terms in "The Other Concentration Camps," one of his public lectures. That discussion survives the test of time—and his own test of balance, historical context, and absence of judgement. It is published here, a fine tutorial on the topic.

Betty Sims and the team she gathered to help with this project began with a mission statement: to illustrate the power of one person's research, writing, and community engagement to move the cause of social justice forward, effect enduring changes in public policy, and influence individuals to care about and preserve our civil liberties. Bob would, I think, want his readers to realize that we ourselves have that same power.

Bob Sims in June 2007. *Photo by John Kelly courtesy of Boise State University.*

# An Introduction to Bob Sims

## Betty Sims

Robert C. Sims devoted nearly half his life researching, writing, and educating himself about the unjust incarceration of Japanese Americans during World War II. He brought deep empathy as well as intellectual rigor to his scholarship on the experiences of those incarcerated. What might account for his interest in and sensitivity to that somewhat then-neglected topic in United States history? Once discovered, why did he take on the topic with such passion and tenacity, and work to mitigate that neglect and preserve the Minidoka site?

Bob was raised by three generations of women in Fort Gibson, a small eastern Oklahoma town. Soon after his birth, Bob's father left the family and divorced his young mother, leaving her with their two small sons and no financial support. She moved the family into her own parents' small two-bedroom house, which housed Bob's great-grandmother as well. Bob once wrote about the economic instability the family experienced during this time as his mother, with a high school education and no work experience, struggled to find paying work. She did in time find steady work, was finally able to support the entire household, and later even served as mayor of the town.

Bob credited his grandmother with having the most influence on him. He once wrote, "I was very fortunate that I had a grandmother who cared for me and essentially raised me...[she] was a saint...and to the extent that I have any semblance of ethics and morality, it is attributed primarily to her." She raised Bob and his brother, cared for her own ailing husband (who died when Bob was seven) and, later, her own aging mother. She was the one to provide emotional stability and structure to the extended family.

All three of the women so important in his early life—mother, grandmother, and great-grandmother (who lived to be 103)—were members of the Cherokee Nation, as was Bob. He learned about the cruelty and injustice of the 1838 forced removal of the Cherokees from their homelands in the southeastern United States to Indian Territory.

Bob grew up during a time of racism and racial segregation. While he played on an integrated baseball team, his African American teammates went to a segregated school. He often observed that his own neighborhood was racially, culturally, and economically mixed, which he later realized was unusual; he was grateful for that aspect of his childhood experience.

Bob often spoke of particular teachers and parents of friends who encouraged him as he grew up. By high school, most of his friends were developing ambitious educational and professional goals for themselves. These relationships undoubtedly contributed to his own growing interest in further education, and he became the first in his family to enter college.

A shortage of funds, however, forced him to leave college after a year, and he joined the army. The army posted him to Germany and assigned him to legal work in Courts and Boards. The work interested him and he decided to finish his undergraduate work at Northeastern Oklahoma State College as a foundation for law school. He thought he would finance evening law school classes by teaching, so he got a teaching certificate. To his surprise, he discovered that teaching was actually his calling. He started working for an M.A. at the University of Oklahoma, and in 1964 began teaching at a high school in Denver, Colorado, launching a lifetime of teaching history.

By 1968 he had completed his master's degree, taught high school history for four years, and was midway through a doctorate in history at the University of Colorado. He considered himself a reasonably well informed teacher of American history. However, that year he was to learn that there was a part of America's history that he knew nothing about. Dr. Roger Daniels, a guest speaker at the university, was soon to publish *Concentration Camps USA*, a history of the government's 1942 decision to forcibly remove all persons of Japanese descent then living on the West Coast, most of whom were American citizens, and incarcerate them at ten camps in inland western states for the duration of the war. Bob, in Daniels's audience, was dismayed to realize that not once during his entire educational experience to date had he read or heard about this shocking part of American history. Hearing about it at this late date had a profound impact on him.

Bob's knowledge of injustices at the hand of the federal government, his experiences with racism in his community, and his family's poverty all seem to have played an important role in setting the stage for his sensitivity to those facing oppression of any kind. In college and graduate school, he acquired the tools, the understanding, and the insight that prepared him for the role he would play in confronting the incarceration of American citizens during World War II.

At an oral history workshop in Boise sponsored by the Japanese American Citizens League in 1973, Bob elaborated on his reaction to Dr. Daniels' lecture. "My interests [in the wartime incarceration program] can be marked to a time about five years ago when I became aware for the very first time of that entire experience. It seemed to me a sad commentary on the education system of America that would permit an event like that to go unnoticed in the education career of someone who is presumably going to go out and teach American history." After five years, he was still outraged. Anger proved to be a strong motivator; for Bob it transformed to a vigorous commitment to teaching all aspects of our country's history—our worst mistakes as well as our glorious accomplishments. He would be equally passionate about the importance of teacher training. He grabbed every opportunity to speak in classrooms, participated in teacher training workshops, and spoke frequently to public audiences large and small.

His conviction about the balanced teaching of *all* of our history led to his serving on the Idaho State Planning Team for "The Project for American Studies in the Secondary Schools," funded by the National Endowment for the Humanities in 1980–81, an effort of history teachers to define and agree upon standards for elementary and high school history students. It was, he felt, a way of insuring that students and teachers would have a thorough understanding of all facets of our country's history—and teach them.

Soon after he arrived in Idaho to teach at Boise State University in 1970, Bob discovered at the Idaho State Historical Society several neglected boxes of Minidoka-related documents. As a newcomer to the state he wished to get acquainted with Idaho history. He chose the history of Japanese settlement in Idaho and the Minidoka camp as one of his first research projects. Perhaps his early years in Oklahoma predisposed him to focus on those who had experienced the upheaval directly, not just those responsible for defining policy and making the decisions. He therefore reached out to Japanese Americans and the Japanese American Citizens League, encouraging them to speak their memories, record them, and preserve them.

In addition to developing friendships with Japanese Americans in Idaho, he spent time in Portland, Seattle, Bainbridge Island, and California. He listened and learned and then began to speak at conferences, workshops, meetings. He was deeply touched by the stories he was collecting, but of equal importance, he was finding a community eager to have their stories told. While there had been a culture of silence

In the early 1970s, Bob Sims framed this photo of Yuki Okinaga (Llewellyn) awaiting the train that would carry her away from home to Manzanar. He kept it at his desk until his death in 2015. *National Archives and Records Administration, WRA photo by Clem Albers, Los Angeles, April 1942, 210-G-2.*

for many of the incarcerees after their experience, they were grateful to have him as a spokesperson. He often heard the comments, "You can say things we have been unable to say" and "You are teaching us our own history."

After decades of documentary research, asking questions, preparing and publishing scholarly papers, and giving talks and slide shows, he developed an overwhelming belief that the injustice of incarcerating Americans based largely on their race should never happen again. He saw education as a means of avoiding a repetition of such tragic wrongs. He visited the Minidoka site and found most—but not all—of its buildings gone. How would anyone remember that this had been an incarceration center? How could what remained be preserved in the interest of our collective memory of it?

He found and joined a coterie of like-minded individuals who were connected in a variety of ways with Minidoka. In 1988, President Ronald Reagan informed the country that the confinement of Japanese Americans had been "based solely on race, for these 120,000 were Americans of Japanese descent."[1] When an opportunity arose in 2000, Bob and others joined forces to lobby and support the designation of Minidoka as a National Internment Monument, a unit of the National Park Service. After that, he participated in the creation of Friends of Minidoka, Inc., joining its board about a year after its creation. The establishment of the annual Minidoka Civil Liberties Symposiums soon followed. About all this, there is more in this book.

All these activities occupied Bob for over forty years. His reputation for fairness, balance, and a candor that rarely, if ever, led to rancor led him to become well known and highly regarded as the historian of Minidoka. Those same qualities contributed to his approach and involvement in community affairs. He served on the Boise City Planning and Zoning Commission from 1978 to 1984 and on the Idaho Humanities Council from 1978 to 1986. He co-founded the Fettuccine Forum, a feature of Boise's "First Thursday" celebrations downtown.

Bob brought to his teaching at Boise State the same empathy and caring for his students as he did to his work with Minidoka. He seemed to have a particular knack for noticing the individual who needed a shoulder, a nudge, or a little encouragement. One of his sons remarked that when watching sports events, he would "assess the situation, figure out who was playing and inevitably begin cheering for the underdog." He was a man of compassion, of empathy born of early awareness of injustices, and who loved learning and teaching history. A colleague described him as being "all about education in the service of social justice and the public good." He took a ten-year break from teaching and research to assume the position of dean of the BSU School of Social Sciences and Public Affairs, but returned eagerly to the classroom and Minidoka. He retired from teaching in 1999 but stayed actively involved in all things related to Minidoka, including community and school lectures supported by the Idaho Humanities Council, until 2014.

Bob realized that his accumulating scholarly research might be the foundation for a full-length book about Minidoka. He spoke publicly and often of that goal, but it proved to be elusive, which was a disappointment to him as well as the public who was eager for the book. The reasons are many, but underlying all other factors were serious health issues for the last twenty years of his life.

He was devoted to his family. His wife, three children, and nine grandchildren remember a gentle man with a great sense of humor and a love of jazz, as well as being a huge sports fan, and captain of the winning United States European Basketball Team of 1960. In 2003, after twin granddaughters were born in Boise, he went to their house and read to them each morning to their mutual delight, until a couple of months before his death in 2015.

Bob's family is extremely proud that part of his legacy is the rich archive of his research, ideas, and work and that it now resides at Boise State University. It is our hope that students, writers, and teachers will dig into his records and be inspired to continue his work: researching, writing, and teaching about Minidoka.

## Note

1. Ronald Reagan, "Remarks on Signing the Bill Providing Restitution for the Wartime Internment of Japanese American Civilians," August 10, 1988. See Appendix A. Online transcript at www.presidency.ucsb.edu/ws/?pid=36240.

# PART ONE

# ROBERT C. SIMS ON JAPANESE AMERICANS AND MINIDOKA

Japanese Association from Eastern Idaho, circa 1915. Image from Robert C. Sims slide presentation. *Sims Collection.*

# The Japanese American Experience in Idaho

## EDITOR'S NOTE

*After arriving in Idaho in 1970 to teach history at Boise State University, Robert C. Sims soon met Merle Wells, the director of the Idaho State Historical Society. As Betty Sims recalled, Wells pointed Sims to several boxes of material on the Minidoka War Relocation Center (also known as Hunt camp) "just sitting there waiting for someone to get into them." So Bob Sims began his long and particular relationship with Minidoka and the Japanese American community.*

*He also researched the history of Japanese settlement in Idaho and its contribution to the state's economic growth. The persistence and successes of this group occurred despite the racism, legal and otherwise, they encountered. Sims became acquainted with members of the Pocatello-Blackfoot chapter of the Japanese American Citizens League and members of other chapters, establishing relationships that also persisted over time.*

*This overview of the Japanese American experience in Idaho set the foundations for themes that Sims explored in greater detail in subsequent articles.—Susan M. Stacy*

———————

The justification for a review of the Japanese American experience in Idaho is not necessarily that it offers unique features of the Japanese American experience in the United States, but rather that it incorporates most of the significant experience of Japanese in America. Idaho was one of the earliest states to receive Japanese immigrants; it applied discriminatory laws to Japanese; it was involved in the relocation experience because one of the camps was in Idaho; and it received a significant number of relocatees who became permanent residents.

———————

This article by Robert Sims originally appeared under the same title in *Idaho Yesterdays* 22, no. 1 (Spring 1978).

Japanese first came to Idaho in the decade following statehood, the last decade of the nineteenth century. For much of the time since then, Idaho's Japanese have constituted one of the largest minorities within the state. Their contributions have been significant, all the more so because of the discrimination they have overcome.

Significant Japanese immigration into the United States began just about the time Idaho became a state. In 1890, there were only about 2,000 Japanese in the entire country; a decade later, there were almost 25,000. Most of those early immigrants found jobs in agriculture and railroad construction and maintenance. They also found discrimination, for they reaped the harvest of a half-century of anti-Chinese feeling, an attitude white Americans easily transferred to them. When Japanese first came to Idaho—and for decades thereafter—they found legal discrimination in the state's constitution, which had a provision prohibiting "Asiatics" from enjoying full rights.[1] There were other forms as well. In 1892, when Japanese laborers were first present in sizable numbers along the Oregon Short Line Railroad in southern Idaho, local citizens subjected them to harassment and intimidation. Starting in Mountain Home, where a dozen Japanese were chased out of town by the "best citizens" of that community, this attitude spread.[2] By the end of the summer more than 150 Japanese laborers had been driven out of southwestern Idaho.[3] But the railroad company persisted, as did the Japanese. By the end of the 1890s Japanese settlements were common features along the length of the Oregon Short Line, especially in cities like Nampa and Pocatello.

Some of those who came to work on the railroad gradually moved into agriculture, especially in the first decade of the twentieth century with the establishment of the sugar beet industry in the state. As sugar factories were established at Idaho Falls, Sugar City, Blackfoot, and Nampa between 1903 and 1906, a pattern of Japanese settlement in Idaho was set that persists to the present. These enterprises were possible because of Japanese immigration. In announcing plans for the Idaho Falls plant, the president of the Idaho Sugar Company commented that the only drawback was insufficient labor. That would be remedied, he said, by importing 600 to 800 Japanese.[4]

Starting with the population attracted through railroad construction and the sugar beet industry, Japanese built a base in the Gem State from which they gradually moved out into independent farming and occasionally into some trade or commercial enterprise. Particularly in the period just before World War I, with the agricultural development of the Snake River Valley, more Japanese came, settled on farms, and started families. By 1920, the number of Japanese in Idaho had reached 1,569.[5]

A Japanese farm family poses with fruit buckets. *Courtesy of Mrs. Itano Hosoda, Emmett, ID, Sims Collection, Box 22, Folder 6.*

In many ways the personal histories of these early settlers were the same as those of others. And, like pioneers on any frontier, there were sufficient challenges just to survive. But the generation of immigrants, the Issei, had other obstacles as well. Recognition of Japan as a world power following that country's defeat of Russia resulted in a strong anti-Japanese movement in the western United States. Beginning in California, and building on anti-Oriental attitudes from an earlier time when Chinese were the victims, anti-Japanese movements flourished—as evidenced by a California law in 1913 that limited the rights of Japanese to own and lease land.[6] An important element in this situation was the success the Issei had achieved. If Japanese were threats through competition in agriculture, some people sought to limit their opportunity. This movement was reflected in Idaho, and, beginning soon after the California law was passed, sessions of the Idaho legislature regularly considered bills designed to restrict Japanese property rights. There were groups opposed to such legislation, but they were unable to prevent passage of a 1923 law.[7] Although Japanese were not named specifically in the act, it was definitely an anti-Japanese measure. It declared that "Aliens ineligible for citizenship" were not entitled to own or lease land in the state. The federal naturalization statute did not specifically exclude Japanese either, but it did declare that only Caucasians and persons of African ancestry were eligible for naturalization. Although there are cases of local jurisdictions applying this rather loosely and admitting Japanese, most states, including Idaho, did not consider Japanese eligible. In 1905 a judge in Boise denied the application of a Nampa man for naturalization on the grounds that the statute did not permit Japanese to become citizens.[8] Such grounds were confirmed by a United States Supreme Court decision in 1922. Another important step in the anti-Japanese movement was taken in 1924 with the passage of an immigration act that prohibited Japanese from coming into the United States by providing no quota for Japan.

Relegated to such a position, it is natural that Japanese in America would maintain close ethnic and political ties with Japan. In this, the Japanese Association was the most important Issei group. Its particular function was protective, to look out for the rights of those who did not enjoy full rights in American society. Part of the protective power of the Japanese Association lay in its relationship with the Japanese Consulate. The Issei were technically citizens of Japan, so their problems were usually brought to the attention of the Japanese government rather than local officials. The files of the Japanese Association for Idaho contain a heavy correspondence with the Consul General at Portland.[9] Not

The Japanese float in Boise's July 4, 1919, celebration connected the old country and the new. *Sims Collection, Box 22, Folder 12.*

surprisingly, the Japanese Association played a conservative role with regard to acculturation.

By the 1920s, a new generation was coming of age. While their parents were prohibited from enjoying full citizenship rights, they were born in the United States and were entitled to full rights under the Constitution. By the late 1920s this group, intensely aware of their Japanese heritage but strongly seeking identification as Americans, had formed a variety of loose-knit "Citizens Clubs" composed of Nisei, or second generation. By 1930 these had come together in a national organization, the Japanese American Citizens League. Nisei in Idaho soon affiliated with the national group.[10]

In the period between the two world wars, the Japanese population of Idaho remained stable in numbers, but its character was changing.

In 1910 Japanese numbered over 1,300, but only 31 were born in the United States. In 1940, more than 60 percent of Idaho's 1,200 Japanese were native-born Americans. One thing that did not change was the large proportion continuing in agriculture.[11]

Unfortunately, this period saw a continuation of discrimination. The land law remained on the statute books, and isolated instances of racism occurred as well. There was often a correlation between these incidents and international events. Following the Japanese invasion of Manchuria in 1931 and a revival of strong feelings about the "Yellow Peril," the state witnessed a flurry of such activity. In the 1932 gubernatorial election campaign, for example, opponents of Governor C. Ben Ross placed an ad in the *Idaho Daily Statesman* informing voters that Ross had leased his farm near Parma to a Japanese, sufficient proof that the governor was inadequately informed on the peril and did not deserve public office. To the credit of Idaho voters, this did not prevent many from voting for Ross, who won the election. But those who placed the ad presumably had some hope that the people would respond to such an appeal.[12]

As Japan continued its activities in the Pacific and Asia, particularly after its invasion of China in 1937, apprehension grew in this country among Japanese Americans concerning a possible United States–Japan war. As war approached, nativist groups and individuals, in Idaho as on the West Coast, increased their verbal and physical assaults on Japanese. But the Japanese American response was positive. As the nation prepared for war in 1940 and passed a new Selective Service Act, the first Idaho man to register was a Japanese American. When the war began, twelve young Nisei from the Boise Valley area alone were in the armed services.[13]

The attack on Pearl Harbor was a national tragedy, and for some Americans it led to an intensely personal tragedy as well. Japanese Americans were shocked by the event and uncertain as to what the future held. The immediate reaction, locally, was expression of strong support for America in a number of ways. A tragic element of this situation was that more seemed to be required of Japanese Americans; at least, more was expected. The day following Pearl Harbor, Japanese from Middleton to Weiser met at Ontario, Oregon, and pledged their allegiance to the United States. The Japanese Farmers' Association stated in a resolution to the governor that "the action of the Imperial Government" was deplorable and "we do hereby declare our unswerving loyalty to the government of the United States, and we declare our determination to uphold its policies. We appreciate the advantages we have enjoyed here and the friendship manifest toward us by the people of Malheur County, Oregon, and of southwestern Idaho, where many of us were born and others of us born across the Pacific, have made our homes for upwards of 40 years."[14] On December 9, officers of the Japanese American Citizens Club of Southern Idaho and Eastern Oregon purchased a $100 U.S. Defense Bond.[15]

In spite of these and other sincere gestures, Japanese in the area were subjected in numerous ways to acts of discrimination and proscription. By the end of February 1942, approximately 100 Japanese homes had been raided, mostly in the Nampa, Caldwell, and Boise areas. According to a newspaper account, what the "sleuths found was the usual semi-sensational bill of fare, guns, ammunition, cameras, and a few documents whose significance officers said they would be unable to ascertain until they could contact an interpreter of Japanese 'hieroglyphics.'" For those whose homes were entered it was a time of great upheaval. Only one thing was certain—they were in a very vulnerable position.[16]

As agitation mounted on the West Coast to "do something about the Japanese" there gradually developed a plan for removing them. Wartime hysteria, building on the long tradition of the anti-Japanese movement, finally resulted in a presidential executive order issued in February of 1942 making the removal of the Japanese from the West Coast possible. Essentially, the three westernmost states were designated as a defense area from which "any or all persons might be excluded," at the discretion of the military commander. In March President Roosevelt established the War Relocation Board, which had the authority to "remove, relocate, maintain, and supervise" anyone detained by the military commander in the West Coast states. Through a series of military proclamations, the complete evacuation of Japanese and Japanese Americans from the West Coast was ordered as a security measure.[17]

With the relocation program, the history of the Japanese in Idaho entered a new period. That program greatly affected the state through the placement of one of the ten camps within its borders. The effect was felt not only during the war but after, since many chose to remain rather than return to their former homes. In addition, the nature of relocation—the forced removal of 110,000 people in ten concentration camps—was at least in part determined by the people of Idaho, particularly through their governor, Chase Clark.

The early plans for relocation called for voluntary action. That is, Japanese were encouraged to seek out their own opportunities inland. When a congressional committee held hearings in Seattle in late February 1942, to consider the kind of welcome relocating Japanese would find in interior states, they got a clear answer from Governor Clark, who told them that it would be a serious mistake to send "enemy aliens" to Idaho. Clark recommended to the committee that if Japanese were to be placed in Idaho, it could be done only by putting them in "concentration camps under military guard."[18] The governor had a lot of support. Many individuals and organizations revealed hatred for and fear of Japanese, whether American citizens or aliens. For example, representatives of most of Nampa's women's clubs met with Governor Clark in late February to protest movement of Japanese aliens into Idaho; they were assured by him that if "Japs" were sent into the Gem State, armed guards would be requested."[19]

If West Coast Japanese were to voluntarily relocate in Idaho, they would have to lease or purchase homes and land. But they met strong resistance when they tried to do so. A group of fifty Japanese Americans from Monterey, California, sent a representative to negotiate for the purchase of the 3,000-acre Mesa Orchards in Adams County. He was thrown out of the governor's office when he went there to inform Clark of his mission. This representative, a deputy sheriff of Monterey County, was incensed at his treatment and in a meeting with the press declared: "If a democracy is worth fighting for, it ought to be worth practicing. Class hatred and racial discrimination…are the fundamentals of the dictatorships with whom we are at war." Clark responded by saying that he was not ready to sell Idaho to Japanese while Americans were dying to prevent Japan from taking the state of

Idaho by force of arms.[20] In taking that position Clark refused—as he had before—to distinguish between loyal Americans of Japanese ancestry and Japanese in Japan. Many in the state agreed with the governor. Armed with a feeling of support from his constituents, Clark protested to military authorities about voluntary relocation, and he continued to argue against the Japanese coming. In early April 1942, he declared: "When this war is over, I don't want this great Snake River of ours—it is an ideal spot for Japs because it is the greatest garden spot in the country—I don't want ten thousand Japs to be located in Idaho."[21]

Clark took yet another approach to discourage migration to Idaho. Feeling that many who were coming were doing so because they were encouraged by those already in the state, he issued a warning to Japanese in Idaho to "refrain from any activity in encouraging other Japanese to come into Idaho because it might result in the exclusion of all."[22] Members of Idaho's Japanese American Citizens League were in fact searching in March of 1942 for homes for relocatees but admitted that sites were scarce. Under pressure from the governor, they publicly backed away from this effort.[23] In early April, when the governor became aware of attempts by Japanese to purchase land in Kootenai County, he contacted the sheriff there to investigate and attempt to stop the sale. At the same time, he announced that the force of public opinion had brought about the cancellation of sales of three farms to Japanese at Rexburg.[24] At one point he appealed to Idaho citizens "not to sell land to the Japanese. If we let them come now, and by the purchase of land, settle themselves here, we will soon be sick of them."[25] Public opinion was, indeed, the only weapon Clark had at his disposal. Although Idaho had a law prohibiting alien land ownership, most of those trying to relocate were not aliens, but American citizens. Early in his campaign to keep Idaho free of Japanese, Clark was reminded by the editorial writer of the *Idaho Daily Statesman* that Japanese Americans,

> regardless of our personal feelings in the matter, have the same right to live here and hold property here, under the democratic covenant, that citizens do whose fathers and grandfathers were German or Italian. If the American melting pot has failed to melt Jap complexions or habits to the strict American mold, that is too bad, but it still doesn't erase inalienable rights under the Constitution.[26]

Clark disagreed. In a radio address, he spoke to the problem of the "constitutional rights" of the evacuees. He argued that these were nonexistent, for, if they had any such rights at all, they had a right to stay on the Pacific coast. "My only thought now," he said, "is to keep Idaho for Idahoans, and not to sell it to the Japanese. There is nothing un-American about my taking that position. If we permit them to come in here and buy land, there would be one hundred thousand here before summer starts."[27] At another time the governor stated that "recognizing their constitutional rights and being good to them is flowery language, but I am looking to the future of Idaho."[28] With official resistance such as this to the program of voluntary relocation, it is little wonder that it did not work. In fact, by early April only 3,200 had voluntarily relocated.[29]

A conference was called at Salt Lake City on April 7, 1942, at which Army and federal officials met with governors and other top officials from the ten western states. At the conference, Milton Eisenhower, War Relocation Authority Director, made a plea for a relocation program emphasizing voluntary relocation and private employment and resettlement in independent and self-supporting communities. What Eisenhower called for was just such an operation as had been planned for Mesa Orchards. Obviously, Clark was opposed to such an idea. In fact, most of the governors expressed strong opposition to Eisenhower's proposals. Some suggested that the coastal states were using the war as an excuse for getting rid of a long-standing problem by transferring it inland, a point made several times by Clark. Some governors also denied that those who were native-born had any citizenship rights.[30]

With Governor Clark leading the way, federal officials became convinced that the state officials would settle only for concentration camps with armed guards. Clark considered this the only reasonable approach to the problem. In the closed executive session at the conference he spoke candidly on his position and expressed a desire not to be known in history as the person responsible for letting Idaho become full of Japanese. He then went on to admit, "right on the start that I am so prejudiced that my reasoning might be a little off, because I don't trust any of them. I don't know which ones to trust and so therefore I don't trust any of them."[31]

Since he was unable to persuade the governors to endorse his relocation plan, Eisenhower considered the conference a disaster, and he concluded that it was largely Clark's fault. The day following the conference, Eisenhower wrote to the Attorney General of the United States referring to the meeting as a "rather tragic conference," highlighting Clark's resistance.[32] The results of the conference confirmed what WRA officials had already perceived: voluntary relocation had not worked, and would not. Two weeks after the meeting, the War Relocation Authority announced plans to relocate the Japanese and Japanese Americans in ten camps in the western United States, under military guard. One of the camps would be built in Idaho. Until the camps were ready, the relocatees would be detained in a number of "assembly centers."[33]

The possibility of large-scale voluntary relocation had created considerable anxiety among Idaho citizens. As a side effect, even those Japanese who were long-term residents of the state met with increased suspicion and hostility. The decision reached at Salt Lake City relieved this somewhat. In May of 1942, a Japanese American wrote from Caldwell to a friend in Seattle, "The prejudice here has died down immensely since the voluntary evacuation has been stopped."[34]

Perhaps the greatest impact that the relocation program had on Idaho was its provision of agricultural labor. When proposals for removal of Japanese Americans from the West Coast were first made, comments on that removal usually dealt with the labor they might provide to inland states. In Idaho, in early 1942, views were mixed on the advisability of using such labor. At its annual meeting in Boise in February of 1942, the Idaho Grange—which was consistent in its anti-Japanese American position throughout the war—voted to oppose importation of Japanese aliens from coast areas for farm labor.[35] Idaho beet men, looking at the possibilities for the 1942 crop, were told by sugar company officials that acreage would be doubled in 1942 and that they could rely on Japanese workers to provide the additional labor. But the general reaction among farmers continued to be mixed. While Governor Clark attended the Salt Lake City conference to protest against bringing Japanese to Idaho, the head of the Idaho Beet Growers Association also attended and reported that, contrary to Clark's views, Idaho needed the labor that might be provided by relocation.[36]

There was a serious need for additional manpower in agriculture in this region. By May of 1942 the shortage became so acute and pressure became so great that, contrary to the policy announced after the Salt Lake City conference, the WRA permitted evacuees to work in sugar beet areas. Once the sugar beet interests got to work, it was amazing to see how quickly some politicians changed their minds. By May 15, 1942, the WRA concluded an agreement with Governor Sprague of Oregon for the release of evacuees to work in the sugar beet area in Malheur County. At first, the WRA proceeded with great caution; but as the need for labor grew, regulations were gradually relaxed, and by late September of 1942 the release program was quite liberal.[37]

While Sprague and others were changing their minds, Governor Clark was still insisting on his previous points. In a speech in late May he made a statement that has been as much quoted as any other on the issue of relocation. He bitterly denounced Japanese as people who "act like rats," and he told the Grangeville Lions Club that a solution to the "Jap problem" in Idaho and the nation would be to send them all back to Japan, "then sink the island." "Japs live like rats, breed like rats and act like rats. We don't want them…permanently located in our state."[38]

Predictably, Clark's attitude interfered with efforts to attract Japanese labor. The Idaho Director of the U.S. Employment Service found Japanese reluctant to come to Idaho to work because of reports of anti-Japanese sentiment, especially as expressed by Clark.[39] When Idaho sugar beet companies sent recruiters to the Puyallup Assembly Center, they found a clipping of Clark's Grangeville speech posted on the bulletin board and discovered that evacuees were not at all anxious to work in Idaho. When he saw the potential disadvantages of his remarks, the governor modified his stand with a press release, which stated: "In this beet thinning emergency, Japanese living in this country have a fine opportunity to demonstrate their loyalty. Any that are doing this I am ready to give my praise and they should be excepted in any remarks I've made."[40] By the end of 1942 some 9,000 evacuees were working in agricultural areas throughout the west and were being enthusiastically praised. In Idaho, their contribution was essential, and there is no doubt that they were instrumental in saving the sugar beet crop.[41]

Evacuees assigned to the newly constructed camp at Hunt, Idaho—first opened on a limited basis in August of 1942—began almost immediately to obtain work releases. By the end of the harvest, about 2,100 were working in off-project employment, more than double the number of workers from any other relocation center.[42] Early the next year sugar companies began recruitment programs seeking laborers and sharecroppers, including extensive advertising efforts in the camp newspaper. By October of 1943, the number of Hunt residents working in seasonal agriculture was 2,400, a significant addition to the labor force available for Idaho's harvests.[43]

Not all Idahoans were pleased with this turn of events, however, and some viewed the activities with horror. Some continued their insistence that the Japanese be closely guarded. In addition, the work-release program was unpopular with some because it permitted the Japanese to compete in the labor market. Labor unions around the state were particularly concerned, and their attitude was reflected in a number of resolutions against employment of Japanese. Typical of such resolutions was that of the Pocatello Carpenters' Union, which in May of 1943 approved a resolution prohibiting any of its members from working on any job where Japanese were used in any capacity.[44]

General public concern was expressed that good jobs might encourage the evacuees to settle permanently in Idaho. This concern was closely related to activities in the West Coast states to prevent the return of the Japanese at the end of the war. There, many of the groups involved in the removal program initially began to push for a prohibition against the Japanese returning. For example, Grange Masters representing Granges in the West Coast states requested that the federal government prohibit persons of Japanese ancestry from returning following the war, complaining that such persons had "failed to assimilate themselves and can never be assimilated into American community life."[45]

The evacuees were aware of these pressures, and as a result, when permanent relocation became possible by late 1943, many of the younger generation took the opportunity to start a new life. By February of 1944

Hunt relocatees were scattered in thirty-three states, and the camp led all other centers in the number of evacuees out on this type of leave.[46]

One Hunt resident, who had been active in the JACL in Seattle, saw this as a blessing in disguise. In a letter to a friend he wrote:

> The interesting feature about this whole affair is, however, that the second generation constitutes some 85 percent to date of the entire number of persons leaving the relocation centers for resettlement outside. This is what we were leading up to before the war with little success. Now when America is at war with the land of their parents, what was proving not any too successful is now taking place under forced conditions. It is a healthy thing, nevertheless.47

The camp they had come to was the Minidoka camp, at Hunt, Idaho, in the area north of Twin Falls. Most of the residents of the camp were from the Portland and Seattle areas and were not prepared for the physical environment they were coming to. A Caldwell Nisei wrote to a friend in Seattle, referring to the relocatees:

> It sounds like they will be coming to Idaho...I'm afraid it will be dusty and hot because of the uncultivated land and no trees as such. They sure won't think so much of this state, while all along I've been trying to explain to them what a wonderful state it is. They surely won't believe me now after the experience they will no doubt go through.[48]

The movement to Hunt from the assembly centers, which began in August of 1942, was by train. The evacuees all passed through Nampa, where many saw friends who had come in the period of voluntary relocation. One internee wrote: "I thought how ironic it was that we should see...Japanese who were free to do as they pleased while we, by trainloads, were being herded to camps." The same writer also commented on her arrival at the camp: "We finally arrived at Minidoka, and at the sight of dust and rows and rows of barracks, I was ready to cry when I thought that this was to be our home for the duration."[49] Another expressed these feelings:

"When we first arrived here we almost cried, and thought that this was a land that God had forgotten. The vast expanse of nothing but sagebrush and dust, a landscape so alien to our eyes, and a desolate, woebegone feeling of being so far removed from home and fireside bogged us down mentally, as well as physically."[50]

That some were able to have a positive thought in that kind of situation is a tribute to the human spirit. Some did: one young man wrote to a friend in one of the assembly centers, gave him a description of the physical layout, and then added "all in all, the great intensity and extent of work that needs to be done here cannot be overemphasized. There is no denying the fact that the place is a desert now but it can be made into a model community and will certainly be worth a try."[51]

An element among the evacuees, perhaps a majority, could see through the difficulties and sense opportunity. One of the more optimistic wrote a friend:

> The more I think of it, the stronger becomes my belief that the path of the second generation into American life becomes much more clearcut and broader. Placed into a camp such as this, we are prone to feel that our future in America is closed to us, but instead, I believe that this is now a new starting point, from which we can proceed... to become part and parcel of the national life. I am basing this belief upon the fact that by obeying the military order we are proving our loyalty. By our conduct today in these camps will we be judged later as either good or bad timber in the building of America.[52]

The physical hardships and the "testing" might have been better borne if the Japanese Americans had not had to endure other degradations as well. One situation that made relocatees feel unwelcome in Idaho involved the practice of many school districts charging tuition for children of relocatees. When the War Relocation Authority objected, the state superintendent of public instruction requested an attorney general's opinion and was advised that they had to pay nonresident tuition. The superintendent criticized the decision:

> It is unfortunate that such obvious discrimination exists in some districts in Idaho. Such acts are bound to reach the ears of sons and brothers of these people fighting in the American army with other American boys. It is equally astonishing that such charges should be made in the face of the contribution the evacuated people have made to Idaho's outstanding record of agricultural production in war time.[53]

One of the ironies of the situation in Idaho during the war was that Chase Clark, following his tenure as governor, was appointed a federal district court judge. In late 1944 he was the presiding judge in trials for draft evasion of thirty-four internees from Minidoka. At the beginning of the war, there had been no prohibition against Japanese in the armed forces. When enlistment lines formed in Pocatello on the Monday following Pearl Harbor, the first in line was an Idaho-born Japanese. But the opportunity for Japanese Americans to enlist was soon cut off. In May of 1942 the War Department began devising plans for all Japanese American units, and recruitment began at the camps in July. The result was the establishment of the 442nd Regimental Combat Team and a group composed mostly of Hawaiian Nisei, the 100th Battalion. These groups fought with distinction in the Italian campaigns, and the 442nd was the most decorated unit in the war. Largely on the strength of the public support gained by these military groups, Selective Service procedures were by January of 1944 once again applied to Japanese Americans. It was probably predictable that some would balk, and at Minidoka thirty-four refused induction.[54] This must be measured against the approximately 800 residents of the camp who did enter military service. Many other Japanese Americans served in units in the Pacific and distinguished themselves. Slowly some of the bitterness toward Japanese and Japanese Americans was tempered by the realization that they, too, were fighting and dying for America.

When the order excluding Japanese from the West Coast was rescinded in January of 1945, many would not return to their former homes. In the short run, approximately 3,000 Hunt residents were resettled in Idaho by the end of the war. Five years later, fewer than 1,000 remained. With the exception of some who obtained relocation permits in the state, worked in communities where they were accepted, and found friends, the total experience was a tragic one; little wonder few stayed. The last family left Minidoka in October of 1945. They were reluctant to leave, probably because they really had no place to go. The camp director asked the Jerome County sheriff to arrest them, and they spent the night in jail while camp officials packed their personal effects. The following day, they were put on the train for their former coastal home.[55]

It would be too much to say that after the war there was a return to normal. People did not just go back and pick up where they left off. The war and relocation left a heavy mark on Japanese American communities and families. Many took the opportunity to break away from their old life and move to the East or Midwest. Others—like many who stayed in Idaho, either in the period of voluntary relocation or out of the camps—had established roots and were not inclined to attempt to start over again in their old homes.

But the end of the war and the immediate readjustment is not the end of the story. Many Japanese Americans had endured, even tolerated, relocation because of a feeling of loyalty, and saw that time of trial as a way of proving that loyalty. They came out of the experience with a resolve that, having passed the ultimate test, they were now entitled to a full share of the American Dream—they were entitled to equal treatment.

The JACL honors Idaho Issei upon their naturalization as American citizens in 1955. *Sims Collection, Box 22, Folder 16.*

One of the most significant barriers to the realization of that dream fell in 1952 when, with the passage of new immigration and naturalization legislation, alien Japanese became eligible for citizenship. In addition, for the first time since 1924, Japanese were allowed to immigrate. Just a few years later, in 1955, Idaho Japanese organized and successfully obtained the repeal of the 1923 Alien Land Law, which had stood so long as a symbol of racial discrimination.[56]

Through the efforts of many, the Idaho Legislature placed on the ballot in 1962 a proposed constitutional amendment that deleted the section disqualifying Japanese from full citizenship rights. The amendment symbolized a new status for Japanese in Idaho, one won through many struggles and against strong odds.[57]

In the past decade or so, Americans have come to an increased appreciation of their pluralistic cultural and ethnic heritage. Few minorities have as much to celebrate, in terms of both what they have overcome and what they have contributed. In seeing Japanese in our midst, in seeing how fully they have been incorporated into Idaho community, business, and professional life, it is perhaps too easy to forget that their achievements are all the more remarkable because of the difficulties they have overcome. Because of the uniqueness of their experiences and contributions, Japanese Americans make up an important chapter in Idaho's history.

## Notes

1. Article VI, Section 3, Constitution of the State of Idaho (1889).
2. *Idaho Daily Statesman* (Boise), July 13, 1892, 5.
3. Ibid., July 26, 1892, 8.
4. Ibid., January 31, 1903, 2.
5. Harry H. L. Kitano, *Japanese Americans: The Evolution of a Sub-culture* (Englewood Cliffs, NJ: Prentice-Hall, 1969), 162–63.
6. Japanese American Citizens League, *The Experience of Japanese Americans in the United States* (San Francisco: JACL, 1975), 53.
7. Kazuo Ito, *Issei* (Seattle: Japanese American Community Services, 1973), 162–63; Idaho Session Laws, 1923, 160–65.
8. *Caldwell Tribune*, November 4, 1905, 1.
9. The files are located in the Japanese American Research Project Collection, The Research Library, University of California, Los Angeles.
10. *Japanese-American Courier* (Seattle), June 11, 1932, 4; March 10, 1934, 4.
11. 1940 Census of Population, Idaho, 396.
12. *Idaho Daily Statesman*, November 1, 1932, 2.
13. Ibid., December 9, 1941, 6.
14. Ibid., December 10, 1941, 2.
15. Ibid., 8.
16. *Idaho Daily Statesman*, March 1, 1942, 1.
17. These events are best described in Roger Daniels, *Concentration Camps, U.S.A.* (New York: Holt, Rinehart, & Winston, 1972).

18. *Idaho Daily Statesman*, February 28, 1942, 1.

19. Ibid., 3.

20. *Idaho Daily Statesman*, March 15, 1942, 1.

21. "Verbatim Record of Speeches," WRA-WCCA Salt Lake City Conference, April 7, 1942, Japanese American Evacuation and Resettlement Collection, Bancroft Library, University of California, Berkeley (hereafter cited as JERS).

22. *Pocatello Tribune*, March 17, 1942, 1.

23. *Idaho Daily Statesman*, March 27, 1942, 6.

24. "Survey of Public Opinion in Western States on Japanese Evacuation, Idaho" (A 16.03), JERS.

25. *Idaho Daily Statesman*, March 15, 1942, 1.

26. Ibid., March 14, 1942, 4.

27. "Radio Address of Gov. Clark" (C 1.03), JERS.

28. *Idaho Daily Statesman*, March 15, 1942, 8.

29. Remarks by Milton Eisenhower, Salt Lake City Conference (C 1.03), JERS.

30. Ibid.

31. "Verbatim Record of Speeches," JERS.

32. "WRA Correspondence on Meeting and Post-Meeting Policy" (C 1.03), JERS.

33. *Twin Falls Times-News*, April 23, 1942, 1.

34. Letter from Evacuee to Rev. Emery Andrews, May 1942, Andrews Papers, University of Washington Library, Seattle.

35. *Idaho Daily Statesman*, February 13, 1942, 16.

36. John W. Abbott to Robert K. Lamb, April 8, 1942, "WRA Correspondence on Meeting and Post-Meeting Policy" (C 1.03), JERS.

37. Carey McWilliams, *Prejudice* (Boston: Little, Brown, and Company, 1944), 164.

38. *Idaho Daily Statesman*, May 23, 1942, 1–2.

39. Ibid., 1.

40. *Idaho Daily Statesman*, May 26, 1942, 8.

41. Audrie Girdner and Ann Loftis, *The Great Betrayal: The Evacuation of the Japanese-Americans During World War II* (London: The Macmillan Company, 1969), 339.

42. *Minidoka* (Relocation Center) *Irrigator*, November 4, 1942, 2.

43. Ibid., October 23, 1943, 1.

44. Walter Chambers, Recording Secretary, Local 1258, to August Rosqvist, Secretary, Idaho State Federation of Labor, Pocatello, May 12, 1943, "Japs-NYA and Employment, 1943," Box 23, Rosqvist Papers, Idaho State Historical Society, Boise.

45. *Salt Lake Tribune*, August 22, 1944, n.p. Clipping in "Japs-NYA and Employment," Rosqvist Papers.

46. *Minidoka Irrigator*, February 26, 1944, 1.

47. James Sakamoto to Father Mulligan, December 23, 1943, Sakamoto Papers, University of Washington Library, Seattle.

48. Letter from Evacuee to Rev. Emery Andrews, May 1942 (1–107), Andrews Papers.

49. Ibid., August 24, 1942 (1–105).

50. Ibid., n.d. (1–117).

51. Dyke Miyagawa to the Japanese Advisory Council, Puyallup Assembly Center, August 10, 1942, Sakamoto Papers.

52. James Sakamoto to Robert Flanders, July 13, 1942, Sakamoto Papers.

53. *Salt Lake Tribune*, September 8, 1944, n.p. Clipping in "Japs-NYA and Employment, 1943," Box 23, Rosqvist Papers.

54. *Idaho Daily Statesman*, October 3, 1944, 1.

55. *Salt Lake Tribune*, October 29, 1945, 1.

56. Box 306, Japanese American Research Project Collection.

57. *Idaho Daily Statesman*, January 14, 1961, 6.

# Idaho's Governor Chase Clark and Japanese American Relocation in World War II

## EDITOR'S NOTE

*After Imperial Japan attacked Pearl Harbor and the United States declared war against Japan, the subsequent punitive treatment of Japanese American citizens living on the West Coast—their detention, forced removal, and incarceration for the duration of the war—was due in part to war hysteria and the powerful force of racism. Much of this hysteria was fueled by a number of western state leaders, among them Idaho Governor Chase Clark.* \*

*For many years after the war, the general belief among Americans was that the confinement of Japanese Americans was a military necessity during wartime. But a 1982 Congressional examination of the Japanese incarceration, published under the title* Personal Justice Denied, *revealed that military assessments during the early months after Pearl Harbor had denied any such military necessity. The report said that those assessments had been suppressed, and that bureaucrats had deliberately contrived euphemisms to manage the public perception of the mass incarceration of American citizens and their immigrant parents.—SS*

---

During World War II, the United States government removed the entire Japanese and Japanese American population from the West Coast and interned the 110,000 men, women, and children in the interior. The incident was tragic not only for those directly affected but for all Americans, because it constituted a failure of the American

---

This essay by Robert Sims was originally published as "'A Fearless, Clean-cut, and Patriotic Stand': Idaho's Governor Clark and Japanese American Relocation in World War II," *Pacific Northwest Quarterly* 70, no. 2 (April 1979).

system of justice. This subversion of the civil rights of American citizens, justified at the time as a military necessity, has been characterized in recent scholarship as a triumph of racism. Studies have proven that anti-Japanese groups influenced the decision to remove all persons of Japanese ancestry from the West Coast. Overt racism also affected development of the wartime relocation program.

At least partly in response to anti-Japanese attitudes in the interior states, the federal government adopted the harshest and most restrictive solution to relocation that it had considered—concentration camps. Chase Clark, governor of Idaho in 1941 and 1942, was one official who insisted on a program that included detention and armed guards; his demands were strident, persistent, and influential. A look at his role in this regrettable episode in our history will help us to better understand the part played by other officials and individuals from interior states.

Governor Chase Clark, far left, accompanies President Franklin D. Roosevelt circa September 21, 1942, on a secret tour of Camp Farragut Naval Training Station near Sandpoint, Idaho. *Idaho State Historical Society, Idaho State Archives, 72-3-3.*

Before Pearl Harbor, Clark showed little indication that he was capable of his later stand against Japanese Americans. He came from a section of the state which claimed more than half of Idaho's 1,200 Japanese. Many of these families had long been residents of the region, some for forty years or more, and Clark knew and was known by many of them. In late November 1941, he was a featured participant in an intermountain district meeting of the Japanese American Citizens League (JACL) at Pocatello, Idaho. At that gathering, Clark stated: "We must realize that we are all, first and last, Americans." Unfortunately, his commitment to that view was one of the casualties of Pearl Harbor.[1]

By late December 1941, speculation about the relocation of West Coast Japanese was rampant. The issue touched Idaho primarily as a labor question. With acreage controls lifted because of expected demands, Idaho sugar beet growers were concerned about having sufficient labor to meet their needs. Attitudes of Idaho farmers on the possible use of evacuee labor varied, with some farm organizations adamantly opposed.

In an interview in mid-February, Clark referred to Japanese and Japanese American laborers imported from the Coast as "enemy labor," and he indicated that, in his view, Idahoans were opposed to bringing "alien enemy labor to Idaho." In a telegram sent that month to the chairman of a House committee investigating national defense migration, Clark warned that it would be a "serious mistake to send enemy aliens to Idaho," and he urged that any Japanese brought to the state "be placed in concentration camps under military guard."[2]

At that time, the government was still forming its policy concerning Japanese and Japanese Americans. Although there clearly was strong support for removal of the Japanese from the West Coast, officials were undecided about the manner of removal and about what to do with the people after they were moved. Little evidence exists to suggest that federal officials favored placing the Japanese in detention centers under armed guard, as Clark recommended. In fact, an army spokesman indicated that the military could not respect the wishes of Clark and various groups in the inland west on the relocation matter.[3]

Once the government made the decision to remove all Japanese from the coastal areas, initial plans called for voluntary relocation.

Encouraged to seek out opportunities on their own, adventurous souls headed into interior regions where they attempted to find new jobs, homes, and land to lease or purchase. But they met fierce resistance.

When a group of fifty families from Monterey County, California, tried to purchase a 3,000-acre tract of land in Adams County, Idaho, they were opposed by Clark, who sent telegrams to Lieutenant General John L. DeWitt, commanding officer of the Western Defense Command, and to other military and federal officials. When D. A. Storm, a representative of the group and deputy sheriff of Monterey County, asked to speak to Clark, the governor refused to hear him. Storm was incensed over his treatment and in a statement to the press declared: "If a democracy is worth fighting for…it ought to be worth practicing. Class hatred, racial discrimination, slave or convict labor are the fundamentals of the dictatorships with whom we are at war." Clark responded by indicating his unwillingness to "sell the state of Idaho to the Japanese for a few dollars while our American boys are dying to prevent Japan from taking the state of Idaho…by force of arms." The governor exhorted citizens "not to sell land to the Japanese. If we let them come now," he said, "and, by the purchase of land settle themselves here, we will soon be sick of them." He also reiterated his belief that any Japanese brought to Idaho should be kept under guard.[4]

The position Clark took in this and other land sales matters is significant because it indicates that the governor did not distinguish between Japanese in Japan and Americans of Japanese ancestry. Further, it shows that he was willing to restrict the rights of or even deny legal status to some Americans. Among those who found fault with Clark's view was John Carver, U.S. attorney for Idaho. Carver believed that the rights of American-born Japanese were unquestionable. In a public statement he indicated that the Justice Department took the view that enemy aliens could come into Idaho regardless of protest. Carver accused the governor of lack of support for the federal government. He also warned that Clark's actions toward Japanese Americans could have detrimental effects. "We can treat them in such a way as to make them loyal Americans or we can alienate them," he said.[5]

Clark responded to Carver's criticism: "It seems to me that we had our arms around them when they stabbed us in the back at Pearl

Harbor.… Recognizing their constitutional rights and being good to them is flowery language, but I am looking to the future of Idaho." Clark referred to the experience of California with the Japanese and, in doing so, revealed how completely he accepted the views of the anti-Japanese forces in that state:

> Thirty years ago the federal government asked the state of California to soft-pedal the Japanese controversy because they were a sensitive people and worthy of our complete confidence, good will and cooperation.… What is the condition today, 30 years later? The state of California is crawling with Japanese. They contribute nothing to the standard of life but undermine it.

In conclusion, he threatened that "in 100 years they will overrun us to the Rocky Mountains, unless checked."[6]

To justify his attempts to prevent sales of land to Japanese, Clark later argued that he had acted in the best interests of Idahoans. He also expressed his belief that he had been more tolerant with Storm than others might have been. "He accused me," Clark said,

> of Hitler policies because I would not want the people of Idaho to sell Idaho to the Japanese. Would you want me, as your servant, to take any such insult as that and continue to give an interview to a man of this type? I do not believe you would have been as patient as I was. Instead of terminating the interview and seeing that he left the office, as I did, I think you would have made a hospital case out of him.

Clark went to the heart of the matter on this occasion and posed the question all-important to the people of Idaho: "Do you want them living next door to you?"[7]

The editorial writer for the *Idaho Daily Statesman* also chided the governor for his stand and argued that American citizens of Japanese ancestry had a legal and constitutional right to come to Idaho and purchase land if they so desired. But Clark disagreed. "I am not doing anything to the Constitution," he countered.

> It is a sacred document to me. Certainly I am doing no more to it by refusing to sell land to the Japanese, than the Government itself is doing when it requires them to leave the Pacific Coast. The Gov-

ernment is not moving them out of the Pacific Coast area because it
knows they are safe and trustworthy. It is moving them out of Pacific
Coast area because it remembers what happened at Pearl Harbor. It
knows that Japanese, born and educated in America, led some of the
planes that bombed Pearl Harbor. They are being safe.[8]

As Roger Daniels has pointed out, other factors contributed to the
failure of the voluntary relocation program. Although resistance alone
would probably have doomed the plan, the freezing of bank accounts
and a lack of familiarity with possible relocation areas complicated the
plight of Japanese faced with the necessity of leaving the West Coast.
Regions with established Japanese and Japanese American populations
were logical relocation points for evacuees. Idaho, for example, had
acquired Japanese residents by immigration as early as the 1890s; by
1940, Idahoans of Japanese descent numbered about 1,200. They
could have helped friends, relatives, and others establish themselves
in the state. But, as the head of the Pocatello chapter of the JACL
wrote to the organization's national president, the hands of the local
Japanese Americans were "tied so far as helping the Pacific coast mass
evacuation to any great extent." Because of Clark's campaign, he said,
property owners were even reluctant to lease land to resident Japanese
Americans.[9]

Clark kept the pressure on. In mid-March 1942 he warned Idaho
Japanese to "refrain from any activity in encouraging other Japanese
to come into Idaho, because it might result in the exclusion of all."
Local Japanese had been searching for settlement sites but finding
few. In the face of the governor's opposition and threats, they publicly backed away from their efforts. Idaho JACL presidents passed a
resolution "pledging all members of the league in Idaho to discourage
all evacuee relatives, friends, and others" from coming to the state.
Thus, at a time when evacuees needed the aid of their fellow Japanese Americans, Clark contributed to a division among them. Some
Idaho Japanese, finding their own security jeopardized, asked Clark
to distinguish between "coast evacuee Japanese Americans and those
[who]…resided in Idaho permanently."[10]

Although federal officials had not given up on voluntary relocation, by mid-March they were reviewing other possibilities. The for-
midable opposition to the voluntary plan led to growing speculation
that evacuation would be tightly controlled and that large relocation
facilities would be established. On March 19, 1942, Thomas C. Clark,
chief of DeWitt's civilian staff, conferred with the governor on the
possibility of Japanese evacuees being brought to Idaho and housed
in a "reception center."[11]

While military and federal officials worked on plans for evacuation
and relocation, Clark continued his campaign against the Japanese.
And his stand was a popular one, the opposition of John Carver and the
*Statesman* notwithstanding. That month, a delegation of sixty farmers
from southwestern Idaho assured the governor that they supported his
efforts, and they expressed opposition to importation of Japanese for
any purpose. Support also came from most of the state's farm organizations, the American Legion, and some private individuals. One legion
post, located in Adams County, the site of Mesa Orchards, passed a
resolution opposing sale or lease of land to Japanese.[12]

Sensing that he was striking a responsive chord among his constituents, Clark strengthened his anti-Japanese image through his
role in an incident involving Japanese American transfer students
from West Coast universities and colleges. When it was reported that
the University of Idaho had agreed to accept six evacuated Japanese
American students from the University of California at Berkeley, Clark
intervened. As a result, the president of the university repudiated the
story, and the students were not allowed to enroll at that time.[13]

Clark's activities earned him support from anti-Japanese individuals in the state. One man wrote to the editor of a Boise newspaper to
commend Clark for his "fearless, patriotic, clean-cut stand." The writer,
like Clark, preferred to categorize all Japanese together, whether they
lived in Tokyo or Boise. Approving Clark's view that Japanese were
unfit for settlement in Idaho, he wrote: "The perfidious internationally immoral reputation of the Japanese Imperial Government and
her unscrupulous leaders make[s] any member of the Japanese race,
citizen or alien...an undesirable applicant henceforth and hereafter
for American citizenship."[14]

Although aware of anti-Japanese attitudes, federal officials continued to search for an enlightened policy. But it became increasingly apparent that voluntary relocation was not working. Public Proclamation No. 4, issued at the headquarters of the Western Defense Command on March 27, 1942, ended the program by prohibiting any further migration from the West Coast. With the demise of the voluntary plan, the government turned to other alternatives. Even as late as March, according to Milton Eisenhower, director of the War Relocation Authority (WRA), federal officials "had no conception of relocation centers as they finally evolved." Only after they met in April with officials from ten western states did they become convinced that concentration camps were the only acceptable solution.[15] At the conference, held at Salt Lake City on April 7, 1942, most of the governors expressed views similar to Clark's. They echoed his demands for military control of any Japanese brought into the interior. Clark expressed his opinions with remarkable candor. At one point he said:

> I would hate...to have the people of Idaho hold me responsible...for having let Idaho [become] full of Japanese during my administration. I want to admit right on the start that I am so prejudiced that my reasoning might be a little off, because I don't trust any of them. I don't know which ones to trust and so therefore I don't trust any of them.

He went on to declare that those who came into the state during the period of voluntary relocation should be subjected to the same treatment as involuntary evacuees. He also requested that the army guarantee that all West Coast Japanese and Japanese Americans would be returned to their former homes at the end of the war and would not be allowed to reside permanently in Idaho.[16]

The conference also brought forth opinions from people who favored relocating Japanese Americans in the intermountain west. These individuals were motivated by a need for labor. The head of the Idaho sugar beet growers organization, attending a separate meeting in Salt Lake City, indicated that workers were in short supply; in contrast to Clark, he thought evacuees could prove useful as laborers. Sensing the strength of that view, Clark implicitly agreed to the importation of West Coast Japanese by asking the army for assurance that "when they are taken from the reception centers for work…they are taken under guard." However, he continued to insist that evacuees not be allowed to purchase or lease land for permanent settlement. "When this war is over, I don't want this great Snake River Valley of ours, it is an ideal spot for Japs because it is the greatest garden spot in the country—I don't want ten thousand Japs to be located in Idaho."[17]

Dismayed at the reactions of the governors at the Salt Lake City meeting, Eisenhower wrote the following day to U.S. Attorney General Francis Biddle and referred to the encounter as a "rather tragic conference." Clark, on the other hand, explained his behavior in terms of the extraordinary responsibility of citizens in wartime to "sustain our government in every way." He apparently assumed that as governor he had a particular responsibility in wartime to carry out the wishes of the people. "For this reason," he said, "in all discussions of the question of Idaho's position with reference to evacuated Japanese aliens and native-born Japanese from West Coast States, I have adhered to what I believe is the feeling of a vast majority of our citizens."[18]

He restated that he was "unalterably opposed" to land purchases in Idaho by Japanese. "They are being moved out of the Coast area for the very reason that the Government is afraid that they have this fifth column taint…. My only thought now is to keep Idaho for Idahoans." Yet Clark declared that he would be glad to change his position if the people willed it. "Instead of taking the position that I know all, I am trying to listen closely to the voice of the people of my State," he said. In his closing remarks, Clark revealed once again his failure to distinguish between Japanese in Japan and Japanese Americans. "We are recording a page in history today," he said. "Do you want those who come after us to find recorded on that page of history that we sold our State to the Japanese while our soldiers were fighting to defend it?"[19]

Since the people of Idaho apparently supported Clark, he remained active in his campaign to oppose "any relocation of Japanese in Idaho under any program except that of concentration camps" and to prevent land sales or leases to Japanese. He particularly worried about the Japanese who had moved to the state under the voluntary relocation plan, for they might not be regarded as evacuees if a detention program were adopted. Consequently, he cautioned his constituents "not to sell their land, or lease it for permanent settlement, to evacuated Japanese." On at least two occasions, he was able to intervene and stop land sales to Japanese Americans.[20]

On April 12, 1942, the army announced that it would establish a camp in Idaho for 10,000 relocatees. Army representatives assured Governor Clark that the camp would be created only for the duration and that evacuees would have to move after the war. But Clark continued to raise protests. When farmers in the area of the proposed camp objected because of possible jeopardy to their water rights, he called a public meeting to discuss the problem. His contribution was the comment: "I just cannot believe the Japs are any good for any community in any state. I realize we've got to put them someplace but I don't trust any of them." After the meeting, Clark asked the army to review its decision, and he joined with local farmers in an official protest.[21]

Not everyone supported the governor in his crusade, however, and he began to feel pressure from some agricultural interests. In anticipation of serious labor shortages in western farming areas, the army approved plans for use of evacuee labor, contingent upon approval by state and county officials. In early May Clark reluctantly conceded to sugar beet companies' requests, but by mid-month, when he realized that at least 2000 workers would be needed, he fell back on his demand that any Japanese brought in would have to be kept under military surveillance and housed in guarded camps. As plans for using evacuees in Idaho beet fields progressed, the governor gave ground only after considerable resistance. He maintained that local officials of the fifteen counties affected by the plan could veto evacuee labor, and that no Japanese would be sent into an area unless requested.[22]

Mid-1942 was a critical time for growers in the intermountain west. With huge crops ready for harvesting, they needed workers. It seemed logical in the crisis that they should look to the potential labor force gathered in West Coast assembly centers. Since working in the fields was based on voluntarism, evacuees had to be enticed to participate. Although agricultural work might have been preferable to imprisonment in fairgrounds or stables, the Japanese did not respond eagerly. In fact, they hardly responded at all to the first overtures of the agricultural interests. One reason for their reluctance was the blatant anti-Japanese sentiment expressed openly by Governor Clark.

In a speech at Grangeville, Idaho, in late May, the governor made some remarks that have been much quoted. Speaking to the local Lions Club, he bitterly denounced Japanese as people who "act like rats." He proposed a solution to what he characterized as the "Jap Problem": "Send them all back to Japan, then sink the island."[23]

Not surprisingly, A. J. Tillman, U.S. Employment Service director for Idaho, reported that Japanese and Japanese Americans in the assembly centers were reluctant to come to the state because of reports of anti-Japanese sentiment. This situation was confirmed by a WRA official, who reported to Eisenhower that the evacuees were slow to respond to recruitment efforts because of "unfavorable newspaper stories such as Governor Clark's." A former JACL president interned in an assembly center wrote to an officer of the Utah and Idaho Sugar Company, explaining that it was difficult to get workers to respond to requests for labor in the sugar beet areas because of the "statement of Governor Clark of Idaho and the resultant feeling of unrest and uncertainty caused by it."[24]

Eisenhower wrote to Clark and politely reminded him that "it is the policy of the War Relocation Authority and I am sure it will be yours, to demonstrate to the world—to our enemies and our friends alike—that this wartime human problem can be handled by a great democratic nation with kindness, tolerance, and deep understanding." The governor also had more forthright criticism closer to home. An editorial in the *Statesman* faulted him for his intemperate remarks but also blamed the farmers, among others.

> To blame the Governor exclusively is plain demag[o]guery.... [He] had companions in raising the repellant ruckus. As we recall, plenty of erstwhile noise about saving Idaho from the Japs came from some farmers. Now when they could use beige boys in their fields, the growers innocently grumble about why in the Samhill Chase Clark went and raised that rumpus.[25]

Clark apparently knew that the political winds had shifted, and he had already begun to alter his position. In a statement praising those Japanese Americans who were "loyal to the United States," Clark declared: "In this beet thinning emergency, Japanese living in this country have a fine opportunity to demonstrate their loyalty. Any that are doing this I am ready to give my praise and they should have been excepted in any remarks I've made."[26]

The intensity of the labor shortage forced Clark to back down from his insistence that evacuee workers in the beet fields be kept under guard and returned to camp each night. Along with the evacuees' exemplary conduct, the enormous need for Japanese labor silenced the governor's demands; eventually, despite Clark's efforts, there was broad acceptance of—and even appreciation for—evacuees as agricultural workers in the intermountain west. When the Idaho camp opened in August 1942, work releases were easily obtained, and few people worried about maintaining security for those Japanese Americans who volunteered to work outside the camp.[27]

Clark's demands for the removal of Japanese at the end of the war also subsided. Although removal was still a live issue in 1945 when the camp closed, no official action was taken to insure that Japanese did not remain in the state. In fact, attitudes in Idaho had so changed toward evacuees that more than a thousand Japanese Americans stayed on and became permanent residents.

Acting as spokesmen for their constituents, Clark and other public officials not only influenced the government's decision to set up concentration camps but also helped determine their character. They must therefore bear some responsibility for the detrimental effects of the months, even years, that evacuees spent behind barbed wire and under armed guard. It is not unreasonable to suppose that internment might have been avoided altogether and the trauma of relocation mitigated had more enlightened minds prevailed.

In addition, Clark's public expressions unnecessarily compounded the anxieties and fears of the Japanese and Japanese Americans. The governor ignored Eisenhower's admonition to "kindness, tolerance, and…understanding." Instead, he joined in the racist rhetoric that flourished during the early months of the war, spreading the notion that Japanese Americans were the enemy and encouraging discriminatory treatment of them. Unwillingness to distinguish between and among persons of Japanese ancestry, whatever their nationality or residence, was a hallmark of racism prevalent in the West, and Clark's actions fit the pattern of racism perfectly.

Like Roger Daniels's study of the leaders of the anti-Japanese movement in California, this essay treats a single episode in the public career of Chase Clark. Daniels cautions against evaluating the total career of a public official on the basis of one situation, no matter how significant. It would be particularly inappropriate to so evaluate Clark. The governor's behavior in the wartime relocation situation stands in sharp contrast to his otherwise capable and benevolent public service. His political success—he had served several terms in the Idaho legislature and had been mayor of Idaho Falls—is attributable more to his friendly, open political style and sound administration than to bombast. Although it is possible that political expediency motivated Clark to take a strong anti-Japanese position, it is likelier that, at a time when wartime sentiment outweighed tolerance and reason, he reacted emotionally to an unfamiliar and pressing situation.[28]

Clark's stand appears to have been popular, yet there is no evidence that it was a strategy for gaining political support. To the contrary, in other wartime matters the governor showed that he was willing to take political risks. Despite spirited public resistance, for example, he released inmates of the Idaho State Penitentiary who were eligible for military service, and refused to back down from his decision. Moreover, the admission at the Salt Lake City conference of his prejudice and faulty reasoning on the Japanese relocation issue suggests that he realized he was responding uncharacteristically. Had Clark followed conscience rather than emotion, he might have heeded Milton Eisenhower's appeal, regardless of popular opinion. As it was, his anti-Japanese activity stands out as an aberration in a record of fair-minded, competent leadership.

In any case, Clark apparently neither benefitted from nor suffered politically for his actions. When he sought reelection in 1942, he was unopposed in the Democratic primary, then faced Republican C.A. Bottolfsen in the general election. Bottolfsen had been the incumbent governor when Clark defeated him in 1940 by more than 2,000 votes. During his campaign to regain the governorship, Bottolfsen tried to use Clark's prisoner release program against him, but he made no issue of Clark's position on Japanese relocation. The 1942 contest was even closer than its predecessor; Bottolfsen's victory was not announced until nearly a week after election day.[29]

Following his defeat, Clark was appointed federal judge for Idaho, a position he filled with distinction until his death over two decades later. During his judicial service, he greatly improved the process of naturalization of new citizens, thereby aiding alien Japanese who sought American citizenship after the enactment of a new naturalization statute in 1952. Perhaps because of this involvement, Idaho's Japanese Americans forgave Clark for the part he played in the relocation episode. When a group of Japanese Americans held a dinner celebrating their naturalization under the new law, they invited him to address them.[30]

Although Japanese Americans in Idaho were able to forgive Clark, their experience and Clark's place in it should not be forgotten. To some, the position he took during the early days of the Second World War may have seemed fearless and patriotic, but in retrospect it appears to have been nothing more, or less, than a combination of xenophobia and racism. His reaction to the evacuation and relocation of Japanese and Japanese Americans was but a reflection of the persistent racism that has flawed the history of the United States. Chase Clark deserves to be remembered for his commendable public service and for his conciliation with Idaho's Japanese American community; it is worthwhile, however, to remember—and reflect upon—his shortcomings in World War II, for they were not his alone but America's as well.

### Editor's Note

\* Idaho was not the only western state with a racist governor. Roger Daniels discussed California leadership in his books *The Decision to Relocate the Japanese Americans* (1975) and *The Politics of Prejudice: The Anti-Japanese Movement in California and the Struggle for Japanese Exclusion* (1962). Among all the western governors, only Governor Ralph Carr of Colorado, a conservative Republican, objected publicly to the incarceration of Japanese Americans. See Adam

Schrager's *The Principled Politician: The Ralph Carr Story* (Fulcrum, 2008). Carr welcomed anyone displaced by the forced removal to Colorado and saw to it that no Japanese American residents of Colorado were deprived of their basic freedoms. Carr had insufficient power to refuse the federal decision to locate one of the ten camps, Granada War Relocation Center, also known as Amache, in his state.

## Notes

1. *Salt Lake City Tribune*, November 22, 1941.
2. *Idaho Daily Statesman* (Boise), February 28, 1942 (hereafter cited as *Statesman*).
3. *Twin Falls Times-News*, March 2, 1942.
4. *Statesman*, March 13, 15 (quotations), 1942.
5. Ibid., March 5, 14 (quotation), 1942.
6. *Statesman*, March 15, 1942.
7. Radio Address by Gov. Chase Clark, transcript, WRA-WCCA Salt Lake City Conference, April 7, 1942 (C1.03), Japanese American Evacuation and Resettlement Collection (JERS), Bancroft Library, University of California, Berkeley (hereafter cited SLC Radio Address).
8. *Statesman,* March 14, 1942; SLC Radio Address (quotation).
9. Roger Daniels, *The Decision to Relocate the Japanese Americans* (Philadelphia: Lippincott, Williams, and Wilkins, 1975), 55; Paul Okamura to Mike Masaoka, March 3, 1942 (quotation), Box 308, Japanese American Research Project Collection (JARP), Research Library, University of California, Los Angeles.
10. *Pocatello Tribune*, March 17, 1942 (first quotation), clipping in "Japs-NYA and Employment," Box 23, August Rosqvist Collection, Idaho State Historical Society, Boise; *Statesman,* March 27, 1942 (second quotation); Okamura to Clark, March 29, 1942 (third quotation), Box 308, JARP.
11. See "Jap Base of 10,000 Predicted for Idaho Between Caldwell and New Plymouth," *Twin Falls Times-News*, March 24, 1942; *Statesman*, March 20, 1942.
12. *Statesman*, March 20, 29, 1942.
13. Ibid., April 1, 1942; *Twin Falls Times-News*, April 7, 1942.
14. *Statesman,* April 5, 1942.
15. Daniels, 128; Jacobus tenBroek, Edward N. Barnhart, and Floyd W. Matson, *Prejudice, War and the Constitution* (Berkeley: University of California Press, 1954), 123 (quotation).
16. Verbatim Record of Speeches, WRA-WCCA Salt Lake City Conference, April 7, 1942 C 1.03), JERS (hereafter cited SLC Speeches). In a summary of Clark's statement, a WRA clerk wrote: "Gov. Clark stated that perhaps his logic was disturbed because of his strong feelings in the matter"; see "Summary of SLC Conference," mimeograph, 19 (C 1.03) JERS.

17. Roger Daniels, *Concentration Camps USA: Japanese Americans and World War II* (New York: Holt, Rinehart and Winston, Inc., 1971), 94; SLC Speeches (quotations).

18. WRA Correspondence on Meeting and Post-Meeting Policy (C 1.03), JERS (Eisenhower quotation); SLC Radio Address.

19. SLC Radio Address.

20. "Surveys of Public Opinion in Western States on Japanese Evacuation," May 1, 1942 (A 16.01), JERS (first quotation), and Report for Idaho (A 16.03), JERS; *Statesman*, April 9, 1942 (second quotation).

21. *Twin Falls Times-News*, April 12, 23, 30, 1942; and *Statesman*, April 26, 30 (quotation), 1942.

22. *Twin Falls Times-News*, May 3, 1942; *Statesman*, May 15, 16, 1942.

23. *Statesman*, May 23, 1942.

24. Ibid.; E. R. Fryer to M. S. Eisenhower, May 31, 1942, Correspondence, Reports on Employment and Proposals—Employment in Sugar Beet Industry (C 1.07), JERS (first quotation); James Y. Sakamoto to Paul Kirker, June 26, 1942, Box 10-20, Sakamoto Collection, University of Washington Libraries (second quotation).

25. Eisenhower to Clark, June 16, 1942, Correspondence, Reports on Employment and Proposals—Employment in Sugar Beet Industry (C 1.07), JERS (first quotation); *Statesman*, May 27, 1942 (second quotation).

26. *Statesman*, May 26, 1942.

27. Ibid., May 18, 20, 21, 1942.

28. Roger Daniels, *The Politics of Prejudice: The Anti-Japanese Movement in California and the Struggle for Japanese Exclusion* (Berkeley and Los Angeles: University of California Press, 1962), v. Following Clark's defeat in 1942, the *Statesman*, which had opposed his reelection, conceded that Clark had "made Idaho a satisfactory governor. He has shown the faculty of quick and open decision, the hallmark of executive ability. He has steered clear of half-baked ideas. He has indulged in no spending sprees. Above all, he was invariably friendly and ready to hear any man's woes" (November 10, 1942).

29. *Statesman*, September 28, October 26, November 9, 1942.

30. Henry Fujii, Oral History Workshop, JACL Northwest-Intermountain Regional Convention, November 23, 1973, Boise.

# 3

# Japanese American Evacuees as Farm Laborers During World War II

EDITOR'S NOTE

*The sugar-beet industry in Idaho and Utah was busy in the 1940s try-ing to mechanize production in order to reduce requirements for human labor. As the war began, it had not found a solution to the fact that each sugar beet seed was actually a seedball containing many germs capable of sprouting. When these emerged in the spring, severe thinning was required so that only one sprout be left to grow and thrive without competition. The best technology available to do this was human labor—hand thinning the plants one by one. Then during the growing season the fields needed human hands for weeding. In the fall, human labor was the only option for topping the beets (removing the green part of the plant) and loading the heavy beets onto trucks.*

*The war forced the government to compete for sugar against all others who demanded it for chocolate and other sweets. Warfare required sugar to help make the alcohol needed to manufacture smokeless ammunition. The ensuing sugar shortage resulted in the rationing of sugar for civilians. But in 1942, it was the immediate labor shortage for sugar-beet field labor that aroused sugar producers to blame Governor Chase Clark for the difficulty they were having attracting Nikkei to work in Idaho.*

*By 2000, when Bob Sims published this paper on Japanese American farm laborers and their role in saving Idaho's sugar beet crops in 1942 and 1943, he was particularly interested in the experience as lived by the Minidoka workers.—SS*

O n March 6, 1943, the Utah-Idaho Sugar Company placed a four-column, page-long advertisement in the *Minidoka Irrigator*,

This article by Robert Sims originally appeared as "'You Don't Need to Wait Any Longer to Get Out': Japanese American Evacuees as Farm Laborers During World War II," in *Idaho Yesterdays* 44, no. 2 (Summer 2000).

the newspaper of the Minidoka "relocation center," the United States War Relocation Authority camp in Idaho. The company appealed to residents to sign contracts with the company and "be part of America again." The ad, which had at its top a bleak drawing of a concentration

The Utah-Idaho Sugar Company advertises in the March 6, 1943, *Minidoka Irrigator* encouraging Nikkei to work in its sugar beet fields. *Sims Collection, Series 2.*

camp, listed the presumed benefits of such an action, which included the "opportunity to produce more food for freedom, thereby helping America win the war and the peace to follow."[1]

Camp Minidoka (or Hunt, as it was sometimes called) was one of ten internment camps to which Nikkei—persons of Japanese ancestry—were sent as part of mandatory relocation from the West Coast in 1942. The camp, in south central Idaho, was made up primarily of Nikkei from the Seattle and Tacoma areas of Washington and from Portland, Oregon. While agriculture had been a traditional pursuit of Nikkei in the United States, the Northwest had a much smaller percentage so employed in 1940 than did California. In the latter, 47.8 percent of employed Nikkei worked in agriculture; for the Northwest the figure was only 31.4 percent. In addition, many of those in agriculture in the Northwest were essentially urban: 80 percent of the Nikkei population of Washington lived in King and Pierce counties, which contain Seattle and Tacoma.[2] After they had spent several months in assembly centers at North Portland and Puyallup, Washington, the internees began moving to Minidoka in mid-August and continued to do so through mid-September of 1942. Although original plans for these camps called for incarceration for the duration of the war, demands from agricultural interests for utilization of the labor of the imprisoned people brought a change in policy and significantly altered their experience.

By late January of 1942, strong sentiment had developed for the removal of the Nikkei from the West Coast. The first result was a program of voluntary relocation, in which persons of Japanese ancestry were encouraged by the U.S. Army and other federal agencies to leave the military zone that had been established along the West Coast and relocate. While up to 8,000 attempted to do so, many met bitter opposition inland. Principally because of this opposition, General John L. DeWitt, commander of the Western Defense Command, discontinued voluntary relocation on March 29, 1942.

Meanwhile, interest was growing about the employment of Nikkei in seasonal agricultural work in the western states. With acreage limitations lifted and with the drain of manpower out of the region to war industries and the military, growers had a serious problem. As early as February, sugar-beet interests were worrying about how they were going to meet their labor needs. They had an opportunity to express their concerns in early April in Salt Lake City. On April 7, 1942, the War Relocation Authority and Wartime Civil Control Administration authorities met with officials from nine western states to discuss the issue of relocating the Nikkei inland.[3] That the use of the relocated peoples as agricultural labor was a major issue was apparent from the full list of those invited to the conference. In addition to governors of the affected states, they included state extension directors, chairmen of state agricultural war boards, state directors of the Farm Security Administration, representatives of farm organizations, and sugar-beet growers. In fact, fifty-four of the seventy-four individuals at the meeting had some direct relationship to agriculture.[4]

Tom C. Clark, special assistant to the United States Attorney General, opened the meeting with remarks that highlighted the possibility of using the relocated people as agricultural laborers. He said that "the Army cannot win this war unless...we who are in the back, raise things, produce and give them the support that is necessary."[5]

Persons representing the agricultural interests, particularly the sugar-beet growers, expressed a strong desire to use evacuees—all still in West Coast assembly centers—for farm work. The Army, for its part, was open to the possibility if done on a voluntary basis and if state and local authorities would guarantee the safety of both evacuees and the communities and would maintain law and order. The overwhelming response of the governors was that such a condition could not be met; if evacuees were brought into the region, the Army should supply troops to guard them. In concluding remarks to the conference, Milton Eisenhower, who had been director of the WRA for only two weeks, stated that "military guards are not available to provide the necessary supervision.... I can say to those representatives of the sugar beet industry here, and who have been requesting the transfer of evacuees for work in these sugar-beet fields, the answer is no. I don't think you should count on it."[6]

However, shortly after the conference, sentiment among state officials grew more favorable to the employment of evacuees on terms that had been specified by the military. The shift was clearly caused by the crisis facing farming interests and their ability to get public officials to have a change of heart and mind. In response, the Army and the War Relocation Authority established a set of conditions and a procedure for the voluntary recruitment of evacuees from assembly centers for seasonal employment. On May 5, 1942, the first private employment agreement based on these conditions was signed by the governor of Oregon, officials of Malheur County, and the Amalgamated Sugar Company. Four hundred workers were requested for sugar-beet thinning. Recruitment in the North Portland Assembly Center started off well; but when transportation arrived for the first group of recruits, only fourteen would board the train. Most of those who had signed up apparently feared for their safety if they left the assembly center without military protection.

Recruitment was next begun in the Puyallup Assembly Center and was progressing favorably until local newspapers carried a story that Idaho's governor, Chase Clark, had strongly opposed the entrance of any evacuees into the state. After agricultural interests applied pressure on the governor, he softened his stand. His reversal was a dramatic change for Governor Clark, who had been among the most vocal at the Salt Lake City conference in opposition to allowing Japanese into his state. By late May, a WRA official noted: "The past week we have had two governors—Oregon's Charles Sprague and Idaho's Clark—yelling to high heaven that Japanese should have the choice between beet fields and concentration camps." According to this official, "Clark... has been rounded up by the beet growers and has taken a hell of a beating from them for his inflammatory remarks when they wanted the Japanese to come into the state."[7]

During the period of the operation of the assembly centers, the flow of workers to agricultural areas was relatively small; but after the establishment of the main camps, including Minidoka, recruitment of labor began in earnest. The movement from the assembly centers was essentially complete by late September 1942, just in time to meet the fall labor needs of the agricultural regions in which the camps were located. In the harvest season of 1942, Minidoka led the camps in numbers on seasonal leave, although all camps contributed. The call for evacuees to work on the area farms came at a time when many were psychologically inclined to accept outside jobs: initial enthusiasm for making a home in the camps "for the duration" soon waned, and the opportunity to leave for the freedom of the outside was appealing to many.[8]

This aspect of the desire to leave the camp should not be minimized. As one resident recalled in a memoir, "[t]he climate [at Minidoka] differed greatly from that of Portland. Windstorms, sagebrush, unpaved streets and coyotes were new experiences for those of the inner city."[9] A student at Hunt High School wrote: "The war has brought to me many changes, as it has to other people. From a world of sidewalks and tall buildings to another place with dust, sagebrush, and uncomfortable living."[10]

Minidokans who left the camp for agricultural work fell into three categories. The first were those who continued to live in the camp and commuted to the fields each day—an arrangement possible for only a small number. The second group included those who lived on the farms where they worked, with housing provided by the farm owners. The final group, and the largest, included those who lived at labor camps, supervised by the Federal Employment Service or by other government agencies. One such camp was the Twin Falls Migratory Labor Camp, located several miles south of Twin Falls—which was itself some eighteen miles from Minidoka. The camp consisted of 224 unheated units, some of which were small barracks and some family units "about the size of an average trailer."[11]

From this site, hundreds of Minidokans, as well as workers from some of the other camps, went daily to the area fields to work in sugar beets, potatoes, onions, and other area crops. The camp residents were not entirely Nikkei; they included migratory workers from the Midwest and South and Mexican and Jamaican workers as well. An item from the Minidoka newspaper captures some of the cosmopolitan nature of the labor camp:

Louie Sato and his Harmonaires are going to town. Following their Hallowe'en eve debut before the Twin Falls High School Alpha Nu Sorority dance at the IOOF Hall, the Harmonaires made their second appearance at the Filer High School pre-Thanksgiving formal Nov. 16 and more engagements are being lined up by business manager Kaz Shitama. The boys have sweated in the onion and potato fields of Eden, and are now working the frozen grounds of the Twin Falls beet fields... Saturday evenings the Harmonaires treat nisei farm workers with real swing—to dancing at the camp's spacious community hall—and as the weeks rolled on and the fame of the youthful musicians fanned out, more and more jitter-bugging Caucasian youths as well as the more sedate oldsters from Twin Falls and surrounding communities join the Saturday evening dances. Enthusiasm abounds from all who hear of the "kids from camp." A woman taxi driver from Twin Falls and the deputy sheriff are but a few of the more enthusiastic boosters—never failing to attend a session. Sales clerks in the Twin Falls stores ask about the Harmonaires who, with the lanky figure of Louis Sato swinging the baton, brought something new and exciting—the rhythm of the big cities to the migratory labor camp which had hitherto known only the strumming of guitars and the yodellings of the migrant farm workers.[12]

Women from Minidoka harvesting potatoes. *National Archives and Records Administration. Minidoka Relocation Center, 210-CMA-MK-146.*

Many ages and backgrounds were represented in the farm work crews that left Minidoka on buses and trucks provided by their employers. They included young high school students and both men and women. Many, from urban Seattle and Portland, were tackling hard farm work for the first time.[13] Letters to friends recount the experience. "Maggie," released from Puyallup to work thinning sugar beets in Wyoming, wrote to a friend in Seattle early in the summer of 1942:

> They really keep me busy here on the farm. I gradually believe farm life is not fit for a girl like me, especially extensive farming since I last wrote I told you about thinning beets, or did I? I don't remember. Maybe the farm life has got me absent minded. Anyway, after the sugar beet thinning was over, I was laid flat on my back for two solid days. Every time I moved I hurt all over. The work was pretty hard. My knees were red for a week after because I used it [sic] to crawl on. My back ached and boy my wrists hurt from swinging the hoe. I wished you could see how they do it. My cousin took me to the mineral hot springs and that helped a lot.[14]

Since many of the workers were inexperienced, the labor was arduous and unprofitable until they became accustomed to it. Farmers who were patient with new workers were repaid by their diligence and productivity later on.[15] And the farmers whose crops they saved appreciated their efforts. At the end of the harvest season in 1942, the camp newspaper solicited comments from those who employed labor from Minidoka. One southwest Idaho farmer wrote one of the most positive reports:

> The fifteen workers and one chaperone who signed my contract and fulfilled it, satisfied me so much that I decided to write to you. You see, my workers were girls. And although most of them were raised in the city of Portland, they did good conscientious work. During the twenty days of actual work topping beets, they averaged a little over three dollars a day. Many days they worked less than eight hours. Altogether they topped about 950 tons. I think that this crew of Japanese American girls was the only one comprised of girls around Nampa that worked as long as they did topping beets. The Amalgamated Sugar Company is proud of them too. They took movies of

them topping and loading and gave them a special permit to make a tour of the factory....I'm glad that I had the opportunity to meet these young women. Not only because they helped save a large part of my crop, but because of the friendship that has been formed will help to strengthen our country to unity again.[16]

The transition from urbanite to farm laborer was hard on many, and not solely because of the work involved. A Minidokan who worked in the sign shop at the camp followed the enticement of more money in the potato fields but found that there were tradeoffs. In his words, the work "was backbreaking... and I was soft. One thing I didn't like about the place was that it didn't even have a bathtub or shower."[17] As this account reveals, one of the issues important to the workers was living conditions—a matter fully discussed before a contract was signed. According to a camp report: "There probably was some truth in the saying around Hunt that many Idaho farmers had gotten

Farmers bring trucks for the early morning call to collect workers from the Nyssa, Oregon, Farm Security Administration labor camp. *Library of Congress, FSA/OWI Collection, LC-DIG-fsa-8a31248.*

along for years without a bathtub or shower until they wanted to hire Japanese workers."[18]

There were other problems in the field as well, to the extent that the Japanese American Citizens League (JACL) dispatched a team of observers to travel through the area checking on conditions for workers. This effort was initiated because of reports of poor living conditions, some instances of violations of contracts, and conflicts between workers and local people. The observers "found the morale to be fairly high, although they stated that the work was very hard and that they were not used to it." The group traveled through sugar-beet areas of the intermountain west, where they found the workers staying mostly in Farm Security Administration camps and living in tents. Their report observed that tents were "adequate for summer housing, but the tenants were not satisfied with them as late autumn domiciles. We found several laid up with colds and a number of women in rather depressed moods." In general, they found that workers were not satisfied with the living conditions and found it somewhat ironic that, "having been accused so often of lowering the living standards on the Pacific coast, these workers were surprised to find quarters and basic facilities provided that even to them are intolerable."[19]

The report included observations on the conflict occasioned by the mixing of populations. In a discussion on this issue at a special JACL meeting, Mike Masaoka, a longtime official of that organization, expressed a strong view on the matter: "many of these people [the workers] are not aware that the people of this area are not accustomed to seeing so many Japanese who smoke, and drink and conduct themselves in the manner so characteristic, shall we say, of certain Los Angeles elements which we all know."[20]

One important area of conflict was between longtime Nikkei residents of the region and evacuee workers. An Idaho Falls farmer, Mr. Kasai, expressed the view that there had "been some hard feelings between the evacuee beet workers and our local fellows. The evacuee boys do not measure up to our standards and so the local farmers feel they are not receiving their money's worth. Most of the evacuees are more satisfied to work for Caucasians than for Japanese."[21]

One group of workers available for Idaho farm work was found in the schools of Minidoka and the larger labor camps. High-school students were recruited in the fall of 1942 to work in the harvest. The response was so overwhelming that, because of the absence of most of the student body, the Minidoka high school did not begin classes until late November. The next year, following the pattern of all schools in the area, a three-week harvest "vacation" was scheduled to permit students to leave the camp and engage in such work. It began on October 1 and was extended to six weeks, further disrupting the education of over 300 students.[22]

In an effort to encourage camp residents to go out to work in agriculture, camp officials, public officials, and agricultural interests made a specific plea to their "patriotism." The ad cited at the beginning of this article made a direct connection between the willingness to work in sugar beets and patriotism.[23]

An editorial in the *Rupert* [Idaho Farm Labor Camp] *Laborer* made the connection even more explicit when it expressed the view that beet workers were "soldiers." According to the editor, Arita Ikegama: "The beet knife is your sword and the potato basket is your knapsack...at last 'they' know you want to help; 'they' know you want to see the harvest through.... For no one compelled you to do this work. You asked; you even begged for the privilege that is now yours. THIS IS YOUR CHANCE TO DO FOR AMERICA!"[24]

This ploy was not always accepted by the workers. The JACL team that conducted the beet-area survey found growing irritation toward the sugar companies for "their practices of coercion, intimidation and other tactics to force [the workers]...to work after their contracts had been fulfilled." According to the report,

> often the term is employed, "you have an obligation as patriotic American citizens to save the sugar beet crop." The boys feel that exploitation of patriotism on the part of sugar companies is not patriotic in itself....The indications gathered from various sources showing that the sugar lobby is working in Washington to have the Government draft Japanese American citizens for labor in the beet fields is not helping the situation at all.[25]

Minidoka was not the only camp from which evacuees found their way to the farms of the intermountain west, but it led all other camps in the fall of 1942, with over 2,000 out on seasonal leave. It is estimated that as many as 9,000 from all camps were involved in agricultural labor in that year. As the first opportunity to "taste freedom" after the assembly centers and the concentration camps, this was a significant part of the Nikkei wartime experience. For some, it was an opportunity to earn much needed money for more permanent relocation opportunities elsewhere, when those became available. It was also important in that it led to interactions with people outside the camps that were, for the most part, positive. As an editorial in the *Minidoka Irrigator* put it, "fear and distrust are born of ignorance and the unknown."[26]

In many cases, relocation to the agricultural areas of the region became a permanent one. When it became possible to return to the West Coast in early 1945, few took the opportunity immediately. This reluctance was due in part to the fact that some had found new homes and new lives for themselves. Some who did return found too many problems and chose to resettle in the intermountain west. Thus one of the effects of the wartime experience of Japanese Americans was a redistribution of that population. For some, this meant taking up a new life in Idaho or eastern Oregon. A 1946 report on a group of Nikkei at the Caldwell, Idaho, labor camp found that few were considering a return to their old homes. Most of them did not have anything to go back to and were considering putting down roots elsewhere, in some cases giving up their urban life for a rural one.[27]

Even though most who spent time in rural Idaho and in the intermountain west returned to the coast following the war, they were nonetheless shaped in part by that experience. Jim Tanaka was ten years old and living in Portland when the war began. After a few months in the North Portland Assembly Center, the family went directly to the Twin Falls Labor Camp. The family lived there until 1946 when they moved to Ontario, Oregon, where they remained for two years. In 1948 the family moved to Los Angeles, where Jim lives today. Although an urban family before the war, they spent about six years in agriculture. While that was but a small portion of his life, for Jim it was extremely important because of the period of his life in which it occurred, and today he regards it as the most formative of his life.[28] There are many others like Jim whose lives were significantly affected, not only by the camps, but by their experiences outside barbed wire as farm workers in the rural west.

### Notes

1. *Minidoka Irrigator*, March 6, 1943.
2. U.S., Congress, House of Representatives, 77th Congress, 2d sess., House Report 2124, *National Defense Migration*, May, 1942, 104.
3. The WCCA was an agency of the War Department with responsibility for managing the forced removal from the West Coast and the administration of the assembly centers. The WRA was established to conduct and manage the resettlement of the Nikkei, including the administration of the so-called "relocation centers."
4. "List of Those Attending Wartime Civil Control Administration War Relocation Authority [sic] Meeting, Salt Lake City, April 7, 1942," WRA-WCCA Salt Lake City Conference, April 7, 1942, (C 1.03) Japanese American Evacuation and Resettlement Collection (hereafter JERS), Bancroft Library, University of California, Berkeley.
5. "Conference on Evacuation of Enemy Aliens," April 7, 1942, JERS.
6. Ibid., 40.
7. Informal memorandum, Ed Bates to John Bird, San Francisco, May 30, 1942, in "Offices of Governor, Secretary of State and Attorney General and County Grand Juries," (A 15.10) JERS.
8. Harry L. Stafford, Project Director, and John Bigelow, Reports Officer, Minidoka, to E. R. Fryer, Regional Director, WRA, December 24, 1942, Minidoka Report No. 13, (3.95) JERS. By late 1942, the federal government was already looking for ways to move internees out of the camps and resettle them permanently outside the exclusion zone; and students who could enroll in institutions outside the zone were encouraged to do so.
9. Laura Maeda, "Life at Minidoka," *Pacific Historian* 20, no. 20 (Winter 1976).
10. Student essay reproduced in Jerome T. Light, "The Development of a Junior-Senior High School Program in a Relocation Center for People of Japanese Ancestry During the War With Japan," unpublished PhD diss., Stanford University, 1949. Light was principal of the high school at the camp.
11. B. M. Bryan, Lt. Col., Chief, Aliens Division, Office of the Provost General, War Department, to McGill, March 19, 1942, memorandum reproduced in Roger Daniels, editor, *America's Concentration Camps: The Relocation and Incarceration of Japanese Americans, 1942–1945*, vol. 3 of 9 (New York: Garland Publishing Company, 1989).

12. *Minidoka Irrigator*, November 25, 1942.

13. Harry L. Stafford and John Bigelow to E. R. Fryer, n.d., Minidoka Report No. 6-Public Relations (2.07), JERS.

14. "Maggie," Kirby, Wyoming, to Mrs. Emory Andrews, Seattle, June 30, 1942, Emory Andrews MSS (Box 2, ff. 30), University of Washington Library, Seattle.

15. Toraichi Sao, Caldwell, ID, to Jimmie Sakamoto, Minidoka, June 2, 1943, Sakamoto MSS (Box 2, ff. 34), University of Washington Library, Seattle.

16. *Minidoka Irrigator*, December 19, 1942.

17. Dorothy Swaine Thomas, *The Salvage: Japanese American Evacuation and Resettlement* (Berkeley: University of California Press, 1952), 524.

18. Minidoka Report No. 13, 12.

19. Minutes, JACL Special Emergency Conference, November 17–24, 1942, Salt Lake City, Utah, Supplement #6, Beet Field Survey, G. F. Inagaki and Scotty H. Tsuchiya.

20. Minutes, JACL Conference, 98.

21. Ibid., 42.

22. *Pacific Citizen*, October 30, 1943.

23. *Minidoka Irrigator*, March 6, 1943.

24. *Rupert Laborer*, November 14, 1942.

25. Beet Field Survey. See note 19.

26. *Minidoka Irrigator*, October 9, 1943.

27. War Agency Liquidation Unit (formerly War Relocation Authority), U.S. Department of the Interior, *People in Motion: The Postwar Adjustment of the Evacuated Japanese Americans* (Washington, DC: Government Printing Office, 1948), 80.

28. James K. Tanaka, interview with author, Los Angeles, CA, July 29, 1995.

4

# The "Free Zone" Nikkei: Japanese Americans in Idaho and Eastern Oregon in World War II

EDITOR'S NOTE

*Bob Sims's early papers described the history of racial discrimination against Japanese and Japanese Americans, as well as highlights of Governor Clark's racism after Pearl Harbor. In 1983 the Commission on Wartime Relocation and Internment of Civilians reported in* Personal Justice Denied *that the broad, historical causes shaping the decisions to force the removal and relocation of Japanese and Japanese American people from the West Coast were "racial prejudice, war hysteria, and failure of political leadership."*

*These three causes are abstractions until someone paints a historical portrait of what those things actually looked like at the time. What does someone with "war hysteria" actually do, for example? Sims revisited Idaho Nikkei experience in light of this trio of the commission's findings. He shows the extent to which racism, leader-authorized civil rights abuses, and "wartime hysteria" helped introduce negative divisions among people and degrade a sense of community. Regrettably for the legacy of Idaho, its own governor was an example of a failure of political leadership.—SS*

---

In August 1942, during the period when Nikkei from the Puyallup Assembly Center were moved by train to Minidoka, their route took them through Nampa, Idaho.[1] In a letter to a friend in Seattle, a young man gave the following account: "At 9 a.m. we stopped in

This article by Robert Sims was published in *Nikkei in the Pacific Northwest: Japanese Americans and Japanese Canadians in the Twentieth Century*, Louis Fiset and Gail M. Nomura, eds., Seattle: Center for the Study of the Pacific Northwest in association with University of Washington Press, 2005.

Nampa and there were two Japanese at the station who had left Seattle long before the evacuation. I thought how ironic that we should see two Japanese who were free to do as they pleased while we, by the trainloads, were being herded into camps."[2]

This account points out the presence of an often-overlooked aspect of the lives of Nikkei during the war years—the different experiences of those from the West Coast who were imprisoned and those who, by virtue of living outside Military Area 1, were not.[3] The latter group lived in what came to be referred to as the "free zone," and persons of Japanese ancestry living there were free of most of the restrictions imposed on the former. The two populations had much in common in their histories and considerable intermingling during the war. In

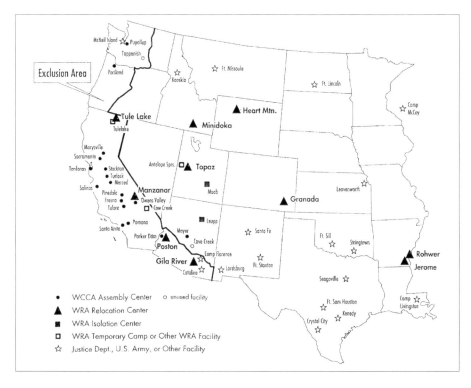

The "exclusion zone," from which Nikkei were encouraged and then forced to leave their homes, was the area west of the boundary line shown through Washington, Oregon, California, and Arizona. *From the book* Confinement and Ethnicity, *Jeffrey Burton et al., Tucson, AZ: National Park Service, 1999*

fact, those from the West Coast who moved inland during the period of "voluntary 'relocation'" and those who left the camps to work in the region became "free zoners" themselves, thus blurring the distinctions between the two groups.[4]

The so-called "voluntary relocation" began following the first announcement that Nikkei were to be excluded from the West Coast and continued until March 29, 1942, when a proclamation by the head of the Western Defense Command halted it. By that time, almost 5,000 people had moved to sites inland, hoping to escape the forced evacuation which was on the horizon. Colorado was the most attractive destination, receiving 1,963. Utah followed with 1,519, Idaho was third with 305, and the eastern portions of Washington and Oregon received 208 and 115 respectively.[5] Those who moved inland represent a significant increase in the number of Nikkei already residing in these areas. Those who moved to Idaho equaled about one-fourth of that state's Nikkei population in 1942. New Nikkei coming into eastern Washington and Oregon almost doubled Nikkei populations in those areas. The circumstances between imprisoned people and those who were already residing in the region often made for stresses and conflicts between the groups as they each tried to cope with their wartime situation. Their relationship was complicated by "voluntary evacuation" and by the leave programs of the War Relocation Authority, both of which resulted in considerable numbers of the excluded people working and living in the "Free Zone."

The areas discussed in this paper are primarily the State of Idaho and Malheur County in Oregon, with occasional references to Spokane County, Washington. The latter two areas are contiguous to Idaho on its western border and, as such, have cultural and economic ties to the state. These areas represent "case studies" that vary in important respects from either Colorado or Utah. One important difference is in the character of the political leadership. Idaho's governor, unlike Colorado's, was openly hostile to the presence of Nikkei in the state, either as "voluntary relocatees" or as incarcerated people. In that, he differed even from Utah's governor, who was willing to accept the presence of the relocated people if they were in camps guarded by the military. This difference had a great deal of impact on the nature of the relationship between the Idaho Nikkei and those who came from the West Coast, particularly during the "voluntary" period. Also, unlike Colorado and Utah, Idaho was contiguous to the exclusion area, and this played a significant role, as people were able to leave the camps but were not yet able to return to their former homes. Many of these chose to move as close as they could in anticipation of an eventual return home. Otherwise, the history of the Nikkei in Idaho and the adjacent portions of Oregon and Washington was remarkably similar to that of their counterparts elsewhere in the Rocky Mountain region.

Japanese railroad workers in rugged terrain. *Sims Collection, Box 24, Folder 4.*

Much of the prewar population in these areas was due to employment of Nikkei in railroad construction in the last half of the nineteenth century and the first part of the twentieth. The development of the sugar beet industry also accounts for some of the early settlement in the region. From those early beginnings, Idaho had about 1,500 Nikkei by 1930. Like their counterparts on the West Coast, they faced a range of discriminations that helped define their status on the eve of World War II. Long before the United States Supreme Court established the principle of no citizenship for the Issei in the 1922 Ozawa case, a federal judge in Boise denied an Idaho Issei's petition for citizenship in federal district court in Boise. In his opinion the judge cited language from the federal naturalization statute, which held that only Caucasians and persons of African ancestry could be naturalized.[6]

In 1923 Idaho passed an anti-Japanese land law patterned after that of California, which passed its legislation in 1913.[7] The state legislature had considered such a law in every session since 1917 before it was adopted. The year before its adoption, an article in the *Idaho Farmer* sounded the alarm against the "Japanese Invasion." It argued that land laws restricting Japanese ownership of land in other states were driving them to Idaho. "A number of Japanese driven out of Oregon and California and Washington, and some who have been driven off of Indian reservations by a recent ruling of the department of the interior, are coming to Idaho and offering rent that it is claimed white men cannot pay and make a profit....It is hoped to evolve some method of preventing the Japanese from invading the Boise Valley."[8] The 1923 land law was designed to do just that. In debates over this legislation in the previous legislative session, the proposed bill was usually referred to as the "Japanese exclusion bill."[9] While small farmers seemed to support this legislation, the region's sugar companies opposed its passage and were successful for several sessions in killing it. The passage of a similar law in Oregon at that time, coupled with Washington's adoption of an anti-Japanese land bill two years earlier, helped overcome opposition to the bill and add credence to the alarmist rhetoric noted above.

In 1922 the state's anti-miscegenation law was amended to include a prohibition against Japanese marrying Caucasians. The original statute had included prohibition against Caucasians marrying "negroes, mullatoes, and mongolians," the latter seemingly referring to Chinese.[10] These laws were reminders of their second-class status.

Meanwhile the Nisei population was coming of age and becoming more visible in the communities. In the Boise Valley, Nisei students were excelling in school. In 1934 a Nisei was the valedictorian of the state's largest high school. In that year and the one following, the valedictorians at another Boise Valley high school were Nisei, children of longtime families in the area.[11] Other area Nisei were achieving success and acceptance in local colleges, including one young man who was

Michi Suyehira and son Henry, circa 1934. *Courtesy of Mrs. Itano Hosoda, Sims Collection, Box 22, Folder 6.*

the head of the cheerleading squad at Northwest Nazarene College in Nampa, and several who played on athletic teams at the College of Idaho throughout the 1930s.[12] There is little evidence that these young people had any realistic hopes of moving into careers other than farming, but in 1935 a Nisei woman passed her examination to practice medicine in Idaho. Dr. Kimi Nojima of Idaho Falls attended college at the University of Utah and studied medicine at the University of Michigan. She opened a practice in Pocatello that year, one of the centers of Idaho's limited Nikkei population.[13]

By 1930, although Nikkei resided in almost all of Idaho's forty-four counties, the population tended to be concentrated at opposite ends of the state. More than a third lived in three counties in the upper Snake River region: Bannock, Bingham, and Bonneville, which reflected the influence of Nikkei involvement in railroad work and early sugar beet operations in that area. About two hundred lived in Canyon County, at the extreme western edge of the state, adjacent to Malheur County in Oregon. A decade later, although this population had been reduced somewhat, it maintained the same general pattern. There was some interaction among the Nikkei in different parts of the state, including baseball tournaments, and some with the development of Nisei clubs, forerunners of the Japanese American Citizens League in the region. As early as 1936 the JACL attempted to organize these clubs as part of that organization and had achieved some success on the eve of World War II, with chapters in Boise Valley, Idaho Falls, Pocatello, and Rexburg, all communities with significant Nikkei involvement in farming. The region also saw two chapters in Utah, at both Salt Lake City and Ogden.[14]

A Nisei team in the 1930s, Mrs. Itano Hosada's son among them, at a baseball tournament. *Courtesy of Mrs. Itano Hosoda, Sims Collection, Box 22, Folder 6.*

Meanwhile, in Oregon, the Nikkei community in Malheur County was growing, due in part to farming opportunities resulting from the building of the Malheur dam in the mid-1930s. That population was at 137 in 1940, barely more than one-half of one percent of the county's total population. But even by 1938, the community was robust and successful enough to build a "Japanese Hall" for community functions.[15] Bimonthly church meetings were held there as well as "dances, parties and occasional Japanese movies or plays."[16]

Even with such advances, the degree of integration into the general community life was limited, and the Nikkei in this area, as elsewhere, were vulnerable at the time of Pearl Harbor. The actions of the United States government against the Nikkei have been judged harshly by history. Justified at the time on the grounds of military necessity, we now know no such necessity existed. But the actions were taken in an atmosphere of hatred and fear undergirded by a history of racism and fanned by the winds of confusion and hysteria in the days following Pearl Harbor. The Commission on Wartime Relocation and Internment of Civilians, in its 1982 report, determined that this unnecessary decision occurred because of three factors: racism, wartime hysteria, and failure of political leadership.[17]

Idaho provided its share of all three. Racism was evidenced by the legal discriminations imposed over the half century of the Nikkei's presence in the state. The general panic that followed the attack at Pearl Harbor contributed to a civil rights disaster of major proportions. The anti-Japan rhetoric of the West Coast made its way inland and resulted in panic headlines in Idaho's newspapers: "Japs May Fly All the Way to Idaho!" Nationalist fervor got out of hand, with treatment of Idaho's Nikkei population at the hands of their neighbors ranging from expressions of support to acts of violence. In Caldwell, a Japanese American home was hit by gunfire; Japanese American homes were raided by the FBI and local police; and various business, fraternal, and "patriotic" organizations passed resolutions calling for the internment of all enemy aliens for the duration.[18]

In Idaho Falls the war brought the closure of the Japanese meeting hall. This building had been used as a Japanese language school and had also served as a meeting place for the community. In Ontario, Oregon, local Japanese signed their community hall over to the city in the hopes that would ensure the safety of the building. They were acting in good faith that, after the crisis, it would be returned to them, which it was. Ontario proved to be a "haven" of sorts for Nikkei relocating during the "voluntary" period, and others arrived on seasonal and later permanent relocation from the camps.[19]

Compounding the problem for Idaho's Nikkei was the capture of over a thousand Idaho employees of the Morrison-Knudsen Construction Company, who were working on construction projects for the military in the Pacific. These men were captured in the days and weeks following Pearl Harbor, and no word as to their condition or whereabouts was received until February 19, 1942.[20] Newspaper accounts of atrocities committed by the Japanese military during this period placed a special weight on the families of those captured in the Pacific, and this situation may account for much of the heightened feelings toward Japanese in the area. A business associate of the head of the company, in a letter to a colleague, argued against bringing Japanese to Idaho for fear that some could be killed, which might lead to retaliation against Idahoans being held by Japan. "Better send the Japs that we intern to some state that does not have workers interned in Japan," he wrote.[21] This was taking place during a period when Governor Chase A. Clark's rhetoric against allowing Japanese into the state reached its highest intensity.

The animosity toward persons of Japanese ancestry occurred in other parts of the state as well. Denny Yasuhara, who later served as national president of the Japanese American Citizens League (JACL), was sixteen years old when the war began, living with his family in Bonners Ferry in northern Idaho. The family was forced to leave their home and relocate to Spokane because of harassment and abuse, including allegations of disloyalty, even from white people who had known the family for years.[22] Idaho Nikkei were confused and concerned in the early days of World War II. They attempted to show their loyalty to the United States through a variety of means, including a telegram to the governor pledging support and the purchase of savings bonds.[23]

A number of the restrictions imposed on West Coast Nikkei affected them as well, including the freezing of bank accounts of aliens from countries with which the United States was at war. In the week after Pearl Harbor, an official of the First Security Banking Corporation wrote to all branch managers in the region confirming that "the property of all Japanese nationals in the possession of the banks are frozen unconditionally until further order." Further, he indicated they were not to pay any checks or allow the transfer of any Japanese nationals' bank accounts in any manner, shape, or form. "For instance, supposing you have bonds as collateral to a Jap's note to you.

You have no authority to accept the payment of the note and release the security. As a practical matter, collect the money to pay the note if you possibly can, but do not release his security."[24]

Although this position was later modified, some restrictions remained and constituted a hardship on many. This included placing a limit on the amount that could be withdrawn monthly from a bank account.

Another form of discrimination occurred at local ration boards. In Twin Falls, a long-time Issei farmer in the county was denied ration stamps to purchase tires for an automobile. He was rejected by the county ration board, which ruled that "rationing regulations allow only American citizens to acquire rubber for motor vehicles."[25]

Other farmers in the region, particularly in eastern Washington and eastern Oregon, reported difficulty obtaining crop loans in 1942 because of the uncertainty of the status of Nikkei in that area. Nikkei were excluded from the eastern part of California, which was part of Military Area No. 2, and some feared that that order might be extended to include the eastern portions of Washington and Oregon as well. Those rumors persisted throughout early 1942.

Throughout the region Issei employees of railroads were dismissed, some having put in decades of service. In Idaho Falls, two men who had worked for the railroad for forty-one years lost their jobs a few days after the war broke out. They were detained and eventually placed in Heart Mountain, the camp in Wyoming.[26]

While the Nikkei in the interior were suffering such hardships, those in California and western Oregon and Washington were bracing for even greater difficulties. Demands for their removal began immediately after Pearl Harbor, and those demands turned into official policy by late winter. On February 19, 1942, President Franklin Roosevelt signed Executive Order 9066, which authorized the removal of any or all persons from prescribed military areas for purposes of national defense. This authority was granted to the commander of the Western Defense Command, Lt. Gen. John L. DeWitt. On March 2 he issued Public Proclamation No. 1, establishing the western half of Washington, Oregon, and California, and the southerly half of Arizona as Military Area No. 1. The initial effort at removal was the so-called voluntary relocation, and from March 2 to March 29, "nearly anyone who was affected by the proposed evacuation program...was encouraged...to leave."[27] As that policy was discussed and put in place, the interaction of Nikkei from the two regions became significant. According to a study done in 1946, "When relocatees were sent into this area [eastern Washington] where there had been no evacuation of the few Japanese who had lived here for years, friction resulted with Caucasians and, to some extent, among the resident Japanese and those who came into the area during this period." This friction, together with that which already existed because of the war with Japan, led to occasional outbreaks of violence. Throughout the intermountain West, local Nikkei communities found themselves in some peril if they were too aggressive in helping friends and family relocate from the West Coast. In Spokane, leaders of the Nikkei community there publicly took the position that they would "discourage any coast Japanese from coming to the Spokane area."[28]

In early March some groups of Nikkei in the Pacific Northwest were formulating plans to find new homes in the interior. However, they found that "inland communities were giving the voluntary evacuees a cold reception." In Tacoma, a Japanese American community leader said, "opposition of Idaho and eastern Washington communities has kept Japanese from evacuating voluntarily."[29]

Meanwhile, in Idaho, Governor Chase Clark continued his crusade to keep Nikkei out of the state. Clark was among the most outspoken and racist public officials over the matter of the removal to the interior, and he was determined to keep the Nikkei out. As West Coast Nikkei sought out opportunities inland, many looked to friends, family, and acquaintances in the intermountain region. But because of intense anti-Japanese sentiment, this proved to be difficult, and it put the region's Nikkei in an awkward position. In early March, Paul Okamura, president of the Pocatello JACL, wrote to Mike Masaoka, the executive secretary of the national organization, telling him that, because of Governor Clark's attitude, the local Nikkei's "hands are tied so far as helping the Pacific coast mass evacuation problem to any great extent." He continued to write "a certain amount of Niseis could come here without causing undue alarm, providing some employment arrange-

ments have been made or that they have relatives here who would
be responsible for them." He also deemed it wise "that these people,
if they come here, come in as small a group as possible at intervals
rather than a large group at one time." He went on to indicate that
they were having difficulty locating a home for a local family who had
been forced to move, and that "some property owners are reluctant
towards leasing ground to the local Japanese."[30]

He had reason to be concerned about Clark, who, less than two
weeks later, issued a warning through the press to "American Japanese
in Idaho that it is better to refrain from any activity in encouraging
other Japanese to come into Idaho, because it might result in the
exclusion of all."[31]

Idaho JACL presidents, meeting at Caldwell a week later, passed
a resolution "pledging all members of the league in Idaho to discourage all evacuee relatives, friends, and others" from coming to Idaho.
"While we sympathize with those Japanese who are required to leave
California and other restricted districts, we can not look at it from an
individual point of view but must consider it from the viewpoint of
public welfare," according to a spokesperson for the organization.[32]
Paul Okamura wrote to Governor Clark asking that he "make a distinction between 'coast evacuee Japanese Americans and those of us who
reside in Idaho permanently.'"[33] There is no record of a response from
the governor, who continued his position in opposition to Japanese
coming into the state.

Local Nikkei had learned to be wary of Clark, for he was a danger-
ous man on this topic. In a letter to a Pocatello newspaper, he said:

> I am not ready to sell the State of Idaho to the Japanese for a few
> dollars, while our American boys are dying to prevent Japan from
> taking the State of Idaho and our entire nation by force of arms. I
> appeal to every citizen of the State of Idaho not to sell land to the
> Japanese. If we let them come now, and by the purchase of land,
> settle themselves here, we will soon be sick of them. …The ones
> who were born here are more dangerous than those born in Japan
> because the latter, to some extent, may appreciate their escape from
> despotism, but those born here are taught that Japan is heaven and
> their Emperor is the Almighty.[34]

These were strange words from a man who, in November 1941, had been the guest speaker at a gathering of Nikkei from throughout the intermountain area, the purpose of which was "to impress upon fellow countrymen their loyalty to the United States." Mike Masaoka, who attended the conference, said that the purpose of the meeting was to explain the policies and objectives of the JACL, a goal he felt to be important because, as he said:

> In these critical days, when the policies of many organizations representing various nationality groups may be viewed with suspicion by certain individuals not intimately acquainted with the aims, ideals and leadership of such associations, it becomes necessary and proper in the public interest that such fraternal and educational orders as the Japanese American Citizens League make clear their policies and objective.[35]

In spite of Clark's objections and the lack of full cooperation on the part of local people, some Nikkei did arrive during the period of

Intermountain District meeting of the JACL, late November 1941, at the Shanghai Café in Pocatello. Governor Chase Clark (back of the room, center) declared at this meeting, "We must realize that we are all, first and last, Americans." *Sims Collection, Box 22, Folder 7.*

"voluntary evacuation," the result of family and friends willing to risk defying the governor.

When that was ended by official order on March 27, 1942, the relationship between the Free Zone Nikkei and the relocatees entered a new phase. A young woman who had come to Caldwell during the voluntary period wrote to a friend in Seattle, "The prejudice here has died down immensely since the voluntary evacuation has been stopped."[36] Part of the new situation involved the imposition of curfews in a number of towns in Idaho and elsewhere in the region. The "rules" were applied rather spottily, with some area towns, like Weiser, Idaho, observing them, and others, like Ontario, Oregon, not. These "town" curfews especially affected farmers because some farm operation activities, such as storage, shipping, equipment repair, and the like, involved going into towns often at the end of a workday.

Within days following the ending of "voluntary evacuation," announcements were made concerning the placement of large "relocation centers" in the region, to be operated by a new civilian agency, the War Relocation Authority, established by an Executive Order 9102 on March 18, 1942.[37] The news brought additional pressure on local Nikkei in that anti-Japanese feelings became even stronger.

The war was not going well for the United States in the Pacific, and each bit of bad news seemed to fan anti-Japan feelings in the region. Vociferous protests were launched over the placement of one of these camps, the Minidoka Relocation Center, in south central Idaho, even though a major force in the placement of the camp was the need for laborers for the region's agricultural industry. Some of these protests came from the same farmers who would later benefit from the presence of the camps. Individual farmers and some organizations protested in part because they were uncertain of the impact of the camp on available water supplies for agriculture.

In a number of curious ways, the Minidoka Relocation Center's construction and placement operated against the local Nikkei. Many local employers and some farmers were upset that the construction of the camp would drain the local labor supply and drive up wages, which they would have to pay to get good employees. Others complained that the camp's operation, which depended in part on Caucasian "appointed personnel," might exacerbate the problem of shortages in critical areas. In fact, a number of local teachers and a local doctor went to work in the camp.

Anti-Japanese attitudes and actions increased with the building of the Minidoka camp.[38] Some of these actions did not affect a large number of people directly, but they demonstrated the strong attitudes present. In the election campaign of the fall of 1942, the opponent of the incumbent Twin Falls county treasurer placed a political advertisement in the local newspaper criticizing the incumbent for employing a young Japanese American woman in her office, claiming that the treasurer obviously did not understand the feelings of families of "boys who lost their lives at Pearl Harbor, Wake Island, Midway, Guam and [the] Solomon Islands..., when they have to walk into the county treasurer's office and pay their taxes to a Japanese." In response the treasurer pointed out that the young woman in question was an American citizen, a native of Twin Falls, and a recent honor graduate of the local high school. But this did not satisfy those who chose to make no distinction between Japanese in Japan and Americans of Japanese ancestry. The incumbent lost the election, and the employee in question was dismissed when the new treasurer took office.[39]

In the summer of 1943 the Twin Falls Kiwanis Club passed a resolution protesting against public use of "languages of countries with which the United States is at war." While the language of the resolution would seem to include the German and Italian languages, the only issue was the use of the Japanese language by individuals in town on passes from Minidoka. While the camp newspaper, the *Minidoka Irrigator*, issued a mild protest, it also printed a letter from an officer of the Magic Valley JACL. The writer of the letter acknowledged that some of the behaviors in question were from those of "nisei from other relocation camps." He continued,

> it has been noted that a good many visitors from Hunt, including families, argue and talk in public... There have been complaints of groups of niseis getting intoxicated and making scenes in public. It so happened that on the Saturday night our last officers meeting was held, the largest group of disgraceful drunks were out. After seeing

with our own eyes these sights, hearing the course [sic] language being used, we feel something must be done about it. This small group is making our public relations work very difficult.[40]

The same writer wrote again to the camp newspaper on this topic. He said a prominent local Caucasian businessman who complained about the continuation of this practice had contacted him.

He knew they were able to speak English because they were talking to the proprietor. To some people it makes little difference but to others it serves to create unnecessary suspicion. The [Japanese] residents of Idaho have always realized the necessity of speaking in English. The Issei parents very seldom go out in public unless they would speak English, and when conversing among themselves they do so quietly. However, these people, both issei and nisei, from the relocation center, do not seem to realize that they are doing themselves harm, and making their positions increasingly difficult in the face of growing anti-Japanese sentiment in this state.

He went on to write, "We must ask all loyal Japanese Americans to 'be Americans.'"[41]

One issue concerning wartime treatment of the Nikkei centers around their use as agricultural laborers. The enormous demand for farm workers had a lot to do with both the existence and the placement of the camps. Even before the large centers were open, imprisoned Nikkei were urged to leave the assembly centers to work in agricultural areas in the intermountain West. The first group to do so went from the North Portland Assembly Center to Malheur County in May 1942. This continued with the operation of the large permanent centers, and thousands more followed in the next two years.

The movement from the assembly centers to the large camps was essentially complete by late September 1942, just in time to meet the fall labor needs of the agricultural regions in which the camps were located. In the harvest season of 1942, Minidoka led the camps in numbers on seasonal leave, although most of the camps contributed.[42] In fact, in most respects, the contributions made by workers released from the camps went a long way toward creating a climate of acceptance for the Nikkei. As one historian has noted, "the Nikkei received praise from nearly all quarters and were credited with saving the beet sugar crop in Idaho, Montana, Wyoming, and Utah."[43] Repeat performances in subsequent years earned a great deal of respect for Japanese Americans.

While the overall experiences of the Nikkei as farm workers were undoubtedly positive, in some instances the tactics of camp officials and employers created bitterness on the part of workers. They often found that promises made to lure them from camp were not met. The complaints arose very early in the process and centered on poor living conditions, violations of the terms of contracts, and conflicts between workers and local people. This led JACL to dispatch a team of observers into the agricultural areas in October and November 1942 to report on conditions. They traveled throughout the sugar beet areas of the intermountain West, where they found the workers living mostly in Farm Security Administration camps and some living in tents. Their report observed that tents were "adequate for summer housing, but the tenants were not satisfied with them as late autumn domiciles. We

Japanese Workers
Win Praise
of
Sugar Beet Growers

Since the Minidoka War Relocation Center was established only slightly over a year ago, thousands of volunteer victory workers from Hunt have helped to thin, cultivate and harvest sugar beets for our growers in Idaho and other intermountain states. Thus precious crops have been saved. Beet growers and other farmers have been able to maintain production despite the manpower shortage; evacuees have been given a start toward relocation when in the beginning, at least, there were few if any other relocation opportunities.

**The Amalgamated Sugar Co.**

Home Office: Ogden, Utah    Factories in Idaho, Utah and Oregon

The Amalgamated Sugar Company thanks Minidoka's sugar beet workers with an ad in the *Minidoka Interlude. Courtesy of Friends of Minidoka.*

found several laid up with colds and a number of women in rather depressed moods." They found it somewhat ironic that "having been accused so often of lowering the living standards on the Pacific coast, these workers were surprised to find quarters and basic facilities provided that even to them are intolerable."[44]

The report included observations on the conflict occasioned by the mixing of populations. In a discussion on this issue at a special JACL meeting in November, Mike Masaoka expressed a strong view on the matter. He believed that "many of these people [the workers] are not aware that the people of this area are not accustomed to seeing so many Japanese who smoke, and drink and conduct themselves in the manner so characteristic, shall we say, of certain Los Angeles elements which we all know."[45] Masaoka, who grew up in Salt Lake City, epitomized some of the cultural differences between the local Nikkei and those who had come from the West Coast, particularly those from urban areas.

Farm Security Administration migrant camps did not ordinarily provide electricity for family tents. Japanese Americans at Nyssa, OR, advocated for it, and the sugar beet companies and town arranged for the wiring. *Library of Congress, FSA/OWI 8c25254u-1.*

One important area of conflict was between long-time Nikkei residents of the region and evacuee workers. An Idaho Falls farmer, Mr. Kasai, expressed the view that there had "been some hard feelings between the evacuee beet workers and our local fellows. The evacuee boys do not measure up to our standards and so the local farmers feel they are not receiving their money's worth. Most of the evacuees are more satisfied to work for Caucasians than for the Japanese."[46]

Some workers also felt pressured into doing agricultural work and felt that the pressure was often unfair. In an effort to encourage camp residents to go out to work in agriculture, camp officials, public officials, and agricultural interests made a specific plea to their "patriotism." An ad for recruiting workers placed in the *Minidoka Irrigator* by a sugar company made an explicit connection between the willingness to work in sugar beet farming and patriotism, calling it "an opportunity to produce more food for freedom, thereby helping America win the war and the peace to follow."[47]

An editorial in the Idaho Farm Labor Camp's *Rupert Laborer* made the connection even more explicit when it expressed the view that beet workers were "soldiers." According to the editor, Arita Ikegami,

> The beet knife is your sword and the potato basket is your knapsack...
> At last 'they' know you want to help; 'they' know you want to see the
> harvest through... For no one compelled you to do this work. You
> asked; you even begged for the privilege that is now yours. THIS IS
> YOUR CHANCE TO DO FOR AMERICA![48]

In the discussion over the agricultural "survey" at the November 1942 special meeting of the JACL, an Idaho Free Zone farmer took the side of the employers over the workers.

> If these people are to be ambassadors of good will, they should be careful
> of unjust demands because they will make the Caucasian elements bit-
> ter and antagonistic....The workers recruited for the beet fields should
> be men who really want to work and not those who want to go out
> and have a good time... If we are going to show the American people
> that we really are going to help out in the labor shortage, we must go
> out with the idea of helping the war effort as patriotic Americans. We

should think of other things than just earning money. We should think in terms of helping this country win this war.[49]

The cautious approach of JACL to the issues facing the Nikkei in this period was also evident in other discussions at the meeting. A delegate from Poston referred to some instances of Nikkei being refused rooms at a hotel in Boise and suggested that such treatment should be challenged. Mike Masaoka cautioned against this:

> I wonder if such practices won't add to antagonisms and other measures which will be worse than the present type of prejudice. I know that in my travels it is not uncommon for me to be refused service or rooms, but I've always personally thought that it was better to forget the matter and go look for another place to eat or stay than to create a scene as it were.[50]

While the important contribution to Idaho agriculture the relocated people made brought about a greater degree of acceptance through the war years, this should not be overstated. With the exception of a few counties in the western part of the state, the relocated people did not tend to permanently settle in the state. In contrast, by 1950, both Malheur County in Oregon and Spokane County in Washington saw significant increases to their Nikkei populations over the 1940 figures. Malheur's 1,170 Nikkei accounted for about 5 percent of the total population in the county, and Spokane County's Nikkei population moved from 362 in 1940 to 1,171 in 1950. The counties in Idaho that saw the greatest increase between the two census years were Canyon and Washington, in the western part of the state, adjacent to Oregon. Canyon County grew from 149 to 413, and Washington County, with no Nikkei reported in 1940, had 163 Nikkei ten years later. Jerome County, the site of Minidoka, saw an increase of only one Nikkei in the ten years between censuses, and in Twin Falls County, where hundreds of workers from both Minidoka and the Twin Falls labor camp toiled during the war, the Nikkei population moved from 46 to 78.

Certainly the assistance and good will of Free Zone Nikkei helped make reestablishment in new places possible. But it should not be forgotten that whatever successes were achieved were not without difficulties along the way. The history of the actions of the Free Zone Nikkei created a heavy burden for some of the West Coast Nikkei.

More than three decades after the war, there was occasional evidence of bitterness over this. In 1979, during the campaign for redress, a Seattle Nikkei noted that Seattle Japanese Americans "remember that the concentration camps might not have been built if Idaho Japanese Americans had not opposed the immigration of Seattleites from the coast."[51] Whether or not such a view is justified, it reveals the depth of feeling remembered years after the experience. Free Zone Nikkei were under considerable pressure to act exactly as they did even if they knew it was not the right thing to do. And some clearly thought that. Years after the war, an Ontario Nikkei confessed that he was "not too proud of some of the things that went through [his]... mind at that time. I never went out of my way to help anybody."[52]

Another area of "humiliation" recalled with some bitterness by some Seattle Japanese Americans was that of "being used as a source of cheap, forced labor in the same sugar beet fields of Idaho farmers who first turned us away."[53]

The bitterness was also reflected in the planning for a service in 1979 at the Minidoka site celebrating its placement on the National Register of Historic Places. As planning for the event proceeded, differences of opinion soon arose over how the site would be memorialized. Some of the former camp residents living in Seattle wanted to build a mock tower that would be burned as part of the service. In the words of one of the planners, the "purifying flames would help lay the past to rest without forgetting or easing the lessons of the internment experience."[54]

Idaho Nikkei had initiated the idea for the memorial and had worked with the Bureau of Reclamation, the agency controlling the site, to organize the event. The Idaho Nikkei refused to go along with the plan to burn a mock tower, essentially telling those in Seattle that if they wanted to do such a thing they would have to organize it on their own. An Idaho JACL member referred to the proposed tower burning as a "worthless publicity stunt that could damage the image of all Japanese Americans." There was nothing new in such caution. In denouncing the position of the Idaho Nikkei, one of those who had proposed the "tower burning" criticized them for their unreasonable fear of a white backlash, an attitude which reflected their position on related issues over three decades earlier.[55]

In speaking of the Nikkei experience in the Pacific Northwest, one would do well to avoid facile generalizations about the population as a whole. While many experiences of those throughout the region are similar, important distinctions mark the different groups. They were shaped by different forces and saw things in different lights. That Free Zone Nikkei had a different perspective on problems related to the removal and imprisonment of the West Coast Nikkei should not be a matter of surprise. What is less clear is just how far one can go in condemning any group for how they cope with a situation. Free Zone Nikkei acted in what they considered their best interests, even when they clashed with the interests of others. I prefer to think that fear and uncertainty also influenced their behavior, even when that behavior was nothing more than standing by and doing nothing. Recently I asked a Nikkei friend who was living near Nampa in the summer of 1942 if he had gone to the train station during the time of the transfer from North Portland to Minidoka. He told me, with great emotion, "I just didn't have the heart."

## Notes

1. The term Nikkei refers to persons of Japanese ancestry, whether aliens or American citizens.
2. Anonymous to Andrews, 24 August 1942, Emery E. Andrews Papers (Accession No. 1908), University of Washington Libraries, file folder 1105. The inmates at Minidoka were comprised primarily of former Seattle and Portland residents who earlier had been placed in the Puyallup and North Portland assembly centers.
3. Military Area No. 1 was defined as the area lying to the west of the Cascade and Sierra Nevada Mountains in Washington, Oregon, and California; and the southerly half of Arizona. Military Area No. 2 comprised the eastern halves of Washington, Oregon, and California.
4. Initially these involved farm workers, but when leave programs were expanded in 1943, they involved many other types of employment as well.
5. U.S. War Department, *Final Report: Japanese Evacuation from the West Coast, 1942* (Washington, DC: GPO, 1943), 111.
6. *Idaho Register*, November 10, 1905, 3.
7. Oregon passed similar legislation in the same year, and Washington had done so in 1921 with an amendment in 1923 to align it more directly with that of California.
8. *Idaho Farmer*, March 23, 1922, 4.
9. *Idaho Statesman*, February 22, 1921, 5.
10. *1921 Idaho Session Laws*, Section 4596, Article I, Chapter 182.

11. *Japanese American Courier*, May 12, 1934, 4; June 9, 1934, 4; May 11, 1935, 4.

12. Ibid., February 3, 1934, 4; May 4, 1935, 3.

13. Ibid., April 6, 1935, 1.

14. *History of IDC-JACL, 1940–1965*, (n.p.; n.d.), 53.

15. *Japanese American Courier*, December 24, 1938, 4.

16. John deYoung, "Japanese Resettlement in the Boise Valley and Snake River Valley, Sept. 1946," Japanese American Evacuation and Resettlement Collection (JERS), W2.04, Bancroft Library, University of California, Berkeley, 6 (hereafter, JERS followed by file number).

17. Commission on the Wartime Relocation and Internment of Civilians (CWRIC), *Personal Justice Denied: Report of the Commission on Wartime Relocation and Internment of Civilians* (Washington, DC: Government Printing Office, 1982), 18.

18. *Idaho Daily Statesman*, December 28, 1941; March 1, 1942; February 28, 1942.

19. deYoung, JERS, W2.04, 27.

20. *Idaho Daily Statesman*, February19, 1942, 1.

21. E. W. Rising to J. W. Crowe, Chairman, Pacific Island Workers Association, Boise, February 23, 1942. Idaho Reclamation Papers, Idaho Historical Society.

22. Laurie Mercier and Carole Simon-Smolinski, "Idaho's Ethnic Heritage," *Historical Overview* 1 (March 1990), 83–84.

23. *Idaho Daily Statesman*, December 10, 1941.

24. Letter from J. L. Driscoll, Executive Vice President, First Security Bank Corporation, "To All Branch Managers," December 12, 1941. See Robert C. Sims Collection, Box 47, Folder 9 at Special Collections Library, Boise State University.

25. *Twin Falls Times-News*, March 15, 1942, 5.

26. Wayne Yamamura, "Notes on Meeting With Idaho Falls JACL," unpublished typescript, 1976.

27. U.S. War Department, *Final Report*, 102.

28. "Survey of Public Opinion in Western States on Japanese Evacuation, Washington, May 18, 1942," JERS, A16.08, 14.

29. Ibid., 15.

30. Paul Okamura, President, Pocatello JACL, to Mike Masaoka, San Francisco, March 3, 1942, box 308, Pocatello JACL Papers, Japanese American Research Project, University of California, Los Angeles Library (hereafter, JARP).

31. *Idaho Daily Statesman*, March 18, 1942, 1.

32. Ibid., March 27, 1942, 6.

33. Paul Okamura to Chase Clark, Pocatello JACL, Papers, JARP.

34. *Pocatello Tribune*, March 17, 1942.

35. *Salt Lake Tribune*, November 21, 1941, 10.

36. J. to Andrews, May 1942, Emery E. Andrews Papers, file folder 1107. See Robert C. Sims Collection, Box 57, Folder 2, Correspondence of Emery E. Andrews, at Special Collections Library, Boise State University.

37. U.S. War Department, *Final Report*, 50.
38. The camp was built on land controlled by the Bureau of Reclamation, approximately eighteen miles northeast of Twin Falls, the largest community in that region of the state.
39. *Twin Falls Times-News*, October 28, 1942, 3; October 30, 1942, 4.
40. *Minidoka Irrigator*, June 19, 1943, 4. Area residents also knew Minidoka as "Hunt." There was an existing town named Minidoka approximately thirty miles to the east of the camp; "Hunt" was the designated post office address of the center.
41. Ibid., December 18, 1943, 2.
42. Robert C. Sims, "'You Don't Need to Wait Any Longer to Get Out': Japanese American Evacuees as Farm Laborers During World War II," *Idaho Yesterdays* 44 (Summer 2000), 9.
43. Louis Fiset, "Thinning, Topping, and Loading: Japanese Americans and Beet Sugar in World War II," *Pacific Northwest Quarterly* 90, no. 3 (Summer 1999), 134.
44. "Minutes," JACL Special Emergency Conference, November 17–24, 1942, Salt Lake City. Supplement #6, "Beet Field Survey," by G. F. Inagaki and Scotty H. Tsuchiya, box 13, James Y. Sakamoto Papers, Special Collections, Manuscripts, and University Archives Division, University of Washington Libraries (hereafter, Minutes).
45. Ibid., 98.
46. Ibid., 42.
47. *Minidoka Irrigator*, March 6, 1943, 6.
48. *Rupert Laborer*, November 14, 1942, 3. The *Rupert Laborer* was published by the residents of the Rupert Farm Labor Camp, operated by the Farm Security Administration to house workers engaged in agricultural labor in the region. Although most of the residents were on seasonal leave from Minidoka, the camp contained Nikkei from other camps as well. It was located approximately thirty miles east of Minidoka.
49. Minutes, 57–58.
50. Ibid., 35.
51. Frank Abe, "Pride and Shame: Japanese Americans and the 38 Years' Journey to Justice," Seattle Sun, December 5, 1979, 2.
52. J. S., Ontario, Oregon, 4-3-71, University of Washington Library, Special Collections, Tape 216.
53. Abe, "Pride and Shame," 2.
54. Ibid.
55. Ibid.

# 5

# Loyalty Questionnaires and Japanese Americans in World War II

## EDITOR'S NOTE

*As Bob Sims examined the experiences of those who lived inside the prison camp, he found evidence that they endured constant reminders of the contradictions and illogic inherent in their circumstances, and that they were subjected to arbitrary policies concerning their civil rights. While the government had failed to accuse any individual Japanese American of disloyalty, for example, it nevertheless felt that it could positively establish a person's loyalty by means of a poorly worded pair of questions.—SS*

---

During World War II, Japanese nationals and Japanese Americans imprisoned in camps in the western United States were subjected to "tests" of their loyalty. This might seem improbable, since they were placed in these camps initially because of a presumed disloyalty. In his final report on the removal of Japanese Americans from the West Coast, General John L. DeWitt wrote that "the Japanese race is an enemy race," and "there is no ground for assuming that any Japanese… though born in the United States, will not turn against this nation when the final test of loyalty comes."[1] Closer to home, we also have the account of Idaho Governor Chase Clark, in a meeting of western state officials in Salt Lake City in April 1942, saying: "I don't trust any of them [Japanese Americans]. I don't know which ones to trust and so therefore I don't trust any of them."[2]

---

This article by Robert Sims originally appeared as "Loyalty Questionnaires and Japanese Americans in World War II: Assessing the 'Loyalty' of Japanese Americans by a Questionnaire," in the Idaho Bar Association *Advocate*, November 2007, without footnotes. Sources have been added for some quotations.

By early 1943 certain developments had occurred that brought about the administration of loyalty oaths to those in the camps. By that date, interest had grown in an all-Japanese American unit in the U.S. Army, and the army sought some means to identify those who could be shown to be "loyal" to the United States. At about the same time, the War Relocation Authority (WRA), the civilian agency operating the large camps housing Japanese Americans, wished to respond to a growing interest in releasing people from the camps to meet labor needs around the country and to allow young, college-age Nisei (American-born Japanese Americans) to continue their education in colleges away from the West Coast. The result was a two-questionnaire system, one for the army and one for the WRA, to be administered to all inmates seventeen years of age and older. The army questionnaire was given to Nisei males and the WRA version to Nisei females and Issei (immigrant generation) of both sexes.

## Problems with the "Oath"

While most questions were innocuous, numbers 27 and 28 on both forms became the center of attention. Question 27 on the army form was, "Are you willing to serve in the armed forces of the United States on combat duty, wherever ordered?" The corresponding question on the WRA form was, "If the opportunity presents itself and you are found qualified, would you be willing to volunteer for the Army Nurse Corps or the WAAC (Women's Army Auxiliary Corps)?" Keep in mind that the WRA form was intended for all Issei, male and female, so this was puzzling to many. How were elderly Issei women to respond? What did the question mean to Issei men?

Question 28 presented even greater problems. The army version read, "Will you swear unqualified allegiance to the United States of America and faithfully defend the United States from any or all attack by foreign or domestic forces, and forswear any form of allegiance or obedience to the Japanese emperor, or any other foreign government, power or organization?" For young Nisei men, this was a troubling question, particularly since none felt they had any allegiance to the Japanese emperor in the first place. The three-part construction on the question led to further confusion. Many Nisei men were troubled by the third part of the question, forswearing allegiance to the emperor. Would answering yes imply that they had been or still were loyal to a foreign government?

It was also a problem for many that, soon after Pearl Harbor, many Nisei sought to enlist in the army but found that all Japanese Americans were reclassified as 4-C, the same classification as that of enemy aliens. This was an affront not easily overcome and many continued to harbor irritation over it and thus were not eager to volunteer at that point.

Mrs. Mesa Sakura and her family gather for a snapshot. Her sons Kenny, Chester, Ted, and Howard volunteered for combat with the U.S. Army. All survived the war. *National Archives and Records Administration, Records of the War Relocation Authority, Central Photographic Files, 210-G-15-B911.*

The WRA version of question 28 presented further problems. It read the same as the army version but did not ask respondents to affirm that they would "faithfully defend the United States from any and all attack by foreign or domestic forces." Even with that deletion, the question posed serious issues for the Issei. By 1922 court decisions in the United States found that Issei could not become naturalized citizens. Although they had made their lives here without citizenship, they had obviously cast their lot with this country. What would happen at war's end? Might they be sent back to Japan and, if so, what would the Japanese government do with the information that they had "forsworn" allegiance to that country? Since they were not allowed to be United States citizens, would answering this question in the affirmative mean that they were "stateless persons"?

Because of these issues, question 28 of the WRA version was later modified to read, "Will you swear to abide by the laws of the United States and take no action which would in any way interfere with the war effort of the United States?" Although clearly making it easier for Issei to answer affirmatively, much harm had already been done.

The entire process of the administration of the questionnaires had a number of important implications. As Allen Bosworth, one of the early historians of this issue, has written:

> In retrospect, the entire registration program appears to have been a sophomoric and half-baked idea, if not, indeed, a stupid and costly blunder. In the long run, nothing could have been more certain or more simple than this: If there had been any actual Japanese agents or spies in the Relocation Centers in February 1943, they would have been the very first to profess their loyalty on paper, so that they could carry on their work.[3]

## THE "OATH" RESULTS IN SEGREGATION OF THE "LOYAL" FROM THE "DISLOYAL"

The two questions, in whatever form, became known as the Loyalty Questions, and the overall response to the questionnaires led to several important outcomes. One of these was the development of a segregation program for the inmates of the WRA prisons. The Tule Lake camp, in northern California, was named as the site to house those presumed to be loyal to Japan. Negative answers to questions 27 and 28 were part of the information used to assign individuals to this segregation center. Even those "yes" responses, if the respondents qualified their answers in any way, were regarded as "no." By September 1943, the administration of the "oath" was complete. Overall, 87 percent of the respondents answered affirmatively on both questions. About 5,300 (about 7 percent) answered "no" on at least one of the questions and approximately 4,600 (6 percent) did not respond at all or qualified their answers. Not all who responded negatively were assigned to Tule Lake.

## TRIALS FOR DRAFT EVASION

One other important result of the loyalty questionnaire had to do with military service. When the army initiated its program in February 1943, it sought to determine who would be accepted as volunteers. One year later that changed when the Nisei were made eligible for the draft. By that time a label had been given to those who replied negatively. They were called "No-No Boys," and even they were eligible for the draft. In early February 1944, young men in the camps began receiving their draft notices and were ordered to appear for their pre-induction physical examination. The decision as to how to respond to this situation was one of the most wrenching and painful for the young Nisei to make. Should they resist the draft and refuse to yield to the government's demands while their parents were kept in the camp? Why should one capitulate to this demand when that same government had initially classified them as the equivalent of aliens?

Most masked whatever resentment they felt and responded to the draft call as yet another test of their patriotism. Others chose not to comply and resisted the draft. In all ten camps, about 300 chose the latter path. For most of them, their defense was straightforward: If they were loyal enough to serve in the United States military, why were they imprisoned in barbed wire camps?

Throughout the spring and summer of 1944, federal marshals went through the camps and arrested those who insisted on draft evasion. In late summer and fall of 1944, their trials were held in federal courts in western states. If the "resisters" placed any hope in the federal courts, they were soon disappointed. The judges who heard their cases dismissed their arguments on the legality of drafting internees whose only crime was being of Japanese ancestry and conducted what one scholar has termed "shoddy trials."[4] There was an exception: Judge Louis E. Goodman of the Northern District of California, who dismissed the government's charges against twenty-six Nisei and called the decision to prosecute them "shocking to [his] conscience" and a violation of due process. But he was the lone exception.[5]

More typical was Federal Judge Chase Clark, appointed to the federal bench after he was defeated for re-election as governor of Idaho in 1942. Thirty-three draft resisters from the Minidoka camp in south central Idaho stood before Judge Clark in September 1944 without counsel. To deal with the problem the judge ordered available attorneys to appear in his court. Each was appointed to represent one or more of the defendants, which they did, apparently, without enthusiasm. One week after the arraignments, the first of the trials opened. Clark dismissed early efforts by the defendants to present motions regarding the legality of the proceedings. The thirty-three trials were conducted over the following eleven days, with the only issues being whether the individual charged was classified 1A for the draft and whether he had failed to appear for the required physical. The typical defense involved each defendant attempting to express his reasons for resisting the draft. One young man from Seattle later recalled the reaction by Judge Clark to his attempt at explanation, and that was to inform the jury to disregard any statements concerning their treatment at the hands of the government. They were all convicted. In late September and early October, Judge Clark sentenced them. Those who had pled guilty received sentences of eighteen months and most of the rest received terms of three years and three months in prison.

## From "No-No Boys" to "Resistors of Conscience"

The heroic sacrifices of those Nisei who served in the military in World War II—for example, those in the 442nd Regimental Combat Team in Europe and in Military Intelligence Service in the Pacific—brought about a grudging acceptance of their loyalty to America. Conversely, those who refused to cooperate with the U.S. government by acquiescing to the draft were usually seen as pariahs and treated badly, even within the Japanese American community. This continued for some time in spite of the fact that, in 1947, President Harry S. Truman granted full pardons to the Japanese Americans convicted under the Selective Service Act, an action that restored their citizenship rights.

By the 1980s people began to take a more measured look at that experience. Those who resisted came to be called "resisters of conscience." Increasingly they were recognized for taking principled stands in demanding more justice under the U.S. Constitution. For them, fidelity and loyalty to the principles of the Constitution demanded such a stand.

## Notes

1. Quoted in *Personal Justice Denied*, 6.
2. Verbatim Record of Speeches, WRAWCCA Salt Lake City Conference, April 7, 1942 (C 1.03), Japanese American Evacuation and Resettlement Collection (JERS). In a summary of Clark's statement, a WRA clerk wrote: "Gov. Clark stated that perhaps his logic was disturbed because of his strong feelings in the matter." See "Summary of SLC Conference," mimeograph, 19 (1.03) JERS.
3. Allen Bosworth, *America's Concentration Camp* (New York: W. W. Norton and Co., 1967), 69.
4. Eric L. Muller, *Free to Die for Their Country: The Story of the Japanese American Draft Resisters in World War II* (Chicago: University of Chicago Press, 2001), 5.
5. Quoted in Muller, 143.

## Other Sources

Tetsuden Kashima, *Judgment Without Trial: Japanese American Imprisonment during World War II* (Seattle: University of Washington Press, 2003).
John Okada, *No-No Boy* (Seattle: University of Washington Press, 2001).
Jeffrey Thompson, *Nisei Paradox*, unpublished 2017 stage reading in Boise of a dramatized No-No Boy trial in the court of Federal Judge Chase Clark. Copy available at Boise State University Special Collections and Archives.

A Nisei kindergarten teacher greets her students. *National Archives and Records Administration, 210-CMA-E-010c.*

# 6

# "Good Schools are Essential" The Education Program at Minidoka Internment Camp

## EDITOR'S NOTE

*The War Relocation Authority (WRA) removed whole families, orphans, and adopted children from their homes along the West Coast, including pregnant women, infants, toddlers, and schoolchildren of all ages. The WRA had to plan for their continuing education during their imprisonment. The percentage of people under the age of nineteen at the ten camps has been estimated at about 40 percent. At Minidoka, school enrollment in the fall of 1942 was about 30 percent of all residents.*

*Bob Sims participated in the development of curriculum standards in Idaho, so education was a natural subject for his Minidoka research. He investigated WRA school curriculum guidelines and how their ideals fared at Minidoka. Sims presented this paper orally at the Pacific Northwest History Conference in Portland, Oregon, April 21, 2001. He did not subsequently prepare the paper for publication, so I have edited it and completed his abbreviated notes.—SS*

---

In July 1944, the Minidoka Project Efficiency Rating Board upheld the "unsatisfactory" rating of Jerome T. Light, the high school principal, and removed him from his position. The action, only briefly noted in the official records of the camp, reveals much about the educational history of Minidoka. Light was a strong advocate for the progressive educational philosophy expressed in the curriculum

---

Robert C. Sims, "'Good Schools are Essential': The Education Program at Minidoka Internment Camp," paper presented at Pacific Northwest History Conference, Portland, OR, April 21, 2001.

guidelines for the camps. His persistent advocacy of that philosophy in the face of changing conditions and administrative attitudes ultimately led to his dismissal.[1]

Once the War Relocation Authority (WRA) decided to remove evacuees from "assembly centers" to concentration camps instead of dispersing them inland in small groups, it faced the enormous task of planning those communities. One major part of the task was to provide education programs for children and to consider what ideals their curricula would express. A progressive philosophy originated during the summer of 1942.[2]

Much of the WRA's early educational planning took place that summer in its Western Regional Office in San Francisco. The regional director, E. R. Fryer, came to his position from being head of the Navajo Indian Reservation. He chose Lucy W. Adams to lead the education section of the agency. She had directed the Navajo Reservation school system in the 1930s and was an advocate of the "community school" idea which had been part of that system. This idea, which became the model for the curriculum in the camps, was premised on the notion that schools should be integrated with the life of the communities in which they exist. The curriculum for such a program would employ the philosophy of "progressive education" through a "core program," and add courses and programs sufficient to meet state and college entrance requirements. Work experience and vocational education for students were important elements for implementing this philosophy.[3]

Many of the people involved in developing this enterprise came out of New Deal programs of the 1930s and reflected their experience with some of the social programs of that period. They felt that their educational efforts might lessen the burdens of the abrupt dislocation of Japanese Americans. It became a working assumption that the plight of Japanese Americans was due in part to a cultural pathology that the education systems of the camps should address. They might do this most effectively through practices that would promote and strengthen patriotic citizenship. In words taken from the curriculum guide for the camps: "Good schools are essential if the children and youth of these Relocation Centers are to continue their growth toward American ideals during the war."[4]

In creating an education system, the WRA called upon educators for assistance. They looked to Paul Hanna, a professor of education at Stanford University and an expert on community schools. He conducted a graduate seminar in the summer of 1942 to lay out a plan and propose a curriculum for the WRA that would be based on elements of the community life and work directly related to the lives of the students and their families.

The seminar participants spent two days at Tule Lake Relocation Center in northern California to observe life in the camps firsthand, hoping this would help them make their recommendations. A special work session took place in July 1942, involving all the educational administrators on staff at the camps up to that time. Their aim was to clarify the statement of purpose and to develop strategies for putting their philosophy into practice at each of the centers. They produced a document, "Proposed Curriculum Procedures," that was sent to all the camps to help them develop their own programs.

The centerpiece of the curriculum at the junior and senior high school levels was a combined English and Social Studies core course which was to teach ideals of democratic citizenship. After the special work session, the staffs from each center were to discuss the application of these guidelines to their particular situations. The Minidoka staff, in its workshop, developed a set of general aims, the purpose of which was to implement the overall purpose of the education program of the WRA.[5]

For the Minidoka staff, curriculum proved to be only one concern among many others. When the Army had done the initial facility planning for the ten relocation centers, it had provided no plans for school buildings or school equipment of any kind. The WRA, when it began operating the centers, did include plans for educational buildings. While the WRA managed to provide buildings at Manzanar, Tule Lake, Granada, Gila, and Colorado River, it built no classroom buildings at Minidoka. However, a shop building was constructed and a combined auditorium/gymnasium was partially constructed. The latter building was available for limited use only during the last semester of school in 1945 and never was used as a gymnasium. An account by a teacher at the camp captured the austere setting of Minidoka:

When school first opened at Minidoka...the children walked hesitantly into the tarpaper shacks that were to be their classrooms. They looked around for the familiar blackboard and found none; for desks and found only rudely constructed tables and benches without backs; for books and saw a heterogeneous collection unrelated to their needs.[6]

Minidoka had two elementary schools, each occupying one-half of a barrack building, a space of 1,200 square feet. The high school was originally provided little more than half of a centrally located block or about 2,000 square feet. Eventually the high school expanded into an entire barrack (2,400 square feet) plus several other buildings.

The education staff negotiated for the construction of school buildings appropriate to their needs, but Harry L. Stafford, the camp administrator, decided that the elementary school space was adequate. He agreed that a special building would be constructed for the combined junior-senior high school, but took no action on this decision, which was reversed in late spring 1943. It was determined that the high school, too, would have to use remodeled residence barracks. The

Minidoka Relocation Center, Hunt Idaho. Hunt High School students clean and rake areas between classroom barrack buildings preparatory to planting rye grass. *National Archives and Records Administration, 210-G-G243.*

elementary school could use the barracks with a minimum of remodeling, but for the high school, extensive work was required to convert the 20-by-120-feet barracks, with their six or eight apartments, into space more suitable for high school classes. Eventually, those barracks designated for classroom space were reconfigured into classrooms of 800 square feet each.

Elementary school classes began on October 19, 1942, but the high school delayed its opening until November 16 due in part to the remodeling. Enrollment in the elementary schools was 737; in the combined junior-senior high school, 1,296. In addition, nursery schools, operated entirely by the internees themselves, enrolled 266 children.[7]

One of the greatest problems facing the schools in the camps was recruiting teachers. Nationally, the wartime demands for labor and the notoriously low pay for teachers resulted in a shortage amounting to 50,000 to 60,000 people. This problem only grew as the nation continued to mobilize for war. At first, the WRA controlled teacher recruitment, but when its efforts did not yield enough teachers, it gave more autonomy to each camp. The minimum qualifications for Civil Service teachers in secondary schools was a bachelor's degree, two years of satisfactory teaching experience, and a valid certificate to teach in any of the states. At Minidoka, the Education Section administrators wanted teachers with higher qualifications, such as a master's degree or its equivalent. The Section hired most of the teaching staff at Minidoka during the first year and a half of the center's existence. Then in July 1943 the WRA established a centralized Personnel Management Section with total responsibility for teacher recruitment. As that system was being put into place, a six-week delay passed before it became operational. Consequently, no recruiting at all took place at a critical time: just before the opening of school for the 1943–1944 year.[8]

The central recruiting style produced new problems. In its first recruitment package for Minidoka, Arthur Kleinkopf, the Superintendent of Education, had described the camp and the educational plan for the camp schools. This was an attempt to "attract candidates on the basis of the challenge to render a service, to pioneer in the development of a community, and to participate in the development of an educational program that would serve the special needs of the relocation center." Thus, the view of living and working conditions at the camp was a realistic one. The new centrally run recruitment made no such effort, and the realistic circumstances of the camp were no longer included in recruitment packets. As a result, new staff recruits did not fit in very well or last very long. By contrast, the teachers who had initially been recruited for the first school year had a relatively low resignation rate.[9]

All plans for a teaching staff assumed that the camp population would provide at least 20 percent of the staffing needs. It proved to be a poor assumption. When the camp opened, only one person met the certification requirement. Because of the shortage of recruited staff, camp residents actually supplied a much higher proportion of the camp's teachers than expected. In the first year they comprised 41 percent of the faculty, with others working as teaching assistants. Without their contributions, it would not have been possible for the school to offer as full an academic program as it did. But capable Nisei with college degrees eventually began to leave the camp after the spring of 1943, when they were encouraged to relocate elsewhere. The supply of able replacements for them dwindled. On the other hand, the camp population also decreased, reducing the need for teachers. In the 1944–45 school year, the percentage of Nisei teachers was exactly 20 percent; not one had a teaching credential.[10]

What did the students make of these conditions? Robert Hosokawa, a college graduate with a degree in journalism, assessed the school situation several weeks after the first semester got underway. After interviewing several dozen students, he concluded that the students were dissatisfied with their school, and that they were most dissatisfied with the Nisei teachers and assistants.[11] While this might have been an accurate view of student attitudes toward the high-school staff, a different view prevailed at the elementary level, where a number of Nisei were called into service and were well received. One was a fourth grade teacher who proved to be popular with students, parents, and administrators alike.[12]

Initially, this dissatisfaction extended to the appointed personnel staff as well. Some students wondered if "the teachers…could be any good if they had taken jobs 'teaching us Japs'–surely a good teacher would be able to get a job in a 'real' school."[13]

Although students responded to the challenges of their new environment in different ways, most experienced some degree of difficulty. This excerpt from a student essay demonstrates the difficulty for this individual:

> [The] discouragement and the absence of a proper school from the first day of evacuation until the school started in this Minidoka Project has stalemated my once brilliant brain. I find that I cannot concentrate on study no matter how hard I try. My want of education is still wanting, [sic] but my powers of study have declined to an alarming extent. I think that this strange, new environment is the chief cause of my decline.[14]

With the change in recruiting policy, the character of the teaching staff also changed; subsequent hires were not as temperamentally suited to the task of teaching at such a place as Minidoka. The turnover rate accelerated. The last school year opened with no permanent teacher at all for the ninth grade core class. The first substitute for this class was the wife of a new high school teacher who had been hired as an elementary teacher. She had difficulty controlling the class and gave up in about a week. A second substitute from the elementary school worked well for about two weeks. Then a young man arrived to be the permanent teacher. According to the Guidance Director for the school, "he was rather eccentric and had considerable difficulty establishing rapport with his students." One day, while he was detaining several students after school in his room, he got in a fight with one of the boys. When it became apparent that the teacher was at fault, he resigned. According to the report, he was followed "by an equally peculiar woman."[15]

Caucasian teachers, in addition to facing the initial disappointments of students and the harsh environment of the camps, also had to face the problem of their own low status within the camp administration. While their status separated them from the evacuees, they were also set off from the other appointed non-teaching personnel.

Of all the workers at the camp, teachers were the ones most immersed in the world of the barracks through the children. When issues were disturbing adult residents, it was the teachers who wrestled with the effects on the children. Camp administrators expected teachers to disseminate information about camp policy so that the children could convey the information to their parents. At various times they were asked to promote "work programs, community government, draft registration, Americanization, resettlement, and other policies." When this teacher-to-child-to-parent strategy fell short of desired results, the administration often felt that the teachers were not carrying out the larger educational purposes of the camp. Teachers felt that they were being asked to subvert the educational purposes they were trying to achieve in favor of larger and sometimes contradictory administrative ones. The schools absorbed and reflected any community conflict that ensued.[16]

## Contradictory Messages

*In the midst of these difficulties, what became of the ideals of a community-based progressive education with a core curriculum? The fundamental circumstance at Minidoka and the other camps—that an entire ethnic group of American citizens and their parents had been uprooted and forced to live in rough camps with no due process—was ready-made for conflict and contradictions when it came to teaching adolescents about what it meant to be patriotic Americans living in a democracy. Sims discussed a few of them.—SS*

### Issei vs. Nisei

One goal of camp administrators was to promote "community government." In some respects, the educational program meshed with that goal. The intent of both was to provide practice in democratic government so that students would "experience their citizenship" and thus gain a better understanding of life in a democracy. But imagine how difficult that task was: The teachers were attempting to accomplish this with people who had been deprived of their civil rights. Like the effort to establish community government in the camp, this was a paradoxical situation, one in which an authority is attempting to "cultivate self-determination in a dependent population." This impacted schooling in a number of ways. At the beginning of the school year in 1942, the WRA ruled that Issei would be excluded from participating in the self-government arrangements at the camps. So children began the school year with the compounded irony of going off to school in a prison camp, one in which the "principle" of self-government was to be in force, but with their Issei parents excluded from participation. This produced attendant confusion about the role of "traditional leadership and paternal authority" in family life.[17]

The educational purposes of the schools placed them at the forefront in a long-standing, pre-evacuation struggle within the Japanese American community over the question of identity, or the conflict between the Issei and Nisei generations. It would be easy to dismiss, as some have, the efforts of the educators at Minidoka and elsewhere as nothing more than "cultural destruction," since it involved the prohibition of Japanese language and culture, thought to inhibit the Americanization process. But the situation was threaded with other complexities and conflicts as well.[18]

## *Japanization vs. Americanization*

At Minidoka, Jimmie Sakamoto, a former president of the Japanese American Citizens League (JACL), spoke to the teachers' workshop prior to the opening of school in 1942, providing them with his organization's views on the problems faced by Nisei. The idea that schools should promote Americanism as one of its functions certainly meshed with the goals of the JACL. This placed schooling right in the middle of the controversies over the role of the JACL in the forced removal and imprisonment of West Coast Japanese. In early April 1942, Mike Masaoka, the JACL national director, wrote to Milton Eisenhower offering advice on the type of education program needed at the camps. He urged that all classes should be so integrated that every student "will be inculcated with the spirit of Americanism and democratic process."[19]

Conflicts over Japanization versus Americanization persisted throughout the life of the camp, and school was a primary arena for them. Minidoka's new elementary teachers were urged to understand that their students "wait hopefully for some assurance that those fundamentals which you are explaining are workable principles of democracy necessary for post-war readjustment in a world where minorities have equal rights with majorities." However, the stress in the curriculum on Americanization created a situation where adherence to traditional Japanese values and practices might be seen as evidence of disloyalty. In the minds of administrators and some teachers, "the enemy became the family itself."[20]

## *"Loyalty" vs Patriotism*

The loyalty oath and military draft enlistment crises brought this issue to the forefront at Minidoka. School administrators at the camp had just begun to feel that they had made progress in overcoming the damage done by the forced removal and imprisonment when the military draft registration program was announced in February 1943. They were confident that, by having the core classes study the "whole problem of Japanese in America," that they had provided the opportunity for emotional catharsis by talking, thinking, and writing about the process.

The registration program threatened that progress. Schoolchildren reflected the disturbance that ran through the community. The registration program required that each person answer a questionnaire and declare for the record where their loyalties lay. A simultaneous enlistment program for an all-Japanese American combat unit added to the confusion of emotions and loyalties. Some students had parents indicating their loyalty to Japan and desiring to return there, some had friends enlisting (eleven high school students were among the 308 volunteers from Minidoka), others had parents who refused to give their consent for enlistment. A WRA report indicated the significance of this event:

> In a very real sense, this program was a fork in the road for the evacuated people—a testing of fundamental loyalties and democratic faiths in an atmosphere of high emotional tension. It brought to the surface grievances that had accumulated over a period of months and laid bare basic attitudes that had previously been submerged and indistinct. On the whole, this was one of the most exacting experiences the [WRA] has ever undergone.[21]

People who declined to register for the draft were deemed "disloyal." The WRA segregated them and sent them to Tule Lake. At this point, the character and tone of life in the camps changed dramatically. In the schools, absenteeism rose sharply and there were more disruptions. Students struggled to understand how the government's demands for "loyalty" related to their lessons concerning democratic citizenship.[22]

## SHIFT IN ADMINISTRATIVE POLICY

The loyalty crisis marked the beginning of a shift in WRA administrative policy, with important consequences for the education programs. The fall season of 1942 had seen a strike at the Poston camp in Arizona, demonstrations and deaths at Manzanar, and the end of any significant role for JACL leadership in any of the camps. Far from being the smoothly operating communities envisioned by the planners, those "communities" were veering out of control. Minidoka, although sometimes referred to as the "nice camp," had its share of conflict, as we have seen.

The eruption of tensions within the camps had impacts outside camp fences. Public awareness of the difficulties in the camps emboldened critics, including Congressional committees and a hostile press, who did all they could to restrict the social services of the camps. Inadequate budgets certainly meant that planned school buildings did not get built at Minidoka. By the spring of 1943, with the decision made that emphasis would be placed on resettlement of people out of the camps, the WRA was even less inclined to allocate what resources it had to improve life in the camps.

And so, we return to the split between Minidoka high school principal Jerome Light and his superiors. The restriction in budgets initiated the split. Light was convinced that schools were not being fairly treated in the allocation of resources in the camp, for they were often at the mercy of other administrators in other sections. Purchasing, construction or alteration of buildings, and administration of fiscal accounts were among the functions managed by sections outside education, handling these matters for the entire camp. Schools were rarely given any kind of priority. Indeed, the principal often felt that schools were penalized in that they "were not considered to be very essential in certain quarters, and the limited supplies would go to other more favored sections regardless of prior commitments." Light had a point. When typewriters requisitioned for typing classes for the high school arrived they were allocated to various departments around the camp.[23]

Following the draft registration crisis, the major administrative drive in the camps was to promote resettlement: the voluntary departure of people from the camps to locations and schools in states easterly of West Coast states. According to a WRA publication, "evacuees must be stimulated to healthy discontent with the limitations of the center, or they will never move." This certainly affected school operations. Camp administrators expected the schools to be instruments of the resettlement policy, so they encouraged the use of student academic work that fostered resettlement. Teachers were to introduce more information about life "on the outside" and to focus less on lessons oriented to the internal community, as the original curriculum had required.[24]

In the core classes, students wrote essays on resettlement, reflecting a wide range of acceptance of the idea. This is part of one student's view:

> When we do relocate, as others have done, we must build a very close understanding with the neighbors and the community in which we shall live. By doing good deeds to our neighbors, schools, and other organizations within the community, it will broaden our name as well as all of the Americans of Japanese ancestry. At home in Seattle and in Portland, we all lived happily. Again, when we relocate, we shall live in real homes and start a new life without making the mistakes we have made previously.[25]

At this point the schools were in disarray, caught between two approaches to an educational program that caused confusion among teachers as well as students. One analyst describes the situation facing the schools by the second year of operations as no longer one of forming "ideal communities or even carrying out an enlightened program of dispersing a racial minority into new homes. Merely to survive as minimally productive instructors was enough for the mortals who sat face to face with their classes each day." They found refuge in just teaching their subjects. The "shift" of educational emphasis piled up

The administration provided the community library with books and posters promoting its resettlement policy. The shelves contain books with information about various sections of the country. *National Archives and Records Administration, War Relocation Authority, 210-CMA-R-001.*

on insufficient school budgets and formed the backdrop for the firing of Jerome Light.

Light remained committed to the original philosophy and goals; he continued to pursue that approach. During the second school year (1943–44), it was clear that his superiors did not share his views. By then it was evident that the type of teachers that the WRA was hiring were not "trained in the core curriculum program." As the superintendent of schools indicated in his final report, even by the second year, "it became necessary to employ practically anyone who could qualify as a secondary teacher." It was also evident that the superintendent did not appreciate, and perhaps did not understand, the philosophy behind the core program. He concluded that a change was necessary because "the direction in which areas of learning were headed was becoming more and more cloudy." In his view, the philosophy behind the core program and the practices it called for, "lent themselves towards a rather loosely organized school system," and that "many unsound practices were associated with the program."[26]

Another view of this development was written by Helen Amerman, who, by all accounts, was one of the finest educators at Minidoka, and one of only three teachers who remained all three years. Her account is as follows:

> Throughout the fall semester [1944] there was a general unrest. In classes there was much confusion resulting from an unusually high turnover in teachers and in the abandoning of the core program at midterm. In some core classes, as many as three different teachers had charge of a single group in one semester.[27]

Camp administrators faced a serious dilemma, one of their own making, in that they established schools and presumed to teach about democracy. If they allowed the schools to decline it might encourage people to leave the camp and re-enter a real "democratic" society. But this approach might also indicate to those in the camps that, with the poor quality of education, they could hardly be said to prepare individuals for responsible citizenship. If the schools did a good job of preparing students for a productive life as citizens in American society, then that would make life in the camps more bearable and cause the families to decide to stay until the West Coast opened to them again. Thus, this effort to create good citizens might merely foster continued dependence on the government.

In the second semester of the 1943–44 school year, the administrators sought to remove Light from his position. With the deteriorating environment in the camps, student behavior worsened. Problems with attendance and delinquency increased. Light attributed these problems and the move to dismiss him as the administration's antipathy for those who sympathized with the interned people. Light was clearly one who was willing to support them. He had chosen to live at the camp, and his four children all attended the camp schools. Helen Amerman, the teacher in charge of the guidance program at the school, described how these events affected the students:

> Project politics impinged upon the lives of the students in the form of dismissal proceedings against the high school principal and an assistant project director who had been active among the young people of the Federated Christian Church. There was an atmosphere of uneasiness and dissatisfaction throughout the school, nurtured by the feelings of both faculty and students. Since it was generally believed that the principal's case stemmed from a conflict in educational philosophies, there was a tendency to be unusually conscious of the school's practices and policies. Because of the administrative organization of Civil Service, the principal's case did not technically concern either the faculty or the students, no direct information concerning the affair was released, and rumors, suspicions, and animosity toward the administration flourished. When the Student Body spontaneously organized a petition to the Project Director requesting that the principal be retained, the delegates who presented it were told that they were un-American and that it was none of their business. Such reception was disillusioning and frustrating to a group of students who, for two years at least, had been urged to develop the qualities of good American citizens.[28]

Community analysts who studied these events at Minidoka referred to this situation as a "factional cleavage" in the educational system. Light had championed a progressive system of education, but this system was difficult to operate effectively with the conditions that prevailed at Minidoka.

One analyst reported that the action against Light "caused quite a commotion within the high school and junior high school student body." Their petitions of protest convinced Minidoka's Community Council to express its support for Light, but to no avail. Light was given an unsatisfactory rating and dismissed. He appealed his case to WRA headquarters and was transferred to the Colorado River Project (Poston), where he became the principal at the high school at Camp Three.[29]

Historian Thomas James wrote, "No single image or argument can convey the complexity of experience bound up in the institution of schooling within the camps."[30] The case of Minidoka certainly supports his generalization. Educational practices centering round the effort to inculcate patriotism intermingled with issues of one's identity. The long-term effects of the educational experience children had in the camps (and the larger experience of camp life), are still unknown, but disturbing patterns are becoming known. Camp experiences were laden with questions of identity—of who they were, and who they are. For the survivors today, many of the questions about one's place in this society are as relevant now as they were half a century ago. Those years in camp schools were a time for children to "decide how they would live in the future." Central to that decision was wrestling with the conflict between the traditional culture of their parents or grandparents and the idea of Americanization. More than any other issue, these conflicts dominated the educational experience at Minidoka.[31]

## Notes

1. "Project Director's Weekly Report, July 2–8, 1944," 1.11. Japanese American Evacuation and Resettlement Collection (JERS), Bancroft Library, University of California, Berkeley.
2. Verbatim Record of Speeches, WRA-WCCA. Salt Lake City Conference, April 7, 1942, C 1.03, JERS.
3. Thomas James, *Exile Within: The Schooling of Japanese Americans, 1942–1945* (Cambridge: Harvard University Press, 1987), 36–37.
4. "Proposed Curriculum Procedures for Japanese Relocation Centers," 3, in Jerome T. Light, "The Development of a Junior-Senior High School Program in a Relocation Center for People of Japanese Ancestry During the War With Japan," EdD diss., Stanford University, 1947, vol. 4, Part 2. (Hereafter cited as Light.)
5. Light, vol. 4, chapter 2, 1 in Appendix M; "General Educational Aims," Light, vol. 1, 54–58.
6. Eunice Glenn, "Education Behind Barbed Wire," *Survey Midmonthly* 80 (December 1944), 347.
7. O. D. Cole, curriculum advisor, "A Report on School Progress and Needs," December 17, 1942 (2.56), JERS. Part of the delay in beginning high school classes was due to the general call for labor to harvest sugar beets.

8. James, 47; Light, vol. 1, 117–18.
9. Light, vol. 1, 117–23.
10. Light, vol. 1, 138.
11. Robert Hosokawa, "An Evacuee's Opinion of the Minidoka High School," December 1942 (P3.95), JERS.
12. Ayako and Masako Murakami, interview by Dee Goto and Alice Ito, December 14, 1997, Densho: The Japanese American Legacy Project. (Used with permission.)
13. Helen E. Amerman, "Hunt High School Final Report. Pupil Morale," June 1945, Light, vol. 3, Appendix E.
14. Student essay in Light, vol. 3, Appendix C, "Education for Relocation."
15. Light, vol. 1, 120; 107–108.
16. James, 55–56; 71.
17. James, 67.
18. Light, vol. 1, 244–45.
19. Letter, Mike Masaoka to Milton S. Eisenhower, April 6, 1942, (T 6.10) JERS; Light, vol. 2, 462.
20. Nannie Lee Bauman, "Philosophy of the Elementary Schools," in "Minidoka Project Schools," September 10, 1943, Washington Office Records Documentary, NARG 210, box 73. Quoted in James, 86.
21. War Relocation Authority, "Semi-Annual Report, January 1 to June 30, 1943," 8. Washington, DC: Department of the Interior, 1943. Quoted in Light, vol. 1, 99–100.
22. James, 103.
23. Light, vol. 1, 192.
24. "Reconditioning Procedures," WRA Handbook, 30.3.22.B. (Quoted in James, 132.)
25. "Student Essay" in Light, vol. 3, Appendix C, "Education for Relocation."
26. "Historical Narrative Report," Community Management, Education Section Dec 15, 1945. (P 2.50) JERS.
27. "Report by Helen Amerman" in Light, vol. 1, 108.
28. "Report by Helen Amerman" in Light, vol. 1, 105.
29. James Minoru Cecity, "Minidoka: An Analysis of Changing Patterns of Social Interaction," PhD diss., University of California, Berkeley, 1949; Elmer Smith, "Factors for Consideration in Analyzing the Minidoka Community and Seeing Possible Trends," July 8, 1944, WRA Community Analysis Section (P 4.00), JERS.
30. James, 79.
31. James, 171.

Young girl carrying buckets at Minidoka. *National Park Service, Yamaguchi Collection.*

# 7

# Minidoka: An American Story

## EDITOR'S NOTE

*Bob Sims co-founded the Minidoka Civil Liberties Symposium in 2006, a project of Friends of Minidoka. As of this writing the symposium has continued as an annual Idaho conference held either at Twin Falls or Boise. The theme of the second symposium, held in Twin Falls in June 2007, was "Presidential Powers in Wartime." Among the attendees were students who Sims expected knew little about Minidoka; the purpose of his speech was to make a connection between the people who experienced the Minidoka story and the fate of their civil rights during wartime. I have edited his remarks to accommodate readers.[1]—SS*

It may seem a curious way to start but I want to begin with Edgar Rice Burroughs. Many of you may not know that Idaho—particularly Pocatello—has a claim on Edgar Rice Burroughs, the creator of Tarzan. Burroughs spent part of his youth and a good portion of his young adulthood in Idaho, and although he's best known for his Tarzan series, Burroughs was also the author of fantasy literature and early science fiction. His titles, for instance, include *A Princess of Mars*, *At The Earth's Core*, and *The Eternal Savage*.

I mention him in the context of today's event because he also wrote a fantasy titled *Minidoka*. Like most of his works, this is a work of expansive imagination, a work about people, things, places, events that in reality could not exist or happen; about people persecuted by their gods, gods who sent plagues and fevers and then more fevers. His story is set in this region of Idaho but is quite unbelievable. There is another story we call Minidoka about a people persecuted and upon whom were visited great calamities. Like Burroughs's story, this one can be read with great incredulity and a suspicion that these things never could have happened. If a visitor from another time and place looked at this nation, studied its basic documents and its values, it would seem impossible that what happened actually did happen.

And yet in 1942 about 120,000 people were removed from their homes and sent to distant isolated and harsh places in an action by our government that the Attorney General of the United States at the time characterized as unnecessarily cruel. One of those places was a site about eighteen miles northeast of here, the Minidoka War Relocation Center. It happened in the context of wartime when war fever often translates into xenophobia. That fever peaked on February 19, 1942, when President Roosevelt signed Executive Order 9066. Over the next few months those 120,000 persons of Japanese descent were ordered to leave their homes in California, Washington, Oregon, Arizona, and Alaska. Two-thirds of them were American citizens. No charges were brought against them, and there were no hearings.

Initially, they didn't know where they were going, how long they would be detained, what conditions they would face, or what fate might await them. First sent to temporary detention camps set up in converted race tracks and fairgrounds, they lived in crowded, often unsanitary conditions with barbed wire fences and armed guard towers surrounding the compounds. From there they were transported to one of ten permanent camps, including Minidoka, where most remained for three years. It was a story line worthy of Burroughs' most extreme fantasies.

The Minidoka camp opened in August 1942 and ultimately housed 13,000 Nikkei, mostly from the Seattle and Portland areas. The camp filled up at the rate of about five hundred people a day in the heat of summer. The first group arrived from western Washington and Portland by train on a day of 112 degrees.

Those first arrivals found a camp still under construction. There was no hot running water; the sewage system had not been installed. The initial reaction to this harsh landscape by many was one of discouragement. Upon arriving one internee wrote, "When we first arrived here we almost cried and thought that this was a land that God had forgotten. The vast expanse of nothing but sagebrush and dust, a landscape so alien to our eyes and a desolate woebegone feeling of being so far removed from home and fireside bogged us down mentally as well as physically."

Underneath this reaction to the extremes of heat, cold, and dust was a feeling of being abandoned by this country. How Nikkei conducted themselves in this tragic situation is testimony to their inner strengths and courage. One must remember that it was more than just the physical hardship and deprivation that they endured. It was also the rejection by and the loss of liberty within their own country—the country with which the Issei had cast their lot and in which the Nisei had been born. As one writer put it: "There was the hurt of the thing." That seems to capture the essence of it.

Yet in spite of their treatment at the hands of their government, Japanese Americans remained loyal to the United States, and many demonstrated that loyalty by volunteering for military service. They were segregated into an all-Japanese American combat unit and fought in France and Italy. Some served with the military intelligence service in the Pacific. The story of the 442nd Regimental Combat Team is one of the great historic stories of World War II.

Well, why did this happen? Why were the constitutional rights and civil liberties of these people so easily disregarded? Many things contributed to it. After Pearl Harbor, fear of possible Japanese sabotage and espionage was rampant, and an outraged public felt an understandable desire to lash out at those who had attacked the nation. For many, that target expanded to those of the same nationality here in the United States. But these anti-Japanese feelings did not just appear overnight. The imprisonment of Japanese Americans was in many respects merely an extension of more than a century of racial prejudice against the "yellow peril." Laws passed in the early 1900s denied immigrants from Japan the right to become naturalized citizens, to own land, and to marry outside their race. In 1924 immigration from Japan was halted altogether. Idaho had its own episodes of expressing xenophobia: the legislature passed a 1922 anti-miscegenation law, prohibiting Japanese from marrying Caucasians; and in 1923, passed a law forbidding people of Japanese descent to buy land.

In the action implementing the intent of Executive Order 9066, where was the concern about keeping faith with the Constitution? Only a few raised questions. Attorney General Francis Biddle, who called the action ill-advised, unnecessary, and unnecessarily cruel, was one of very few voices. J. Edgar Hoover opposed it. Secretary of War

Henry Stimson had grave doubts about the constitutionality of a plan based on the racial characteristics of a particular minority group. In his diary he wrote that he doubted the military necessity of such an action and that the removal of all Japanese Americans from the West Coast would "make a tremendous hole in our constitutional system."

One of our keynote speakers [Greg Robinson][2] will deal with Franklin Roosevelt's role in this. I can add little to his scholarly contributions but I do want to comment on the matter. Robert Jackson, Biddle's predecessor as Roosevelt's attorney general, once observed that Roosevelt was "a strong skeptic of legal reasoning" and, despite his reputation, was not a "strong champion of civil rights." Later, Biddle speculated that Roosevelt did not think the "constitutional difficulty plagued him." He went on to observe that "the constitution has never greatly bothered any wartime president."

World War II propaganda poster. Artist Theodor Geisel (Dr. Seuss) defined the German enemy with a caricature of Hitler, a single individual; the Japanese enemy, with a race-based caricature of an entire people.
*Dr. Seuss Collection, Special Collections & Archives, UC San Diego.*

Opposition to this action was very limited. Very few public officials, among them Senator Sheridan Downey of California and Mayor Harry Cain of Tacoma, opposed it. Even most civil liberties groups kept relatively quiet, presumably in the interest of national unity. In the years immediately after World War II, attitudes about the Japanese incarceration began to shift, and over time many participants in that action have reflected on the roles they played. Some had misgivings at the time that it was unconstitutional and immoral. In April of 1942 Milton Eisenhower, who was the National Director of the War Relocation Authority—the civilian agency responsible for running the camps—lamented that "when this war is over we as Americans are going to regret the injustices we have done."

Throughout the 1950s most of the legal discriminations against Japanese Americans were lifted, including the bans on Japanese immigration and naturalization. One by one, state laws against alien Japanese owning or leasing land were also set aside as was Idaho's law in 1955. In 1959 Idaho lifted the racial intermarriage ban. In 1967, the U.S. Supreme Court ruled all anti-miscegenation laws unconstitutional (Loving v. Virginia, 388 U.S. 1).

The immorality and unconstitutionality of the internment have continued to reverberate. In 1970 the Seattle Chapter of the Japanese American Citizens League sponsored a Seattle Evacuation Redress Committee that initiated the first legislative plan for redress for those imprisoned in the camps. During the celebration of the bicentennial of the Constitution in 1976, President Gerald Ford issued Presidential Proclamation 4417 in which he acknowledged that we must recognize our national mistakes as well as our national achievements. February 19, he noted, is the anniversary of a sad day in American history; he observed that we know now what we should have known then—that the evacuation and internment of loyal Japanese Americans was wrong.

In 1980 the U.S. Commission on Wartime Relocation and Internment of Civilians was established to review the implementation of Executive Order 9066. The Commission was made up of former members of Congress, the Supreme Court, the cabinet, and distinguished private citizens. It heard testimony from more than seven hundred witnesses. It reviewed hundreds of documents that previously had been unavailable. In 1983 the commission concluded that the factors that had shaped the internment decision were "race prejudice, war hysteria and a failure of political leadership and not as had been claimed, military necessity." It recommended that Congress pass a joint resolution to be signed by the president which recognizes that a grave injustice was done and offer the apologies of the nation for the acts of exclusion, removal, and detention.

That same year, Fred Korematsu, Gordon Hirabayashi, and Min Yasui filed petitions for writs of *Corum Nobis* [in Latin, the "error before us;" this writ orders a lower court to correct an original judgement upon discovering a fundamental error] to have their convictions set aside for manifest injustice. Their claims were based on the result of research by Peter Irons, an attorney and legal historian, and that of researchers working for the commission. They found what Irons described as a "legal scandal without precedent in the history of American law." This "scandal" included suppression of evidence, acceptance into evidence of a military report that contained information known not to be true, and destruction by War Department officials of crucial evidence. In pursuing the original cases, government lawyers had relied upon the War Department for critical supporting records. The U.S. military had justified their application of the roundup, removal, and detention orders to all Japanese Americans on the grounds their "racial characteristics" predisposed them to acts of espionage and sabotage.[3]

Late in 1983, Federal Judge Marilyn Patel granted Korematsu's petition and found that the government had knowingly and intentionally failed to disclose critical information that contradicted the government's claims. She declared that the Supreme Court's decision in Korematsu "stands as a constant caution in times of war or declared military necessity that our institutions must be vigilant in protecting constitutional guarantees. It stands as a caution that in times of distress the shield of military necessity and national security must not be used to protect governmental actions from close scrutiny and accountability. And it stands as a caution that in times of international hostility the judiciary must be prepared to exercise its authority to protect all citizens from the petty fears and prejudices that are so easily aroused." In 1987 the Federal Court of Appeals granted Gordon

Hirabayashi's petition and vacated his conviction. Min Yasui's case was in the process of moving in the same direction but he died before its final resolution. In the last year of his presidency, Ronald Reagan signed the Civil Liberties Act of 1988 which officially declared the internment as a grave injustice.

In his [2004] book *Perilous Times: Free Speech in Wartime from the Sedition Act of 1798 to the War on Terrorism*, Geoffrey R. Stone, former dean of the University of Chicago Law School, commented that in times of war fever we are likely to lose our perspective and needlessly sacrifice fundamental liberties, particularly the fundamental liberties that those we fear already despise. In World War II the president, the Congress, and the Supreme Court all failed in their responsibility to preserve and protect the Constitution. The public sat silently by, or worse, cheered them on. Stone asks: How do we get it right in the future? Part of the answer he offers is that a critical determinant of

Dorothy and Jack Yamaguchi, pictured in a Minidoka barracks with their children and the children's grandmother, were from Seattle. When they returned to Seattle after WWII, they developed a slide show and book, *This Is Minidoka*, which they used to educate schoolchildren about the camp experience. *Wing Luke Museum, Hatate Collection.*

how a nation responds to the stresses of wartime is the attitude of the public. Citizens in a self-governing society are responsible for their own actions and the actions of their government. They cannot expect government officials to act calmly and judiciously without regard to their own response. In 1944 the eminent jurist Learned Hand wrote, "I often wonder whether we do not rest our hopes too much upon constitutions, upon laws and upon courts. These are false hopes. Believe me, these are false hopes. Liberty lies in the hearts of men and women. When it dies there no constitution, no law, no court can save it."

Minidoka has played a continuing role in the discussion of these issues. For many years after the camp closed, most associated with that experience seemed intent on letting the memories die. By the mid-1970s interest was quickening nationally to revisit the decision imprisoning Japanese Americans, including those milestones I just referred to. By that time only a limited number of acres of the original site remained in federal hands. Because of very enterprising and dedicated members of the Pocatello/Blackfoot Japanese American Citizens League (JACL) working with the staff of Senator Frank Church, the site was listed on the National Historic Register. Interest in Minidoka grew throughout the 1980s as the Commission on Wartime Relocation and Internment of Civilians continued its work and issued its findings in 1983. Other landmarks included recognition by the Idaho Centennial Commission in 1990 and President Bill Clinton's naming of the site as a National Internment Monument in 2001.

What else is there to do? It seems that should be enough. Unfortunately the answer is that it is not. We need only look at the public reaction to the 2001 naming of the site as a National Monument to see that it is not enough. It was painfully clear. Much of the early public reaction as evidenced in the newspapers was negative—ranging from a rather benign view that it would be better just not to talk about those things to a repetition of the arguments used in 1941 and 1942 supporting the decision. Consider this letter to the editor of the *Twin Falls Times-News*, which the newspaper titled, "Concentration Camps were Justified":

> It is unrealistic to think that racism was a factor in the government's
> decision to relocate West Coast Japanese Americans to camp. Only

extremely naive people would not suspect that there were Japanese secret agents among them since Japan had been planning to bomb Pearl Harbor for years.

You'll note a lot of disconnects there but I think you get the idea. Unwittingly perhaps, that letter writer and others actually helped underscore the need for Minidoka as a National Monument and for its historic and educational mission. There was clearly a need for public education on the subject.

In his proclamation, President Clinton echoed the sentiment embodied in the last words of the plaque erected there in 1979 when it was placed on the National Register. "May these camps serve to remind us what can happen when other factors supersede the constitutional rights guaranteed to all citizens and aliens living in this country." After the designation the National Park Service assumed control of the site and undertook to develop a general management plan. I had the good fortune to be a small part of that interesting process as a member of the planning team. The most persistent concerns related to civil liberties and constitutional rights violations. As a result, Minidoka is a venue for engaging in a dialogue concerning those violations. The plan also intends to help visitors reflect on the incarceration experience and the relationship of this experience to contemporary and future political and social events. Early in the life of the monument a nonprofit organization called Friends of Minidoka was organized to support the Park Service in the management of its site. This symposium itself is an embodiment of the goal to continue public education.

We believe it is critical that citizens understand and internalize the value of civil liberties and why we must protect them. They must understand that, in wartime, even well-meaning individuals can be swept along by the mentality of the mob and the current-day McCarthys of the media whose rants appeal to the worst rather than the best in the American people.

In every war there is always a struggle to balance security and liberty. Much responsibility for that rests in the president's office. Our record as a nation shows that security outweighs liberty. In order to achieve a proper balance we need strong political leaders with a sense of right and wrong; judges who can stand up to public pressures; members of the press, bar, and academia who help us see the issues clearly; a Congress safeguarding the separation of powers; and most of all an informed and tolerant public who will value not only their own liberties but the liberties of others as well. I hope we can accomplish some of this last item in these two days. Thank you very much.

### Notes

1. Robert C. Sims, Minidoka Civil Liberties Symposium Remarks, June 2007, Boise State University Special Collections and Archives, Robert C. Sims Collection, Box 52, folder 14. Also online as an Idaho Public Television special "Homefront" program.
2. Keynote speaker Greg Robinson, author of the 2001 book *By Order of the President: FDR and the Internment of Japanese Americans*, titled his talk "Why President Roosevelt Signed Executive Order 9066: Sites Along the Evidentiary Trail."
3. This paragraph, inserted here, was part of a talk, also titled "Minidoka: An American Story," that Bob Sims presented at the Sixth Annual Civil Liberties Symposium on June 30, 2011, Sims Collection, Box 58, Folder 9. See also Peter Irons, ed. *Justice Delayed: The Record of the Japanese American Internment Cases*. Middletown, CT: Wesleyan University Press, 1989.

8

# Idaho and Minidoka

## EDITOR'S NOTE

*When the Commission on Wartime Relocation and Internment of Civilians published its report* Personal Justice Denied *in 1982, Japanese Americans, scholars, and others widely considered the report as a "step toward redress." The concept of redress is found in the First Amendment to the Constitution of the United States: "Congress shall make no law...abridging the right of the people to peaceably assemble, and to petition the Government for a redress of grievances." The movement for redress of the wrongs done to Japanese Americans had begun in the early 1970s; Dr. Roger Daniels and others decided to organize a conference aimed at boosting the idea forward. The resulting International Conference on Relocation and Redress took place at Salt Lake City in March 1983.*

*After the conference, Daniels and others published* Japanese Americans: From Relocation to Redress, *a volume collecting some of the papers given at the conference with others added to round out the book with historical perspectives. One section compares the reactions of three states upon becoming hosts of one of the camps and its Nikkei population. In three parallel essays, the authors sought to answer the question, "How did Utah, Idaho, and Wyoming each respond to the presence of the camp and its occupants?"*

*Daniels asked Bob Sims, by this time a well-regarded authority on Minidoka, to prepare the Idaho paper. Sims examined how the initial hostility towards people of Japanese ancestry moderated as contacts of an everyday sort—working the sugar beet fields, baseball competitions, army enlistments—gradually reduced fears and misunderstandings.—SS*

On April 23, 1942, the U.S. Army announced that a relocation center for Japanese Americans would be established on the

Robert Sims, "Japanese Americans in Idaho," in *Japanese Americans: From Relocation to Redress,* eds. Roger Daniels, Sandra C. Taylor, and Harry H. L Kitano (Salt Lake City: University of Utah Press, 1986).

113

Minidoka reclamation project in southeastern Jerome County, near the town of Eden, approximately sixteen miles from Twin Falls, Idaho. The center occupied a federally controlled site approximately two and one-half miles long and one mile wide adjacent to a large irrigation canal.[1] Minidoka, or Hunt, as the camp was called, affected both the state and the region in both positive and negative ways. Because the evacuation occurred at a time when emotions were high and reason often wanting, injustices inevitably took place. Ultimately we are left with only inadequate explanations for the removal of more than 70,000 American citizens from their homes and for their placement in detention camps. The total impact of that program may never be known, but in recent years historians have probed for explanations for why it happened. The Minidoka experience may provide some insights into that question.

Relocating 10,000 Japanese Americans in a county with only slightly more than 9,000 residents was bound to cause disruption. However, Japanese were not unknown in this region—about 1,200 lived in Idaho in 1940.[2] Two things had attracted them—railroad construction and farming. Virtually all of Idaho's early Japanese residents came with the development and extension of railroad lines in the 1890s, serving as a principal source of railroad labor until 1910.

Beginning in 1903 and continuing until about 1912, when a factory was built in Cassia County at Burley, the developing beet sugar industry attracted Japanese Americans to the state. Cassia County, which had eight Japanese residents in 1910, had forty-one a decade later. Twin Falls County, with forty-four in 1910, almost doubled that figure by 1920.[3] Although these early residents helped meet important economic needs for the developing region, they often encountered contempt and opposition, and their presence was sometimes seen as a threat to local residents. Almost from the beginning, they met instances of discrimination and occasional acts of violence.

By the second decade of the twentieth century, Japanese had become increasingly successful as merchants and farmers in Idaho and throughout the west. This success triggered opposition that first found expression in California in 1913 when a law was passed prohibiting aliens ineligible for citizenship from owning agricultural land. The

Idaho legislature soon began considering similar bills and, by 1923, Idaho also had such a law. In the 1917 legislative session, when the bill was debated in the Idaho House of Representatives, a Wendell newspaper editor commented, "Members of the House [in voting unanimously for the bill] declared unequivocally for Americanism and American rights over those of foreign birth who do not, while in this country and enjoying its rights and benefits, become naturalized citizens."[4] This reflects several important aspects concerning anti-Japanese attitudes in this period, but primarily it reveals the misunderstanding that prevailed, for Japanese could not become naturalized citizens.

Idaho's Japanese continued to thrive, however, in spite of misunderstandings and overt discrimination. By 1940, the Japanese community of the Magic Valley region (Twin Falls area) had grown to about 150 to 200, with approximately 65 percent of these native-born Americans.[5] Like other Japanese American communities, the Magic Valley Japanese Americans experienced some tension between their identity as Japanese and as Americans. In the 1930s, when the Japanese American Citizens League began its organizing efforts in south central Idaho, there were spirited discussions about efforts to become Americanized at the cost of losing one's Japanese cultural heritage. Although some counseled that local Japanese should create a "little Japan," others resisted.[6] The lack of a large Japanese population center and the dispersed nature of Idaho's Japanese enhanced their "Americanization."

In 1936, an article in the *Japanese-American Courier*, a Seattle paper, commented on the Idaho Nisei: "The majority of the second generation are engaged in farming. The general outlook for them seems bright in this field and many who at one time believed the work both hard and tedious, are now finding it profitable and best suited to them."[7] Life in Idaho in the mid-1930s involved association with other Japanese. Japanese youths from communities throughout the state participated in sports tournaments, and various cultural events drew Idaho Nikkei from a wide region.

For both the first and second generations, the developing tension between the United States and Japan was a constant source of concern. Older Japanese were faced with the dilemma of supporting their chosen land, which, while offering them some economic opportunity, denied them the rights of citizenship, or maintaining some loyalty for the land of their birth. For the Nisei, the choice was already made: they were Americans. In November 1940, when the new Selective Service act went into effect, the first Idaho Japanese to volunteer for army duty was a young man from Rupert, a graduate of the University of Idaho.[8]

On the West Coast, the more than 110,000 people of Japanese ancestry living there felt the approaching war sharply. Agitation against their presence on the coast continued to build in the weeks after Pearl Harbor and soon received official support. In February 1942, the decision came to remove all Nikkei from the West Coast. The specific nature of the removal program was determined during the following weeks. Japanese would be placed in ten camps in the interior, one to be located in Idaho.

Attitudes among Idaho's residents toward Japanese Americans were mixed. Governor Chase Clark contributed considerably to anti-Japanese feelings by generally displaying a racist attitude toward Japanese and Japanese Americans alike. Before the decision was made to relocate the Japanese to the camps, an early proposal called for voluntary relocation on an individual basis. Clark strongly opposed this plan and became personally involved in thwarting several cases of attempted relocation. His rhetoric contributed to an anti-Japanese attitude.[9]

One of the most important effects relocation had on Idaho was in providing labor for the state's agriculture industry. Idaho farmers, faced with an increased demand for farm products and a sharply reduced labor supply, had a serious problem. The first reaction to the possibility of using Nikkei labor was largely negative. At a farmers' congress in Twin Falls in late February 1942, south central Idaho farmers voted 371 to 41 against using such labor. According to a newspaper account, "One man…voted…against the importation of alien labor under any circumstances. His reason was short and to the point. He put three words after his mark where he voted against enemy alien labor. Those three words were 'Remember Pearl Harbor.'"[10]

However, not all were opposed; representatives of area sugar companies also attended that farmers' congress, and one "stated that his company had no objections to the use of Japanese labor in beet fields, if properly guarded."[11]

The decision to place a relocation camp in Idaho came amid an atmosphere of strong anti-Japanese feeling. When one reads the local newspapers, it is apparent that most of the excitement about the war, especially animosity directed toward the enemy, was aimed at Japan rather than at the other Axis powers. In early 1942, a nationwide Gallup poll survey showed "that while hatred for Germany is concentrated largely on a few public figures such as Hitler, Goebbels, Himmler, Japanese war leaders have not been clearly identified in the public mind."[12] Thus, for Germany and Italy, Americans tended to think of evil leaders; for Japan, they thought in terms of a hated race. It is possible to see this attitude reflected in Idaho in a newspaper article about the discontinuation of a Christmas decoration contest, which would not be held for the duration because of War Production Board requests to conserve energy. "When Hitler, Mussolini, and the Japs have been blacked out, the project will again shine forth with renewed energy."[13]

This attitude found expression in other ways as well. In a controversy over melting down the cannon on the statehouse lawn to make "bullets," Governor Clark referred to their use for killing "Japs." He later sought to scrap the iron fence around the Soldiers' Home in Boise, "so the metal can be converted to bullets. They [the residents of the home] hate to look at it, they say, when they realize that it could be used for bullets to kill the Japs."[14] Wartime hatred coupled with the general inability of Idahoans to distinguish between Japanese in Japan and those in America, including those who were American citizens, created difficulties for Idaho's Japanese.

Clark, who actively sought to prevent West Coast Japanese from relocating in Idaho during the period of voluntary evacuation, applauded the Twin Falls Chamber of Commerce for supporting his position. In a letter to the chamber he asked them to "keep up the good work" in restraining Japanese from settling permanently in Idaho.[15]

An important event affecting Idahoans' feelings toward Japanese was the capture of more than a thousand Idaho civilians who were employed by the Boise-based Morrison-Knudsen construction company at their Pacific sites on Wake Island and elsewhere. Their treatment by the Japanese army was a source of strong anti-Japanese feelings on the part of their friends and relatives, feelings too easily transferred to Japanese Americans.

Unfortunately, the treatment of those who came to Idaho also reflects this attitude, for individuals and groups in Idaho joined their voices to the chorus of anti-Japanese sentiments. In a meeting in late February, members of American Legion posts for five south central Idaho counties recommended concentration camps for Japanese brought into the state, a sentiment the Twin Falls Chamber of Commerce supported. The justification for such treatment was that Japanese were assumed to be a threat to the country's security; that is, they were expected to support Japan in case of an attack on American soil.[16]

Magic Valley strongly adhered to this assumption. When it was first suggested that Japanese might be brought there, the chairman of the Twin Falls Chamber of Commerce pointed out the danger of being too sympathetic and thus too lenient on any Japanese brought into the state. "Sympathy for Japanese," he said, "will make it easier to sabotage the Magic Valley Irrigation system."[17] The president of the Idaho Farm Bureau opposed their use as farm laborers and declared that "Japanese should be treated as prisoners of war. We have no more use for them in Idaho than they have for them on the coast."[18]

About the same time that decisions were being made regarding relocation, Idaho farmers received some important news: Acreage restrictions were removed on sugar beet production, and Idaho farmers were "implored to raise 100,000 acres in 1942 as compared with 48,000 the previous year."[19] This led to speculation about using relocated Japanese as farm laborers. Almost immediately two Idaho sugar beet refineries "indicated that they could use about one thousand Japanese apiece during the season," according to one account.[20]

One of the first public reactions to the April 23 decision to build the Minidoka camp came from the farmers in the Gooding area who were concerned about irrigation water. They thought that water was already too scarce, that the development of the camp would "deprive permanent residents of long-used water rights," according to a report. Governor Clark responded by holding a meeting in Gooding on April

29 that resulted in "adamant opposition to diversion of irrigation water from the Gooding area" by the 200 farmers present.[21] Yet this appeal had no apparent effect on the War Relocation Authority.

Although impending construction of the camp upset farmers, area businessmen were more favorably inclined. An item in the *Twin Falls Times-News* pointed out that "the camp [was] expected to add materially to South Central Idaho business."[22]

For the construction of the camp, the Morrison-Knudsen company, the contractor, needed a crew of about three thousand men, which immediately affected area labor supply and wage rates, a consideration not always viewed favorably by the region's employers. In addition was the problem of housing the workers. Twin Falls and Jerome responded by providing housing for 1,500 workers each, billeting them in fairground camps and private residences.[23]

The pressures generated by camp construction were added to the growing demand for acquiring Japanese evacuees as sugar beet

A panorama view of the Minidoka War Relocation Authority center, showing partially completed barracks. An advance party of Minidoka incarcerees helped construct camp buildings in August 1942. *National Records and Archives Administration, WRA photo by Francis Stewart, 210-G-D105.*

workers. While waiting for the relocation centers to be built, West Coast Japanese Americans had been gathered in assembly centers. From these, evacuees were recruited for the sugar beet fields. Malheur County, Oregon, adjacent to southwestern Idaho, became the first area to use such labor. By early May, Idaho sugar beet companies received approval to use evacuee labor, an approval contingent on acceptance of a specific plan by state and local officials. A number of groups in Magic Valley voiced strenuous objections to releasing evacuees. The American Legion post at Hazelton, for example, passed a resolution urging that any Japanese released to work on area farms be strictly guarded.[24]

By mid-May, state and federal officials had sent a plan to fifteen Idaho counties for the use of Japanese labor in the beet fields. The county officials were given final say as to whether the evacuees would be used. Governor Clark, relenting ever so reluctantly, declared, "We will not permit Japanese to go into any county that does not want them."[25]

Three counties in eastern Idaho responded immediately with labor requests, the south central counties following the next day. On May 19, it was predicted that a thousand workers would be brought into Magic Valley as beet crew labor and that 600 of them would be housed in the labor camp south of Twin Falls. They were to work the approximately 19,000 acres in Twin Falls, Cassia, and Minidoka counties.[26]

But, because of the governor's anti-Japanese expressions and vocal opposition by individuals and groups in Idaho, the Japanese Americans in the assembly centers were reluctant to enter the state. In early May, the governor had given a speech at Grangeville, characterizing the Japanese as people "who live like rats, and act like rats," adding that Idahoans did not want them. When sugar beet company representatives went to assembly centers to recruit workers for Idaho, they found newspaper clippings of Clark's comments on the bulletin boards and a notable lack of enthusiasm among the evacuees for coming to the state.[27]

The governor and others sought to undo the damage, Clark stating that any Japanese willing to "prove their loyalty" by assisting Idaho farmers would be excluded from his earlier remarks. This apology of sorts resulted in part from local pressures. In an attempt to create a better atmosphere, the *Twin Falls Times-News* called for a "square deal" for Japanese workers: "Japanese workers are not prisoners and come into this area of their own free will. Citizens are urged to see that they are allowed all considerations."[28]

But the mood continued to be uncertain, with some area residents concerned about potential problems if the evacuees came. Not convinced that the federal government was capable of solving all problems, the Jerome County sheriff asked county residents to turn in their "high-powered firearms, to be used in case of emergency."[29]

Nevertheless, by the end of May, meetings with county officials, farm organizations, chambers of commerce, and similar groups "officially opened" every county in south central Idaho to relocatees. Those at the meeting had to vote favorably and to agree to a "written guarantee" signed by the "county commissioners, Prosecuting Attorney, Sheriff, and others."[30]

As evacuee laborers began arriving in early June to work on area farms, construction continued on the camp. Although somewhat behind schedule, the job was nearly complete in late August and early September. An advance party of relocated Japanese Americans arrived in early August; the rest of the camp's occupants began arriving on the sixteenth and came at the rate of approximately 500 a day through the middle of September. A member of the advance crew recorded his impressions upon his arrival that reflect astonishing optimism. After noting that "the great intensity and extent of work that needs to be done here cannot be over-emphasized," he went on to say that "there is no denying the fact that the place is a desert now but it can be made into a model community and will certainly be worth a try."[31]

Another of the same group wrote: "The train stopped at the end of the tracks which was right in the midst of sage-brushes, and dust. It was a desolate looking place and down in the bottom of my heart, I started feeling homesick for the green trees [and]...the Puget Sound.... I could feel the struggle inside of me to keep the tears from coming up."[32]

A reporter from an area newspaper visited the camp in mid-August and wrote:

Fourteen miles from Eden as a truck rolls through sagebrush, and an incalculable distance from anything resembling the garden of the same name, a new home is being built for Tojo [refers to Hideki Tojo, general of the Imperial Japanese Army]. In official circles it is the Minidoka War Relocation Area Project. The common name is Jap Camp.... If Tojos now on the grounds forget why they are 12 miles north of Eden, they can have their memories jogged by looking at a billboard near camp headquarters. It says, "Remember Pearl Harbor."[33]

It may be impossible to appreciate completely the experience of the evacuees. Many seemed committed to making the most of the situation. This is seen in the following editorial from the camp newspaper:

We, the ten thousand, then, can have but one resolve; to apply our combined energies and efforts to the grim task of conquering the elements and converting a wasteland into an inhabitable community. Our obligation to ourselves is to wrest the nearest

Sun Valley Stages had the contract to transfer incarcerees from the train for the bus ride to Minidoka. *National Archives and Records Administration, 210-G-11D-087.*

possible approximation of normalcy out of an abnormal situation....
Our great adventure is a repetition of the frontier struggle of pioneers
against the land and its elements. Our future will be what we make
it; and there is no reason to despair.[34]

Committed to making a viable community at the camp, they soon
found that work leave, while it had certain advantages, created serious problems for maintaining an element of regularity in the camp
itself. Nowhere was this seen more clearly than in the school situation.
Although a staff was recruited and buildings, however inadequate, were
ready, classes did not begin for the high school students at Hunt until
mid-November, for several reasons, chief of which was the absence of
many students on agricultural leave until early November.

That first autumn, some two thousand evacuees left Minidoka to
work in agricultural areas in Idaho, Wyoming, and Utah. As a result,
center residents and camp administrators alike got an early taste of one
continuing contradiction of early camp life—that of trying to make
a community within the camp while supplying agricultural labor for
the region.[35] To accomplish the latter, many Minidoka residents left
the center and worked out of regional labor camps, such as those at
Rupert and Twin Falls. Thus, some evacuees began to have contacts
with local residents. Often they were unpleasant encounters. By early
October 1942, because of such encounters, area towns began imposing
curfews on Japanese workers. Burley, Paul, and Rupert were among
the communities making such restrictions.[36]

But the contacts were not all bad and, as area residents became more
familiar with the workers, there seemed to be an easing in relations. A
group of JACL officials, on a tour of beet areas in late October 1942,
visited the camp at Rupert and found the morale high. According to
their report, they "learned that the boys...were receiving considerate
treatment from the Caucasian people of the area." In Filer, the report
continued, "we called upon a group of young people quartered at the
Fair Grounds. The treatment they were receiving from the town and
farm people was apparently as good as could be expected." Overall,
these officials noted "a growing dissension against the Sugar Companies for their practice of coercion, intimidation, and other tactics,
to force the boys to work after their contract had been fulfilled....

[O]ften the term is employed, 'You have an obligation as patriotic American citizens to save the beet crop.' The boys feel that exploitation of patriotism on the part of sugar companies is not patriotic in itself."[37]

One relocatee gave this version of the experience:

> The Caucasian friend for whom I am working was threatened; they said that they would tar and feather him if he continued to use us. Due to the good work of the evacuees and to the public relations work of such companies as the Amalgamated Sugar, the local people have finally been won over. They are now demanding that we be used. Of course, the shortage of workers may have something to do with this change in attitude; the important thing is that they now want us to work for them. Some barber shops, pool halls, and theatres have discriminated against us, but things are looking up. I predict that very healthy conditions will prevail next spring.[38]

In spite of the difficulties of that first year, it appears that his assessment was correct. The role the evacuees played in saving the sugar beet crop in 1942 was extremely important in gaining acceptance. An editorial in the camp newspaper expressed it this way: "Barred from participation in defense industries, evacuated by 'military necessity' to relocation centers and hooted at, even assaulted by unthinking outsiders the Japanese here have, nevertheless, contributed in no small way to the nation's victory program and have proven they...are loyal Americans."[39]

Another editorial in the camp newspaper expressed a related view:

> Fear and distrust are born of ignorance and the unknown. Once this factor is destroyed, better relationships follow. Those evacuees leaving the center are urged to dispel all false rumors concerning persons of Japanese ancestry. Prove to the people the sincerity of your purpose....By building, brick upon brick and stone upon stone, we may rest assured that the majority of the racist, the hypocrite, and the ignorant will be drowned out by straight shooting Americans.[40]

Although acceptance of the evacuees gradually improved in the Twin Falls area, there were occasional incidents that reflected an abiding anti-Japanese attitude. One example of this occurred during the election campaign in the fall of 1942. In that campaign the eventually successful challenger of the incumbent county treasurer placed a political advertisement in a local paper criticizing her for employing a young Japanese American woman in her office, claiming that the treasurer obviously did not understand the feelings of the parents of "boys who lost their lives at Pearl Harbor, Wake Island, Midway, Guam and [the] Solomon Islands...when they have to walk into the county Treasurers' office and pay their taxes to a Japanese." In response, the incumbent pointed out that the young woman in question was an American citizen, a native of Twin Falls, and a recent honor graduate of the local high school. But even this did not satisfy those who made no distinction between Japanese in Japan and Americans of Japanese ancestry.[41]

Camp administrators, aware of the need for some positive contacts with the community, actively pursued a policy of providing them. One thing that did help improve the relationship between camp and community was the practice of sending student groups to area schools to entertain. Also, camp musical groups, such as the Harmonaires, proved quite popular in the surrounding towns. This group, working out of the Twin Falls labor camp in the late summer and early fall of 1942,

Minidoka's Mass Choir prepares for a performance at one of the neighboring towns. *National Archives and Records Administration, 210-CMA-CA-001a.*

developed quite a following after playing at a Halloween dance at the Odd Fellows Hall and appearing at the formal Thanksgiving dance at Filer High School.[42] In January and February 1943, the Minidoka Mass Choir of eighty-nine voices gave a number of concerts in area towns, including a concert in the First Methodist Church in Twin Falls. In addition, a Hunt High School talent review visited several schools and received warm responses.[43]

Sports provided another form of contact with residents of the region. Baseball teams from Hunt played an extensive schedule with surrounding towns during the summer of 1943. However, it is questionable how much they did for public relations since they had the decidedly undiplomatic knack of defeating most of their opponents.

Also, with "the promotion of better relationship between the center residents and the people on the outside as its aim, an arts and handicraft exhibit, displaying original work of Hunt residents" was held at the Twin Falls Public Library in June 1943.[44]

While all these efforts apparently improved camp/community relations, problems remained. In the spring of 1943, because of a number of incidents in Twin Falls, the local Kiwanis Club passed a resolution protesting the "public use of the languages of countries with which the United States is at war." The resolution condemned such actions as tending to "create suspicion and distrust," and recommended that "ways and means be devised to inform [these people] in no uncertain terms that the spoken words of our enemies grate upon our senses."[45]

This incident also revealed another serious problem. Japanese Americans who were longtime residents of the area often were linked in the public mind with the evacuees and, when the latter created problems, this reflected upon all. In a letter to the camp newspaper, an officer of the Magic Valley chapter of JACL asked that something be done about those from the camp who were coming into Twin Falls and other towns and "getting intoxicated and making scenes in public." "This small group," according to the writer, "is making our public relations work extremely difficult."[46]

Another element of discrimination against Japanese Americans was the practice of local school districts charging tuition for the evacuee children. When this was challenged in 1943, the Idaho attorney general upheld it. When WRA officials and the state superintendent of public instruction continued to complain about it some school districts relented. The state superintendent called the practice "astonishing...in the face of the contribution the evacuated people have made to Idaho's outstanding record of agricultural production in war time." With a change in the attorney general's office in 1945 evacuee tuition was abandoned. Twin Falls, which charged tuition during the 1942–43 school year, dropped it the following year.[47]

Nothing did more for the eventual acceptance of Japanese Americans in Idaho or elsewhere than the military record of the 100th Battalion and the 442nd Regimental Combat Team, two Japanese American units that fought in Europe. Shortly after the war began, Selective Service no longer inducted Japanese. But the War Department soon conceived the idea of these special combat units, and plans for such groups were formalized in late 1942. In early 1943 recruitment began at all the centers. Minidoka led all the camps in the number of volunteers for the 442nd and, by late 1943, Japanese American units were fighting in Italy. There and in the campaigns that followed they distinguished themselves with their valor and became the most decorated American unit in the war.

It is impossible to overemphasize what this did for acceptance of Japanese Americans. The *Minidoka Irrigator* expressed this feeling, noting that because of the excellent record of these units, people of Japanese ancestry were viewed with "a little more respect, a little more courtesy, and a little more equality."[48]

This situation seemed a sharp contrast to that of their parents, many of whom remained in camps until the end of the war. In 1945, four mothers from Magic Valley were six-star mothers, so-called because they each had six sons in the armed services and were entitled to display small flags with six stars. One of these flags hung in the Twin Falls Migratory Labor Camp temporary home of Mr. and Mrs. Takeo Sakuma.[49]

Through their contributions as laborers, their military service, and their overcoming the hardships of relocation, Japanese Americans gradually won considerable respect and support. And, as the editorial writer of the *Minidoka Irrigator* stated, "Day by day the American public is beginning to realize which side of the fence we are on."[50]

In January 1945, the ban excluding Nikkei from the West Coast was lifted and those who wished returned to their former homes. By that time the Magic Valley region had come to depend upon evacuee labor and some were reluctant for them to leave. The *Burley Herald* praised the labor and conduct of the evacuees:

> The Japanese men and women who have worked in Burley have per-
> formed a great service. They have thinned, cultivated, and harvested
> the beets; they have irrigated, picked up and sorted the potatoes,
> they have tended sheep in the winter and herded the fattening beef
> in the summer. They have cooked and served food in the cafes....
> We doubt if any other group of Americans would have acted any
> better under the circumstances. Next year...the need for these good
> workers will be acute here. We hope many of the present residents
> will want to remain here to help us.... We have come to understand
> and appreciate them, and we admit we need them.[51]

In early 1945, it was decided that all the centers would be closed by the end of the year.[52] As the closing process continued, some evacuees returned to their former homes while many relocated in other areas.

Veterans who won the lottery acquired and moved barracks and other buildings from the camp, adding new siding and other improvements. *National Park Service, Hermann Collection.*

Most of those deciding to remain in Idaho chose eastern and southwestern Idaho, with the smallest concentration remaining in Magic Valley. The last family left Minidoka in October 1945 and by that time few evacuees remained in the Twin Falls area. By January 1946, only about 150 Japanese Americans remained at the Twin Falls labor camp, a number that declined rapidly thereafter.[53]

In 1947, camp land began to be divided into homesteads for which veterans could file. Along with their allotments, each received two buildings from Hunt, and the process of its dismantling continued.[54] Today many of these buildings still stand in the camp area, but there are few other visible remains. However, other traces persist. The memories of those who lived through that experience—the evacuees, the camp personnel, and the area residents as well—people whose lives were touched by Minidoka show that for them the camp in the Magic Valley region was of major significance in their lives.

For many years those involved in that experience were content to leave it unexamined. Reopening that part of the past is not intended to reopen old wounds, but rather to shed light on those experiences. Perhaps by doing that we might better understand ourselves as well.

### Notes

1. *Twin Falls Times-News*, April 23, 1942, 1.
2. U.S. Department of Commerce, *Sixteenth Census of the United States*: 1940, Population, vol. 2. Characteristics of the Population, Part 2: Florida-Iowa. (Washington, DC: Government Printing Office, 1943), 440.
3. Ibid.
4. Wendell *Irrigationist,* February 1, 1917, 11.
5. Sixteenth Census, 440.
6. Letter to James Sakamoto, December 1935. Box 1-21, Sakamoto MSS, University of Washington Library.
7. *Japanese-American Courier*, November 26, 1936, 4.
8. *Idaho Daily Statesman*, November 30, 1940, 7.
9. Clark's role in the relocation program is examined in Robert C. Sims, "'A Fearless, Patriotic, Clean-Cut Stand': Idaho's Governor Clark and Japanese American Relocation in World War II," *Pacific Northwest Quarterly* (April 1979), 75–81. Reprinted in this volume, chapter 2.
10. Portland *Oregonian*, February 28, 1942, 10; *Twin Falls Times-News*, March 1, 1942, 3.

11. "Survey of Public Opinion in Western States on Japanese Evacuation: Idaho" (A 16.03), 6, Japanese American Evacuation and Resettlement Collection (JERS), Bancroft Library, University of California, Berkeley.

12. *Idaho Daily Statesman*, July 2, 1942, 5.

13. Ibid., November 25, 1942, 4.

14. Ibid., September 18, 1942, 2.

15. *Twin Falls Times-News*, April 1, 1942, 1.

16. Ibid., February 25, 1942, 1.

17. Ibid., February 24, 1942, 1.

18. Ibid., February 23, 1942, 2.

19. *Idaho Daily Statesman*, February 18, 1942, 4.

20. Ibid., February 26, 1942, 5.

21. *Idaho Daily Statesman*, April 30, 1942, 1.

22. *Twin Falls Times-News*, April 28, 1942, 10.

23. Ibid., May 4, 1942, 1.

24. Ibid., May 4, 1942, 1; May 10, 1942, 10.

25. *Idaho Daily Statesman*, May 16, 1942, 2.

26. *Twin Falls Times-News*, May 19, 1942, 1; May 20, 1942, 3.

27. *Idaho Daily Statesman*, May 23, 1942, 1–2; May 26, 1942, 8.

28. *Twin Falls Times-News*, June 2, 1942, 1.

29. *Idaho Daily Statesman*, June 11, 1942, 8.

30. Ernest J. Palmer, "Historical and Personal Narrative," January 1946, JERS, Bancroft Library, University of California, Berkeley.

31. Dyke Miyagawa to Sakamoto, August 10, 1942. Box 10, Sakamoto MSS.

32. Imelda Kinoshita to Sakamoto, August 14, 1942. Box 10, Sakamoto MSS.

33. *Idaho Daily Statesman*, August 14, 1942, 1, 6.

34. *Minidoka Irrigator,* September 10, 1942, 4.

35. Edward H. Spicer, et al., *Impounded People: Japanese Americans in the Relocation Centers* (Tucson: University of Arizona Press, 1969), 128.

36. The Rupert Farm Labor Camp Laborer, October 21, 1942, 1.

37. "Minutes," JACL Special Emergency National Conference, November 17–24, 1942, Salt Lake City. Supplement #6, "Beet Field Survey."

38. "Minutes," JACL Special Emergency National Conference, November 17–24, 1942, Salt Lake City, 42.

39. *Minidoka Irrigator*, November 14, 1942, 2.

40. Ibid., October 9, 1943, 2.

41. *Twin Falls Times-News*, October 28, 1942, 3.

42. Ibid., October 30, 1942, 4.

43. *Minidoka Irrigator*, November 25, 1942, 7; January 27, 1943, 7; and March 13, 1943, 6.

44. Ibid., June 19, 1943, 5.

45. Ibid., June 5, 1943, 1.

46. Ibid., June 19, 1943, 4.
47. Ibid., May 29, 1943, 1; *Salt Lake Tribune*, September 8, 1944; n.p., clipping in August Rosqvist MSS., Idaho State Historical Society.
48. *Minidoka Irrigator*, September 16, 1944, 6.
49. Ibid., August 12, 1944, 1.
50. Ibid., November 11, 1944, 2.
51. Ibid., January 20, 1945, 2.
52. Ibid., February 3, 1945, 1.
53. Palmer, 13.
54. *Idaho Daily Statesman*, March 15, 1947, 6.

# 9

# Japanese American Soldiers as Part of "The Greatest Generation"

## EDITOR'S NOTE

*The year 2011 marked the 70th anniversary of America's entry into World War II. During that year, commemorations around the country recalled Americans who had served with honor and distinction in battle, on the home front, and as veteran-citizens after the war. Bob Sims was asked to give an account of Idaho's Japanese American soldiers to the Idaho State Historical Society on July 30, 2011. The following stories are excerpts from his speech. He reminded his audience of the particular sacrifices and triumphs of soldiers whose "home front" was like none other in the country.—SS*

## THE HOME FRONT FOR JAPANESE AMERICANS

Initially, they did not know where they were going, how long they would be detained, the conditions they would face, or what fate might await them. In temporary detention camps set up in converted race tracks and fairgrounds, their conditions were crowded, unsanitary, and surrounded with barbed wire and armed soldiers. In the permanent camp at Minidoka, about 13,000 people faced physical hardship for the next three years: extreme heat, extreme cold, mud and dust.

More difficult than all of that, they endured the feeling of being abandoned by this country, a feeling of rejection, the loss of liberty. How they conducted themselves in this tragic situation is testimony to their inner strength and courage. For the Nisei who came from a "home" such as Minidoka and entered battle this is sufficient testimony to count them as part of America's Greatest Generation.

Excerpted from "Japanese American Soldiers as Part of 'The Greatest Generation,'" speech delivered July 30, 2011, Robert C. Sims Collection, Box 35.

A Women's Army Corps enlistee poses before the Honor Roll listing Minidoka men and women who served in the armed forces during World War II. *National Archives and Records Administration, 210-CMB-I2-1353.*

At Minidoka, those serving in the military were acknowledged at the time by placing their names on an honor board near the entry to the camp. That memorial has been replicated and is now on display at Minidoka.

## THE 442ND REGIMENTAL COMBAT TEAM (RCT)

After Japan attacked Pearl Harbor, the War Department declared that Americans of Japanese descent were to have a draft rating of 4-C, a rating for "enemy aliens" and "any group not acceptable." However, this changed when on January 28, 1943, Secretary of War Henry L. Stimson announced that an all-Japanese American army combat unit was to be formed by volunteers. "It is the inherent right of every faithful citizen, regardless of ancestry, to bear arms in the nation's battle," he said.

The 442nd Regimental Combat Team (RCT) was organized on March 23, 1943. It had taken several key events to convince the Roosevelt Administration that these men should be allowed to enter combat for their country. Those events included lobbying from significant supporters of the Japanese American community, the excellent record of volunteers serving the army in Hawaii, and the growing need for more troops.

In spite of the earlier "prohibition," a large number of Nisei already were serving in a military group in Hawaii. This group eventually became the famous 100th Battalion, which had formed in June of 1942. Following Stimson's announcement an effort began to recruit young Nisei volunteers from the mainland's War Relocation Centers. Idaho's Minidoka led all camps in the response, with over 200 volunteering.

The Hawaiian group was brought to the mainland and, along with Nisei from the War Relocation Centers, received training as a combat unit in Wisconsin and at Camp Shelby in Mississippi. Soon they were fighting in Italy where they joined the 34th Division, landed on Salerno Beach, and fought at Cassino, Anzio, and the Battle for Rome. Following their initial action in Italy, the unit was moved to France to join the 36th Division, which was part of the force moving east toward the German border and meeting strong resistance.

Building Block Structure of U.S. Army Organization (Infantry) in World War II

| Name of Unit | Number of Soldiers | Staff Leader |
|---|---|---|
| Squad | About 12 soldiers | Sergeant |
| Platoon | Three squads. About 40-41 soldiers (includes officers and assistants) | Lieutenant |
| Company | Three to four platoons. Up to 200 soldiers | Captain |
| Battalion | Four to six companies. Up to 1,000 soldiers | Lt. Colonel |
| Brigade/Regiment | A few battalions. From 3,000 to 5,000 soldiers | Colonel |
| Division | Three to four brigades. From 10,000 to 15,000 soldiers. Smallest unit capable of performing independent actions. | Maj. General |
| Corps | Two to five divisions. From 20,000 to 45,000 soldiers | Lt. General |
| Field Army | Two or more corps | General |
| Army group | Four to five field armies. From 40,000 to 1 million soldiers | General |

Sources: Various; see online sites discussing "military organization," "triangular organization," and unit names.

## THE RESCUE OF THE TEXAS LOST BATTALION–VOSGES FOREST

In May 1944, the 422nd RCT absorbed the 100th Battalion north of Rome. By fall that year, the RCT was in the thick of the action. In late October, operating on little rest after days of front-line duty, the unit was ordered to rescue the first battalion of the 141st Regiment of the Texas 36th Division, 275 men, which had become isolated in the Vosges Forest, completely surrounded by the enemy. Two other battalions of the division had attempted and failed to rescue them. The rescue took place over several days under severe conditions. Fighting from tree to tree and ridge to ridge, the 442nd fought for yards at a time through dense woods shrouded with fog and rain. On October 30 they broke through the German lines and rescued the surviving 211 men of the Lost Battalion. The Nisei had suffered 800 casualties.

The Nisei soldiers were the first to make contact with the Texans, who crawled out of their deep foxholes with bearded, bewildered looks. Suffice it to say the bond between the Nisei soldiers of the 442nd and the Texans is a strong one that continues to this day.

## HEADCOUNTS AND GOLD STARS

After the rescue ordeal, Companies K, L, and I of the 442nd were each down to less than twenty men standing, out of two hundred at full strength. After liberating the surrounding towns, Maj. Gen. John H. Dahlquist asked for the 442nd to pass in review. When he saw how few men were present he reportedly became angry and reminded the commander of the 442nd that he had ordered the entire unit to appear, to which the reply was, "Sir, this is everybody."

Meanwhile, the families left behind at Minidoka spent anxious days wondering if their sons or husbands would return, or whether a blue star on the flag might have to be replaced with a gold one. Some mothers had particular reasons for concern; they had six sons in the military. At Minidoka, as at the other camps, each day seemed to bring news of casualties. Funerals and memorial services were commonplace.

Following the actions in the Vosges forest and the liberation of the Lost Battalion, the 442nd was sent to southern France for rest and recuperation, awaiting new replacements. When they were at

Six Minidoka mothers whose sons died during the war accept American flags for their fallen sons. *National Archives and Records Administration, 210-CMB-MS1-1315.*

full strength, they re-entered Italy and fought in the final battles in the spring, ending with the German surrender there on May 2, 1945.

## NISEI IN THE PACIFIC THEATER

While there has been considerable notice taken of the 442nd by military historians and others, another part of the Nisei contribution is not so well known. More than a month before the war began, the U.S. Army opened a Japanese language school at the Presidio in San Francisco which moved in early 1942 to Camp Savage, Minnesota. Other centers included one at the University of Michigan. Graduates from these Army schools served throughout the Pacific Theater as interpreters and interrogators. They were distributed throughout all forces in the Pacific.

Many of you may have heard of the unit referred to as Merrill's Marauders, named after its commander, Colonel Frank Merrill. This unit was given the mission of opening a vital land communication link between China and India, the so-called Burma Road. It was designated the 5307th Composite Unit, Provisional, and was trained in guerrilla tactics. Its mission was to disrupt Japanese activities in the area. The actions of this unit are the stuff of legends. In five months of combat, traveling on foot with pack mules, they had five major engagements with the enemy, and thirty-two overall.

Critical to their mission was the work of the fourteen Nisei in the unit. One of those was Roy Matsumoto, who had volunteered from the Jerome Relocation Center in Arkansas, and whose job was to gather information critical to the mission. As the war came to a close, these Nisei linguists served in important capacities at the signing of the surrender ending the war with Japan. These included a number of Nisei women linguists who later served in the occupation forces in Japan.

Roy Matsumoto on the occasion of receiving the Congressional Gold Medal on November 1, 2011. He and his family were incarcerated at Jerome, Arkansas. His honors also included the Bronze Star, Legion of Merit, U.S. Army Rangers Hall of Fame, and Military Intelligence Hall of Fame. *Courtesy of Hanako Wakatsuki.*

## AFTER THE WAR: NISEI VICTORIES AT THE HOME FRONT

In July 1946, when the 442nd RCT returned to the United States, President Harry Truman awarded it the last of eight Presidential Citations. At the time, he expressed his thoughts on their efforts in the following manner, "You fought not only the enemy, you fought prejudice, and won."

Following the war, Nisei veterans led the way in achieving equal rights for all Japanese Americans. After their sacrifices, it was difficult for anyone to argue that they were not deserving. Throughout the country, including here in Idaho, Nisei veterans lobbied for changes in laws discriminating against Japanese Americans, such as the land law which kept Japanese Americans from owning land, and the law prohibiting marriage with Caucasians. One of the first victories was the McCarran-Walter Act of 1952, which opened citizenship to the Issei, and permitted immigration from Japan.

Over time, additional efforts achieved nearly full equality. In the 1980s, a presidential commission recommended a national apology for the forced removal and incarceration of the Nikkei. This resulted in Ronald Reagan signing of the Civil Liberties Act of 1988. (See Appendix C.)

In 2000, after a Senate bill requiring the review of military records of Asian Americans, President Clinton awarded twenty-one Medals of Honor to Nisei veterans, all members of the 442nd Regimental Combat Team, three of them posthumously, and one of these to the family of William Kenzo Nakamura, a volunteer whose family had been incarcerated at Minidoka.

In October of 2010, Congress voted to award the Congressional Gold Medal to all members of the 442nd, the 100th Battalion, the Military Intelligence Service (MIS), and the Counter Intelligence Corps. President Barrack Obama signed the bill in the Oval Office. The Congressional Gold Medal, along with the Presidential Medal of Freedom, is the highest civilian award in the United States. The decoration is awarded to those who perform an outstanding deed or act of service to the security, prosperity, and national interest of the United States.

## IDAHO REMEMBERS

Other important commemorations have been made at Minidoka. Not much notice was taken of the site for many years after the war, but since 1979, a number of ceremonies have recognized the historical significance both of the site and the military record of the Nisei. One of most important events was the placing of a plaque in 1990 which bears the names of the seventy-three men from Minidoka who died in World War II. Each year there is a pilgrimage to Minidoka. Part of the ceremony involves reading their names aloud. When the plaque was first placed there, the mother of one of the honorees placed a wreath on the memorial, one of the most poignant moments I have witnessed at Minidoka. One of those names is that of William Kenzo Nakamura, one of the twenty-one Japanese Americans who received the Medal of Honor.

The Hosoda family of Emmett, Idaho, are a part of this story. Issei immigrants Max and Itono Hosoda raised their family on a farm just outside Emmett. They had four sons and two daughters. Three of those sons were in the 442nd RCT. Two died in combat. On Memorial Day 2009 they were honored at the Emmett National Guard Armory with the dedication of a memorial wall, with friends in attendance who remembered them. The oldest son, Max, was a sergeant killed in action in the Vosges Forest in the days leading up to the Lost Battalion episode. He was twenty-nine. His younger brother Earl graduated from Emmett High School in 1943, was drafted in August 1944, and went overseas in January 1945. He was killed in action on April 5, 1945, in northern Italy, just a month before the German surrender there. He was nineteen.

Returning to Roy Matsumoto, now ninety-eight years old.[1] His service with Merrill's Marauders and elsewhere in the MIS earned him the Bronze Star and the Legion of Merit. More recently, he has been inducted into the U.S. Army Rangers Hall of Fame and the Military Intelligence Corps Hall of Fame. Part of the reason that the public awareness of the service of those in the MIS has lagged behind that of the 442nd is that all MIS personnel were instructed not to talk about their service. By the mid-1970s, with the passage of the Freedom of

Information Act, that has changed and we are seeing more books and documentaries about their activities.

## OTHER VIEWS OF THE NISEI

Every year the people of Bruyeres, France, hold a ceremony commemorating the liberation of their town by the soldiers of the 442nd RCT. In 2004, on the 60th anniversary, several veterans of that campaign and many others went to Bruyeres to participate. At that event, Sandra Tanamachi, the niece of one of the men who died there, remarked: "I decided to make this trip, as I wanted to be in the exact location where my heroes, the Nisei veterans, fought and sacrificed, so that we, the future generations of Americans, could live in a more accepting, understanding America in the aftermath of World War II."[2]

Bill Mauldin was one of the most perceptive journalists covering the battle zones of Europe during the Second World War. He gave us a close-up view of the lives of those who slogged through the mud and blood of those battlefields and showed us the humanity in those men who sacrificed so much. He had a special affection for the Nisei soldiers, of whom he wrote: "I know of two such [Nisei] regiments in Italy that never had a case of AWOL, never had a case of malingering, never had a case of cowardice. No one who has not been in the war has a right to mistreat anyone who has been in the war."[3]

With those remarks, what shall I say by way of final accounting? More than 22,500 Japanese Americans served in the U.S. Army in WW II. Of those, 18,000 were in segregated units of the 442nd and 100th Battalions, and the 1399th Engineer Construction Battalion, which served the homeland defense of Hawaii. Most of the remainder served in the MIS. The twenty-one Medals of Honor earned by men of the 442nd RCT stands in distinction with other units. Only four divisions in the Army in WWII had ten or more, and the 442nd had more than twice that many. And it was one-third the size of a division.

The Nisei story is largely one of how those who came of age in the war and its aftermath struggled successfully to acquire an education, to find jobs and careers and places to live, to open businesses, and to win recognition of their civil rights. In all these things, it was the Nisei veterans who led the way.

## Notes

1. Roy Matsumoto died at age 100 on April 21, 2014. Stourwater Pictures produced a short documentary film in 2013 entitled *Honor and Sacrifice: The Roy Matsumoto* Story.
2. Sandra Tanamachi, quoted in an online account, "Niseis invited to French 60th Anniversary of Liberation," at hirasaki.net/Family_Stories/Bruyeres.htm.
3. "Mauldin Tangles with Patton, Defends Nisei...and Hunts House," *San Francisco News*, June 26, 1945, page not cited.

10

# The Japanese American Return to the Pacific Northwest

## EDITOR'S NOTE

*In a talk he gave in 1996, Bob Sims mentioned the book he planned to write about Minidoka and described its theme, at least as he saw it then:*

My approach is to consider the history of the residents of that camp as essentially a community study, describing that "community," and analyzing the history of the group from the time of forced removal from their homes, through the time spent in the assembly centers at Puyallup and North Portland, the wartime experience in camp and the variety of experiences in relocation, and finally, the return to the West Coast and the efforts to establish their former "communities."[1]

*The following paper was prepared two years earlier as a lecture to be part of a proposed traveling exhibit in 1994 called "The Issei Pioneers in Oregon." It provides a glimpse at the research that he already had undertaken to understand the final step in that journey, the return to the Pacific Northwest. His notes are rudimentary, reminders for his later reference. Sources have been added or expanded where possible. Unfortunately, funding for the proposed traveling exhibit did not materialize.—SS*

———————————

The period of the return of Japanese Americans to the West Coast states following World War II is a significant one in the history of this minority group. Although most attention has been given to the evacuation period, during which the entire Japanese and Japanese American population of the West Coast was removed and imprisoned,

Robert C. Sims, "The Japanese American Return to the Pacific Northwest," *Robert C. Sims Collection on Minidoka and Japanese Americans, 1891–2014,* Boise State University, Mss. 356, Box 51, Folder 25.

the post-war years contain the struggle to re-assimilate, to reestablish lives, and to make a place in American society.

While most Japanese in this country lived in California, a substantial number resided in the Pacific Northwest, with the greatest number in and around Seattle. Of Washington's 12,000 Japanese, more than 7,000 lived in Seattle, with several other concentrations, such as the Tacoma district, the farming district immediately south, and in the Yakima Valley.

In Oregon, a similar pattern prevailed, with about one half of the state's approximately 4,000 Japanese living in or near Portland. The most important concentrations outside Multnomah County were in six areas, ranging from about 100 to 500 in Clatsop County, Malheur, Clackamas, Marion, and Washington. Hood River had the largest of these, with almost 500 people.

The efforts of evacuated Japanese Americans to reestablish themselves in the post-war years is the topic of this paper. I consider those efforts to be an important element in the history of Japanese Americans in this country, as well as an important part of the history of this region.

At the end of the war the evacuees did not simply return and pick up where they had left off. Indeed, many never returned at all, and many who did return to the region settled in communities other than the ones they left. The evacuation and the return changed the character of many communities of the northwest and directly affected the lives and fortunes of upwards of 20,000 people. By 1948 a number of distinctive patterns had emerged and, by that time, many of the most important challenges for Japanese American re-assimilation into the Pacific Northwest had been met and overcome. Today, I will describe and assess the significance of some of these factors.

In December 1944, military authorities announced the end of the prohibition against Japanese Americans on the West Coast. This restriction was to be lifted on January 2, 1945, and the evacuees would be able to return to their former homes. But it was not very simple to do that. Many families had become separated during the war, with many of the young Nisei in the military, and thousands of evacuees relocated to the Midwest and the east. This fragmentation and dispersal of families made it difficult to make plans for a return to the

West Coast. In addition, those who suffered extensive financial loss during the evacuation also had an almost insurmountable problem. The available relocation allowance was only $25, and for those with no resources and no immediate prospects for income, it was a serious problem. Japanese American farmers who had owned their own land faced an additional dilemma, for they could not just return at will. Their property had, in most cases, been leased "for the duration, or until the termination of the national emergency." In addition, thirty days' notice had to be given in order to end the lease.

There was also a persistence of anti-Japanese activity, and many early returnees were met with threats, and, in some cases, violence. According to a War Relocation Authority (WRA) report, "One of the most serious problems facing the returning evacuees...was the continued discovery of new incidents, thefts, and vandalism, which occurred to personal and real property." According to that report, hundreds of such incidents occurred in Seattle alone.

Among the early families to return to Seattle were Mr. and Mrs. Shigeo Nagaishi and their three children, who arrived in Seattle on May 11, 1945, from the Minidoka center to reoccupy their house on

Many families returned to Seattle to find that their homes had been vandalized and defaced. *Museum of History and Industry, Seattle, PI28084.*

Walker Street. When they arrived they found a sign painted on the garage doors: "No Japs Wanted Here," and a skull and crossbones painted in bright red on a step leading to the house, along with the word, "death," painted underneath. "The garage doors were battered, the garage windows smashed, and their automobile 'put out of commission.' One window in the house was also shattered with a rock."

In early June of 1945 the director of the WRA, Dillon Myers, testifying before a House Appropriations Subcommittee, identified a major WRA problem as "reluctance, particularly on the part of the old people in the centers, to be relocated because of a feeling of insecurity....They are aliens and they are not sure that they would be accepted. They fear that they would not be able to make a living, and also have a fear of bodily harm."

An article in the *Minidoka Irrigator* for June 9, 1945, quoted someone who had left and reported, "In certain areas...we have had some occurrences such as shooting into dwellings, boycotts, and other atrocities on the part of misguided un-American patriots and a small group of people who have an economic interest in opposing the return of evacuees."

An *Irrigator* editorial a few days later expressed this concern: "Some of us are frightened by the news stories that appear with surprising regularity in the coast papers concerning the hostility of the residents there. We are frightened and sometimes rather hurt and baffled by these stories, because once upon a time we used to know these same people."

Even the more "successful" returns were often tempered with negative elements. Among the first returnees to Portland was the owner of a rooming house. After the return she wrote this to a friend:

> We arrived safely, everything is fine, all the old tenants were glad to see us come back and the new ones like us. [The] manager and housekeeper wanted to scare us away so they could rob us a little while longer.... When I came the manager was so ashamed he couldn't look me in the face. But he has made a good thing out of my being away. The place is dirty, the linens and supplies I've been paying for are all stolen. Even some of the furniture has been taken out. And nothing cleaned or kept up for these three years. It's a shame! Anyway,

everyone is glad to see us back. We have received flowers and presents and even some of the old men had tears in their eyes when they saw us again.... We go everywhere, restaurants, shops, and the like. Old friends glad to see you, strangers too busy to care. The only ones who don't like the Japanese are the ones now robbing them or those who find them too industrious and don't want them as competitors. You should tell people to return home and just act natural.... We feel like kids out of a cage. We are glad to be home.

But the return to Portland was very slow. By late March 1945, only about a hundred had returned.

One of the most disturbing features of the postwar period was the persistence of anti-Japanese sentiment. As before the war, this racism often wore the mask of patriotism, and that approach had a degree of success for a time. Few communities illustrate this situation as clearly as Hood River, Oregon. That community received national attention when, in early December 1944, it removed sixteen Nisei names from the town Honor Roll, which listed the area's men in the armed services. This action was taken by the American Legion Post, and apparently met with the approval of a large part of the community. Two days later the legion post passed a resolution to exclude all people of Japanese ancestry from the Hood River Valley. Shortly after the Japanese were permitted to return, the local legion post published a "Statement on the Japanese," which charged "that the Japanese Americans, with the aid of Tokyo, had managed to obtain the best land in the Valley..." and that "the Japanese in Hood River were all part of a plot of Japan's government for the 'Japanization' of our little valley."

During the second week of January the legion "began running ads in the local newspaper asserting the undesirability of the Japanese Americans." Throughout January and February the ads listed the names of Japanese American landowners and told them not to come back but to sell their land. Those ads also listed about 600 people who signed a petition favoring exclusion. This kind of activity was a factor in the reluctance of evacuees to return. One Japanese American whose name was listed in the ad, read the paper while still at Minidoka and had this response: "It gives you a funny feeling to see your name in your local paper listed with the other Japanese they are trying to keep out and to see the names of people you thought were your friends on a petition saying they want you to stay away. I have seen the names of my neighbors on two sides" (WRA, Community Analysis Report #13).

When the first three Hood River Valley Japanese returned on January 12, 1945, "No Jap Trade" signs began appearing in the store windows. Not until early 1946 did some of the visible signs of prejudice begin to disappear. Even so, as late as 1948 fewer than 200 Japanese Americans were back in the area, compared to about 500 in 1941. Given the strength of the anti-Japanese feelings there, it is remarkable that so many did return. One important element in the return was the factor of land ownership. Virtually all who owned land returned. Those who had leased or rented land mostly did not return. We see this same pattern reflected in several other northwest communities as well. Two that had substantial Japanese American populations that declined significantly were the White River Valley area and the Yakima Valley. An American Friends Service Committee Report in early February 1945 said: "In [these valleys] there is organized resistance of a venomous form.... We know that returning evacuees have been denied entrance to their homes by the tenants and that some have been told to their faces that they are not welcome in the community and would not find it comfortable to remain. We have heard that in one or two cases people have been ordered out of town." Both of these communities had very low return rates, rates that corresponded very closely to the percentage of land ownership in those areas. Two years after it was possible to return, few former White River residents had done so. Many who formerly farmed that area remained in eastern Oregon and western Idaho where they had located during the war.

Although not as well publicized, several communities in these areas also experienced Honor Roll incidents similar to that of Hood River. The parents of a Nisei serviceman returned to their home town to find their son's name omitted and wrote this letter to a friend: "We noticed shortly after returning that Mit's name was not included so we turned it in. Just recently we learned that his name had been up there at one time but had been taken down due to the objections of [some people]. We want to get his name back up there before he comes home even if we have to paint and tack it up ourselves."

The combination of strong anti-Japanese sentiment and low percentage of land ownership both contributed to the low rate of return to these areas. Prior to the war there was a Japanese American population of about 1,200 in the Yakima Valley. Following the war, only about 10 percent returned, the approximate percentage of land ownership.

For many Japanese Americans, western Idaho and eastern Oregon and Washington provided relocation sites during the war and immediately following. That region was important to many as a "stopping-off" place; for some it was one step in the return home. One of the most common features of the Pacific Northwest Japanese American experience was to have spent some time in this region as agricultural labor.

One area most affected by this trend was Malheur County, Oregon. Prior to the war it claimed only 137 Japanese Americans. At its wartime peak, there were perhaps as many as 5,000 evacuees there, working in seasonal agriculture. At the end of the war some of these workers remained and, even as late as 1948, Ontario, the largest town in the county, had 550 Japanese residents.

One impact of the evacuation which persisted into the post-war period was the creation of a type of "displaced person." Although the conditions of their existence were decidedly less severe and harsh than the displaced persons of Europe, it was difficult enough.

There were people who lived in the labor camps on the eastern edge of the restricted zone during much of the war, many of whom remained at war's end. One such camp, near Caldwell, Idaho, had a capacity for 550 workers, and, by late 1946 housed 260 Japanese, mostly in family units, which distinguished them from the migrant workers of an earlier era. A 1946 report on the Caldwell camp included this assessment: "Most of those remaining did not have anything to go back to, for the few that may have had property had long ago disposed of it."[2]

Some of those in the camp at that time had been back to Seattle and returned to work in the fields again, reporting that the only jobs available there were either "in dishwashing or other unskilled service jobs where the pay is fairly low." A few Issei had also made the trip back and "returned with discouraging reports on housing and types of jobs available for Issei.... Families which have two to four members working realize that they will have a much harder time on the West Coast than they have now. Few anticipate leaving at least for the next few years," the report concluded.

One of the big employers of Japanese in Malheur County was the Simplot Company. That company, which dehydrated potatoes and other products and maintained huge packing sheds, hired hundreds of Japanese workers during the war. Its operation at Jamieson, Oregon, about 43 miles from Ontario, hired Japanese almost exclusively. Jamieson was a company town of 350 in 1945, all of whom worked for Simplot except for the postmaster and storekeeper. This number declined after 1945, but there were still about 150 Japanese there at the end of 1946, existing in a company shanty town in conditions decidedly worse than those in the relocation centers. The only convenience was cold water piped into each cabin. There was no social activity at all; few workers had cars; and the train to Ontario ran on an irregular schedule about three days a week. The group living in Jamieson in late 1946 was comprised mostly of older Issei with a few Nisei families. A WRA official analyzing the situation there wrote that: "It is safe to assume that another year or so will see this small Japanese settlement at Jamieson down to several dozen." While it was evident that arrangements such as those at Jameison were on their way out, many evacuees, given their circumstances, lingered on in conditions such as that well into the post-war period.

Since it comprises the largest concentration of Japanese population in the Pacific Northwest, let us consider Seattle. Seattle had a very high rate of return of former residents, in spite of the problems I have already noted.

As elsewhere on the West Coast, the return to Seattle took place with a backdrop of continued anti-Japanese sentiment. Shortly after the West Coast ban was lifted Washington Governor Mon Wallgren "declared emphatically" his opposition "to the return of any Japanese to the Pacific Coast for the duration of the war." He also stated that, "the public has not been fully informed on the extent of underground Japanese (American) collaboration with Japan." When Seattle area Japanese American farmers returned they faced a boycott from produce merchants there. The farmers in that region normally marketed through the wholesale dealers on Western Avenue. The first farmer back was successful in delivering his vegetables on the first attempt, but that evening a representative of the wholesaler called at his farm and told him he would no longer be able to accept his produce. At that time most of the wholesalers displayed "Remember Pearl Harbor League" posters in their windows reading: "We want no Japs here, Hear?" Throughout the spring and summer of 1945 no person of Japanese ancestry was able to deliver his produce to the wholesalers in Seattle.

In non-farm employment, the problems were equally frustrating, and probably more complex. A number of labor unions on the coast refused to admit Nisei members. A report by the Seattle Council of Churches in 1946 concluded: "The labor unions discriminated to such an extent against persons of Japanese ancestry that it was nearly impossible to get service from businesses associated with the unions, or get employment through the unions." Local 7, the AFL Building Services Union, was one of the unions in the city which "allowed Japanese members, however."

Although more extreme than many labor leaders, Dave Beck, vice president of the Teamsters Union, reflected the unthinking racism implicit in that attitude when he said: "We must not permit a repetition of Jap infiltration on this coast, nor the surrender of business enterprises to aliens who hate our people and our institutions."

With these early incidents occurring, those remaining in the camps, and some who had already relocated elsewhere, had reservations about a return to Seattle. A young Nisei woman, writing from Minidoka in early 1945 recorded her feelings: "Well, the evacuation order has been lifted and we are now free to return to the coast where prejudice still runs rampant."[3]

### Notes

1. Robert C. Sims, "Defining the Japanese American Community of the Pacific Northwest," paper delivered to Pacific Northwest History Conference, Oregon State University, Corvallis, OR, April 20, 1996. Sims Collection, Mss 356, Box 51, Folder 25.

2. Likely source: John deYoung, "Japanese Resettlement in the Boise Valley and Snake River Valley, September 1946," Japanese American Evacuation and Resettlement Collection (JERS), W2.04. Bancroft Library, University of California, Berkeley.
3. Likely source: Jerome T. Light, "Development of a Junior-Senior High School Program in a Relocation Center for People of Japanese Ancestry During the War with Japan," unpublished EdD dissertation, Stanford University, 1949.

11

# The Other Concentration Camps: Japanese American Removal and Imprisonment During World War II

*Choosing words to define wartime events is hardly a scholarly issue alone; for words are highly charged with memories and emotions connected with World War II crimes and tragedies. Should an "internment camp" be referred to as "a concentration camp"? Why is it important?*

*Bob Sims took up this matter in a 2000 speech at the Idaho Historical Museum in Boise. He also considered government-originated terms such as "evacuation," "relocation," and "non-aliens." On the topic of language—as with the other subjects he undertook to teach his listeners—he considered it important to consider word usage in the light of the truth about the past. This debate on terminology was reignited in 2019 when detention camps along the U.S. border with Mexico were described as "concentration camps" by New York Congresswoman Alexandria Ocasio-Cortez and others.—SS*

---

Two years ago this week, the Japanese American National Museum moved one of its exhibits to the United States Park Service Museum at Ellis Island. That exhibit, "America's Concentration Camps: Remembering the Japanese American Experience" [at the Ellis Island Museum from April 3, 1997, to January 5, 1998], ignited a controversy which is the focal point of my remarks tonight. The controversy had to do with the use of the term "concentration camp" to describe the experience of this group during World War II, when they

---

"The Other Concentration Camps: Japanese American Removal and Imprisonment During World War II," speech delivered at the Idaho Historical Society, Boise, April, 2000, Sims Collection, Box 51, Folder 32.

were removed from their homes on the West Coast and placed in camps in the interior. Ellis Island officials and some Jewish groups objected to the use of the phrase, contending that most Americans associate the term with the Nazi death camps of the Holocaust, and that using it to describe the experience of Japanese Americans could diminish the horror of the Nazi slaughter. Among those mounting the protest was David A. Harris, the executive director of the American Jewish Committee in New York, who said that the exhibit's title "dilutes what we have come to understand as the meaning of concentration camps. Since the Second World War," he continued, this term has "taken on a specificity and a new level of meaning that deserves protection."

The Ellis Island superintendent for the Park Service, Diane H. Dayson, wrote to Karen Ishizuka, the exhibit curator, and expressed concern that because "concentration camps" today connotes death camps, the "very large Jewish community" in New York City "could be offended by or misunderstand" the title. Dayson told Ishizuka that the exhibit could not appear unless the term was removed from the title.

This was not the first time controversy swirled around the use of this term to describe the Japanese American wartime experience. In October 1944, when the United States Supreme Court rendered its opinion in the Fred Korematsu case, Justice Hugo Black wrote: "Regardless of the true nature of the assembly and relocation centers—**and we deem it unjustifiable to call them concentration camps with all the ugly connotations that term implies**—we are dealing specifically with nothing but an exclusion order" [emphasis by Sims]. In his opinion, Black went on to accept the argument that the action by which Korematsu and over 110,000 people were removed from their homes and imprisoned was justified by military necessity.

At the very beginning of the application of the policy of removal, exclusion, and imprisonment, the term "concentration camp" was frequently used to refer to the places of confinement. It should be kept in mind that, at the time, few could imagine the extent of the horror we later associated with the use of the term in referring to the Nazi camps. If people thought of comparisons at all, it was more likely to be with historical examples such as the Spanish-American War, the Boer War, and even Idaho's own labor wars in the late 19th century.

In these instances the term was used to refer to places of confinement for "enemies of the state."

In the immediate aftermath of the war, there was not only a diminished reference to "concentration camps," but a general disregard or disinterest in the topic. That changed markedly in 1970 with the publication of Roger Daniels's book, *Concentration Camps: USA*. Daniels received considerable flak for the use of that title, but he steadfastly defended the use as appropriate. Gradually, the term, which was widely used during the war years, began to gain a renewed approval. But the approval was not unanimous. When Manzanar, one of the two California camps, was proposed as a state historic site, the controversy was renewed. When Japanese American groups proposed the use of the term on the plaque commemorating the camp, the State Historical Resources Commission voted against it. However, the State Director of Parks and Recreation overruled the commission and, in 1976, the term was used on plaques for both Manzanar and Tule Lake, the other California camp. Four years later, when dedication ceremonies were held at the site of Minidoka, the Idaho camp, the term appeared on the commemorative plaque.

A young woman stands in an evacuation line, San Francisco, April 25, 1942. *National Archives and Records Administration, WRA photo by Dorothea Lange, 210-G-A572.*

This increased use of the term brought a strong reaction from some parts of the public and spawned the creation of a group to orchestrate opposition to the practice. Out of this was formed Americans for Historical Accuracy, an organization arguing against the use of the term and which began a campaign to "set the record straight." One of the leaders of this group is Lillian Baker [died October 21, 1996] who, in a number of publications, appearances at various hearings, and in a concerted media effort, insisted that Japanese Americans were not in "concentration camps." Rather, she places the best possible construction on that experience, overlooking negative aspects. In her book, *American and Japanese Relocation in World War II: Fact, Fiction, and Fallacy*, she presents the high school yearbook from the Manzanar camp as evidence of the normal, even "happy" life led by the camp inmates. The reality was quite different from what she wished to portray. Minidoka also had a yearbook; looking at it, one might assume a normal community and school life. But such was not the case. Students had had their educations interrupted during the spring of 1942, when they were moved to assembly centers. That interruption continued at Minidoka. School did not even begin until November because most of the high school students were out in sugar beet fields helping with the harvest. For most, this meant the loss of yet another semester's credit. The quality of the instruction was limited, at best, and the facilities left a great deal to be desired in both the core subject matter and the extracurricular part of school life. When it became possible for some families to leave camp and move to communities in Idaho, they found they had to pay tuition for the privilege of attending schools inferior to those they had attended in Seattle and Portland.

Minidoka, like all of the other relocation centers, was built using blueprints for an army "field of operations" camp. Amenities one might find in a normal community—such as a high school gymnasium—were not present. Such a gym was promised to the residents but in three and a half years was never completed. In short, things were not as Baker would have us believe.

At the risk of making an unwarranted comparison, one might say that, at one level, the Americans for Historical Accuracy display their own variant of "holocaust denial" by suggesting that the camps might actually have been a positive experience. Or, at worst, benign. Many who object to the use of the term "concentration camps" in this context point to the extensive use of other terms utilized by the army and the War Relocation Authority to describe the experience. What was that experience? Over 120,000 residents of the U.S.A., two thirds of whom were American citizens, were incarcerated under armed guard. No one committed a crime: there were no accusations, no trials, and no convictions. Japanese Americans were political prisoners. To detain American citizens in a site under armed guard surely constitutes a "concentration camp." But what terms did the government officials use while involved in the process? They were using terms Baker found much more acceptable. These were "evacuation," "relocation," and "non-aliens."

Official government policy makers consistently used "evacuation" to refer to the forced removal of Japanese Americans. They called the sites "relocation centers." These are euphemisms: they do not imply forced removal nor incarceration in enclosures patrolled by armed guards. Perhaps the most obvious circumlocution was the use of the term "non-alien," a phrase which appeared on notice sheets affixed to telephone poles announcing the removal orders.

> Pursuant to the provisions of Public Proclamations Nos. 1 and 2, this Headquarters, dated March 2, 1942, and March 16, 1942, respectively, it is hereby ordered that from and after 12 o'clock noon, P.W.T., of Thursday, May 7, 1942, all persons of Japanese ancestry, both aliens and non-alien, be excluded from that portion of Military Area No.1, described as follows....

Exactly what does "non-alien" mean? To whom does it refer? It is a euphemism for "citizen"! Government officials were knowingly nullifying the constitutional rights of Japanese Americans, so it is clear why they did not wish to use the term "citizen." Euphemistic language accomplished a number of objectives for using the terms:

- It sidetracked legal and constitutional challenges.
- It allowed the government to maintain a decent public image.
- It helped lead the victims into willing cooperation.

- It permitted the white civilian employees to work without self-reproach.
- It kept the historical record in the government's favor.

It is also the case, I believe, that use of softer language allows us to continue to think the best of our government's actions toward Japanese Americans and thus to think the best of our country. In reading Lillian Baker it is clear that she sees that insistence on telling the truth about this part of our history constitutes "America bashing," which is exactly the term she uses.

Over the years, I have found a great deal of resistance to the telling of this story by those who consider themselves to be "patriotic Americans" and will brook no tarnishing of the American image. To cite but one example: when I first began to work with this topic, some twenty-five years ago, I gave a presentation to a group of high school students, a gathering organized and sponsored by one of our veterans organizations. After telling the story, in broad outline, of the imprisonment of Japanese Americans, I was met with something between a cold shoulder and hostility by those who had invited me to speak. They made it clear that they were looking for a more uplifting and patriotic message. For a time, many Japanese Americans themselves fostered this approach to their history. Although this is a rather complicated story in itself, for brevity's sake let me just say that, by the early 1960s, Japanese Americans had made such a remarkable "recovery" from their wartime exclusion and imprisonment that they were being hailed as a "model minority." For a long time, they seemed not willing or interested in re-opening memories of that painful experience. In fact, in a curious way, it was even used to validate the appropriateness of their "new" status, and, in the process, celebrate America. Harry Kitano, in the preface of the 1969 edition of his highly regarded, *Japanese Americans: The Evolution of a Subculture*, wrote:

> America likes success stories—the bigger, the better. Therefore, America should enjoy the story of the Japanese in the United States... for it is a story of success, Japanese American style. It has all the elements of a melodrama: the Japanese (the hero) is faced with initial suspicion, mistrust, and hatred by the United States (the heroine).

Starting from this background of hostility and discrimination, the hero begins the excruciating process of winning the hand of the heroine. He pulls himself up by the bootstraps, suffers rebuffs and rejection, and finally gains the grudging respect and admiration of the heroine. Acceptance, romance, and marriage may be in the offing.

Many people read that not as a celebration of Japanese Americans alone, but as a validation of the American Dream and thus an approval of America itself. And, implicitly, it raises the question of how to approach the history of America, or of any American subculture, in essentially "positive" or "critical" ways.

Public memory, like personal memory, is highly selective. Like my veterans organization leaders, we tend to prefer myths that exalt rather than facts that might demean. We like good warm inspiring stories and happy endings. What the historian John Bodner has called "official memory" reflects this tendency to highlight moments of courage, ingenuity, persistence, dedication, sacrifice, triumph, and victory, as in Harry Kitano's story of the "success" of Japanese Americans. Such triumphalism has meant that in the United States commemoration "often becomes celebration." To put it differently, we find it difficult to conceive of commemoration as an activity other than celebration. But this is not why we recollect the experiences of Japanese Americans during the Second World War. We do not celebrate the fact that something like 120,000 people, for no good reason, lost property, their livelihood, and freedom through an arbitrary act of government. We do not celebrate the mass deprivation of constitutional rights.

Commemorations can also be forums on the past, on our culture, identifying and explaining those experiences that do trouble us—or should trouble us. It is in this context and for this reason that we should remember and understand unpleasant parts of our national story. What do we have to gain by digging up the messy past? Many years ago, historian Rodman Paul was in Boise. He told me that he had been on the board of the California Historical Society when they decided to publish a book and sponsor a photographic exhibit on the Japanese American experience during the war. He told me how some of his fellow board members resisted doing that. Paul said he felt the best argument he could come up with was to cite the biblical injunction: "You shall know the truth and the truth shall set you free." More recently, in fact, just this week, I was looking at the Raul Hilberg book, *The Politics of Memory: The Journey of a Holocaust Historian,* and noted his frontispiece quotation from H. G. Adler: "History without tragedy does not exist, and knowledge is better and more wholesome than ignorance."

I do not want to leave the impression that those who were opposing the use of the term "concentration camp" for the Ellis Island exhibit were opting for ignorance over knowledge, so I had best return to that story and conclude it. What is at stake in that debate is that the memory of the wartime camps has become central to the identity of both Jews and Japanese Americans. In this case, a compromise was reached which allowed the exhibit to go on as scheduled, thanks in part to the intervention of Senator Daniel Inouye. The contending parties agreed to place a statement at the exhibit which explained the term "concentration camp" and the differences between the Nazi camps and those in America. When the exhibit opened on April 3, 1997, program pamphlets and a panel at the entrance read:

> A concentration camp is a place where people are imprisoned not because of any crimes they have committed, but simply because of who they are. Nazi camps were places of torture, barbarous medical experiments, and summary executions; some were extermination centers with gas chambers. All had one thing in common: The people in power decided to remove a minority group from the general population, and the rest of society let it happen.

After the compromise was reached, Senator Inouye said that the exhibit and its title in no way diminished the memory of the Holocaust, but provided a powerful and important lesson of its own. "Suffering has many faces," he said. "Jewish suffering has the most terrible face, but suffering is still suffering."

# PART TWO

# THE PATH TO THE NATIONAL HISTORIC SITE

Remains of the waiting room in the reception building near the main entrance at Minidoka. Incarcerees built the fireplace with basalt boulders found in the area. *Courtesy of photographer Teresa Tamura, from* Minidoka: An American Concentration Camp.

# 12

# An Eye to Justice:
# Minidoka National Historic Site

## Susan M. Stacy

At the last Minidoka Civil Liberties Symposium he would moderate—in June 2014—Bob Sims spoke of how, when he began studying Minidoka in 1970, its closing had occurred only twenty-five years earlier, yet felt much farther distant in the past. He began with two favorite quotes about remembering and forgetting. One was from a 2012 poem written by Mark Strand, "In the Afterlife:"

> There was a house, and then no house. There were trees, but none remain. When no one remembers, what is there? You, whose moments are gone, who drift like smoke in the afterlife, tell me something, tell me anything.[1]

Then he referred to a letter written in 1942 by a new arrival to Minidoka who described the place as "a land that God has forgotten."

But that had changed. By 2014 Minidoka was no longer destined to be forgotten. It had been a unit of the National Park System since 2001—a place to remember forever. Sims used his time at the podium to review the milestones by which such change had come about. The following account is based on his own outline but also provides something of his own role in events, which he tended not to report.

After the War Relocation Authority closed Minidoka in 1945, it conducted a homestead lottery and distributed most of the land to returning veterans. The buildings were salvaged and removed. The desert began reclaiming the few acres remaining in the hands of the Bureau of Reclamation, finding little resistance to its erosive winds and invasive plants.

Sims began his academic research into the history of Idaho's Japanese Americans by interviewing them. He found that many people incarcerated at Minidoka continued to hold their painful experiences and memories closely in their own hearts. He met Issei and Nisei who were reluctant to speak of Minidoka even to their children and grandchildren, much less publish or record them. He began to encourage people not only to tell their stories, but write and record them as well.

His research led Sims to descendants of many pioneering Japanese families who had settled in Idaho in the 1890s. Among them were members and leaders of the Pocatello-Blackfoot Japanese American Citizens League (JACL) from whom Sims learned of the organization's history in Idaho. Idaho Nikkei had not been forced from their homes during the war, but had nevertheless been profoundly impacted by anti-Japanese racism and wartime events. The JACL leaders, like Bob Sims, felt strongly about preserving what was left of Minidoka.

## STATEWIDE INVENTORY OF HISTORIC PLACES—1976

In the 1970s, Idaho's JACL chapters and others began inviting Sims to speak about his Minidoka research. In a 1973 discussion with JACL leaders from the Northwest-Intermountain Region attending an oral history conference and workshop, chairman Eugene Furuyama said that he sensed considerable "misunderstanding" of the Japanese American experience by those outside the community. "I think Japanese Americans need to form some type of historical record of their accomplishments despite [their] adversities." Sims asserted that the Japanese American community itself should take the responsibility for recovering its own history.[2] The workshop proceeded with its agenda to teach and encourage potential oral historians. It also foreshadowed other activities that both Sims and the JACL would undertake to preserve the site of Minidoka itself.

Bob Sims had many teaching messages and he delivered them often. He addressed a Boys State gathering in Boise and laid out the facts about this blot on American history. The Boys State organizer thought the presentation "improper" and told Sims he had expected something more "positive."[3] Sims spoke at JACL banquets honoring graduating Japanese American high school seniors and told them, "it is extremely important for each of [you] to know your past as an essential step in self-knowledge....to take a good look in the rear-view mirror—the past—and when you have looked long enough, and carefully enough, I believe that a clear image of yourself will begin to form there."[4]

In 1976, the status of the neglected Minidoka site improved slightly. The Idaho State Historical Society began to compile a Statewide Inventory of Historic Places. With the collaboration of the Pocatello-Blackfoot chapter of the JACL, the inventory listed the Minidoka site (also referred to as the Hunt site). Sims later observed that this modest—but official—status recognition was accompanied by little or no public fanfare.

## NATIONAL REGISTER OF HISTORIC PLACES—1979

By the mid-1970s, the general national public was awakening to the significance of the Japanese American World War II experience. Roger Daniels had published *Concentration Camps USA: Japanese Americans and World War II* in 1969. Jeanne Wakatsuki Houston wrote *Farewell to Manzanar* in 1973. Michi Weglyn published *Years of Infamy* in 1976. The JACL and others were debating and strategizing about reparations and a federal apology; in 1978, the JACL formed a Redress Committee.

Terry Zontec, an archaeologist with the Bureau of Reclamation's Pacific Northwest Region, nominated 6.06 acres of the Minidoka site to the National Register of Historic Places in 1979. In his nomination Zontec wrote that, despite the fact that the camp's entrance area was in ruins and the site much altered by the earlier building removals, "the scattered remnants remind us of what can happen when our country allows fear and racism to overpower our founding principles of freedom."[5] Dr. Merle Wells, the state's Historic Preservation Officer, supported the nomination, and the site was entered onto the National Register on July 10, 1979.

The JACL and its allies felt that this was a moment for public commemoration—for fanfare. A robust energy from many directions came together for a dedication program on August 18, 1979. Over 450 people made the Sunday morning trek to Minidoka. George Shiozawa of the Pocatello-Blackfoot JACL, who had initiated preparations for the dedication, welcomed the guests and speakers. The mayor of Twin

Plaque erected at Minidoka to commemorate its entry on the National Register of Historic Places. *Courtesy of photographer Teresa Tamura.*

Falls greeted the crowd, along with dignitaries from the National and Pacific Northwest District Councils of the JACL, the Idaho governor's office, and Japanese Americans from a half dozen states. Rodney Vissia, the regional director of the Bureau of Reclamation, dedicated the site. Idaho Senator Frank Church spoke and closed his remarks by quoting the wooden marker identifying the site: "May these camps serve to remind us what can happen when other factors supersede the constitutional rights guaranteed to all citizens and aliens living in this country."[6]

Soon, the JACL asked the bureau for help developing interpretive features at the site. High on its list of priorities was to recreate the honor roll camp incarcerees had erected in 1943 to recognize Minidoka's young people who left for military service during the war—and those who had perished. The large wooden three-panel structure, topped with an American eagle, had been lost after the camp closed. But the bureau could not undertake the project at that time.

In 1983, the Commission on Wartime Relocation and Internment of Civilians, created by Congress to investigate what had caused the incarceration of Japanese Americans during the war, concluded that a profound injustice had occurred. The commission's succinct list of causes identified failed leadership, wartime hysteria, and racism. It noted the economic losses of farms, businesses, homes; it described the disruption of education and careers. These findings contributed to the movement demanding a national apology and compensation of at least some of the losses suffered by the uprooted Nikkei.

The JACL organized a pilgrimage to Minidoka in 1985, the 40th anniversary of the closure of the camp, inviting people who had been incarcerated there to attend. Governor John Evans rededicated the place as a National Register site, and many former incarcerees spoke publicly about their experiences.[7]

## Centennial of Idaho Statehood Project—1990

The State of Idaho began in the 1980s to prepare for its 1990 centennial of statehood. Among its goals was to celebrate Idaho's ethnic heritage. An Ethnic Heritage Committee invited applications for grants to support historical or other commemoration projects. In 1987, the Pocatello-Blackfoot JACL, under the leadership of Hiroo (Hero) Shiosaki, and the Bureau of Reclamation, proposed to create pathways through the site, install interpretive signs, and erect a monument honoring those who had been incarcerated. The committee unanimously awarded $5,000 for the Minidoka project on condition that the applicants match the amount. The JACL chapters throughout the region soon raised well over $5,000.[8]

Bob Sims speaking at the dedication of the centennial project improvements at Minidoka on May 27, 1990. *Idaho State Historical Society, Idaho State Archives, photo by Martin Peterson, AR 75, Box 87.*

Shiosaki organized a groundbreaking ceremony at Minidoka in June 1989 to initiate the work on the site. Among those taking part were Idaho Senator Steve Symms, who addressed the group, and representatives of Senator James McClure and Congressman Richard Stallings.

One year later, on May 27, 1990, the completed improvements were dedicated before a crowd estimated at 600 to 700 people. They came from Portland and Seattle, Utah and California, and elsewhere. "There were buses as far as the eye could see," observed Marty Peterson, staff director for the Idaho Centennial Commission.[9]

Dignitaries from all levels of Idaho government were present, many on the stage. Clearly, the State of Idaho was declaring significant ownership of Minidoka and its story. Bob Sims, whose research, networking, and public speaking had contributed to recognition for the site, read from memoirs and oral histories of people who had endured Minidoka, asserting the value of their authentic voices. Sims's emphasis on the personal stories of Minidoka survivors would prove to be prescient.

A woman in the audience at the centennial project dedication. *Idaho State Historical Society, Idaho State Archives, photo by Martin Peterson, AR 75, Box 87.*

## ACHIEVING NATIONAL HISTORIC MONUMENT STATUS—2001

During the 1990s, events beyond Idaho indicated an increasing willingness by the Department of the Interior to recognize places that represented less-than-admirable moments in the nation's history. In his talks, Bob Sims sometimes mentioned how Congress in 1991–92 renamed "Custer Battlefield National Monument" to "Little Bighorn National Monument." A new memorial honored fallen Native Americans and allowed for a more balanced appraisal of the conflict. Issues like this bolstered the case for memorializing Japanese American confinement sites.[10]

In 1992 Congress designated the Manzanar Relocation Center in California as a National Historic Site. As part of that legislation, Congress directed the National Park Service (NPS) to review all of the country's World War II Japanese American confinement sites for potential preservation. The NPS published its findings in a 2000 report called "Confinement and Ethnicity."[11] The title of chapter one, "Sites of Shame," was a vivid signal that the NPS had acknowledged that its mission should include recognizing and preserving all sides of the American experience.

With this report in hand, President Bill Clinton directed the NPS on November 9, 2000, to make recommendations on how to preserve the "existing Japanese American internment sites and to provide more opportunities for the public to learn about the internment." Within the next sixty days—the last sixty days before the end of Clinton's second term in office—the directive required the NPS to consult with other federal agencies, with members of Congress, states, tribes, local officials, and other interested parties; consider expanding partnerships with private organizations and landowners; and to explore creating an interagency team to coordinate federal agencies.[12]

It was a big order. The community of people in and beyond Idaho with an interest in Minidoka quickly mobilized to secure federal status for Minidoka's protection, recognition, and potential role in education. They quickly added to their email chain Neil King, the NPS superintendent of Hagerman Fossil Beds National Monument in Idaho, and got busy making a case for presidential action.

The Department of the Interior contacted King, and asked him to be their representative and local contact for Dan Sakura, White House chief of staff of Clinton's Council on Environmental Quality. Days later, King was escorting Sakura, along with a staffer for one of Idaho's senators, and a couple of others to the Minidoka site. Later, King recalled the visit.[13]

> The first time I visited the old Hunt camp was on a cold, overcast day in late December 2000 or early January 2001. It was a postage-stamp-sized area, with a couple of decaying lava stone structures struggling against nature to retain some integrity against the ravages of wind and extreme temperatures. Some of the most magnificent high-desert big

sagebrush I had ever seen was growing right up against the structures, making a statement about neglect and the passage of time.

The original site had been 33,000 acres; the proposed NPS authority covered only 74 acres. They contained remnants of the military police entrance station and its adjoining waiting shelter, and crumbling concrete foundations. As I meandered through the sagebrush and cheatgrass, I was amazed at the abundance of scattered cultural debris such as broken glass and rusty tin cans obviously from the World War II era. I noticed a broken Ponds cold cream jar, a remnant—as I later understood—of residents' struggles to protect their skin against the drying winds and heat of this climate.

I was not aware, then, of a special site just across the road from the entrance—the Minidoka Victory Garden. It had been designed by Master Gardener Fujitaro Kubota, using large lava rocks to envelop the honor roll. The honor roll had been a prominent feature, facing incoming traffic to the camp, the first thing a visitor would see. It was blunt validation of the incarcerees' rights as United States citizens to serve their country in wartime. Behind the honor roll, looking toward the outside, and with a view of the Military Police Entrance Station partially blocked, was the exact location where Christian and Buddhist memorial services honored soldiers killed in action. Gold Star Mothers and Fathers grieved at this very site honoring their fallen. For most people, the Kubota Garden remains sacred.[14]

Meanwhile, Bob Sims was in the midst of a flurry of emails. He and others weighed in on how much acreage at Minidoka would be "enough" and assessed how they might obtain strong local support from Jerome County and the cities nearby. During the rest of his visit, Sakura assessed the prospects for a successful presidential proclamation concerning Minidoka. He met with several elected officials, along the way hearing from some who extolled Sims's historical research on Minidoka. He also noted the bipartisan political support and the absence of organized objections to preserving the site.

Sims and others recruited the South Central Idaho Tourism and Recreation Development Association, the Jerome County Historical Society, and other interested parties for support. JACL chapters reached out to organizations such as the Idaho Human Rights Education Center and the Four Rivers Cultural Center in Eastern Oregon.

In mid-December, Maya Hata Lemmon, a resident of Twin Falls who had been incarcerated at the Gila River Relocation Center in Arizona, informed the email circle that she had been invited to participate in a telephone conference call two days hence between President Clinton and thirty other people from across the country. Each site could have no more than two or three representatives speaking for it. The call would focus on local efforts to preserve the camps, educate the public about the camps, proposals for legislative and administrative action, and expanding partnerships locally to gain support.[15]

It all paid off. President Clinton signed Proclamation No. 7395 on January 17, 2001, using his authority from the Antiquities Act.[16] The site became Minidoka, an Internment National Monument, a unit of the NPS encompassing 72.75 acres. The case for Minidoka had succeeded because of the highly collaborative efforts among JACL members, the rest of the email circle, survivors of Minidoka, officials from all levels of Idaho's government, well-grounded research in the writings of Bob Sims, and the fact that the proposed site was already in federal ownership and welcomed by the NPS. Minidoka would be remembered forever.[17]

## THE MINIDOKA GENERAL MANAGEMENT PLAN—2006

The designation created big new work agendas. One day after the proclamation, Neil King sent the email circle the first evidence of the crisp new reality at Minidoka: "I have been asked to serve as the superintendent, at least on an interim basis. After we all catch our breath I'll provide additional information."[18]

King was pleased to be asked. "Start-up parks are challenging," he wrote, "because you need everything but have nothing. Yet laying the foundation for a new NPS unit is so consequential that I did not hesitate to accept the responsibility." He would have to organize the complicated preparation of a General Management Plan (GMP), a process expected to take three or more years. He knew from experience that a successful plan would only come of the strong public support of those who had survived the experience and its aftermath in their own lives. Among other things, a consensus would have to form as to Minidoka's "core value." He wrote:

At Mesa Verde National Park, for example, the core value seeks to understand a vanished culture and 5,000 known archeological sites, including 600 cliff dwellings. The people that lived there have been gone for over 800 years. There are no written records—no oral histories.

At Minidoka the core value resides in the oral histories of the Nikkei whose civil liberties were denied without due process, and how they rebuilt their lives in an aftermath that is still rippling. The Minidoka site is essential. It is the real place that provides the context for the stories of the people who endured.[19]

The early months of the planning process, King said, taught him that there was no such thing as a common point of view about the Minidoka experience. Some Japanese Americans thought it had been "unavoidable"; others carried the sting of betrayal as citizens denied their rights. Some viewed the young men who had refused to respond to the military draft as American patriots who profoundly understood how their country had betrayed its Constitution; others found their actions hard to forgive. King saw that there were many different factions to be considered.

King confided this concern to Bob Sims, who agreed. King asked him to stay close to the GMP process as a member of the planning team. Sims agreed and served as a subject matter expert. King also had another reason for asking Sims, as he explained later:

I was impressed beyond Bob's subject area knowledge, primarily with his ability to work with people. He was the essential listener. He was able to absorb the discussion silently, ruminate through his internal filters, and then, with perfect timing, ask the critical question or pin the point, usually with great effect. His credibility was undeniable due to his thorough scholarship and immediate follow-up on any dangling questions. It didn't take me long to realize that Bob was a no-nonsense gentleman who cared deeply about people and his work.[20]

As it happened, Sims's expertise included an understanding of and deep sympathy for the different perspectives among Minidoka survivors. He knew hundreds of their stories, and felt deeply their value in preserving the new monument. As the federal processes for public input and planning for the new national monument took their prescribed course, a large consensus concluded that all of the varied and authentic voices of those incarcerated at Minidoka were indeed the "core value" for preserving and remembering Minidoka.

Meanwhile, King prepared to navigate another sort of concern for budgets and congressional support as part of Minidoka's future success. On a snowy day in late February 2001, he escorted another federal visitor to Minidoka, a staffer from one of Idaho's congressional offices. In the confines of King's truck cab, he was venting his anger over President Clinton's use of the Antiquities Act to designate a protective zone around Idaho's Craters of the Moon National Monument. He felt that Clinton had flaunted his authority; King feared that this anger might also extend to the Minidoka designation as well. King recalled,

> Eventually he quieted, his one-sided conversation running out of steam. The topic drifted and we somehow made a shaky connection. Both of us were military veterans. He was a retired lifer who wished he could do it all over again; I was a one-hitch kid who served in Vietnam. On this slim slice of common ground, I saw a path forward and made my move.
>
> I began to share tales of the 442nd Regimental Combat Team during World War II. His whole demeanor shifted. He focused, actively listening. I began to relax as this matchless American Story was presented to him for the very first time. I had barely begun my own research into Minidoka, but I had come across the stories of the 442nd's honor, bravery, and sacrifices beyond comprehension. The Nisei, as proud U.S. soldiers, lived their motto "Go For Broke." Their commitment to uphold and protect the United States of America cannot be challenged. In the context of this particular field trip in a blizzard to a new national monument, the veterans' connection was golden... I hoped that the political winds would also abate. I have no way of ever knowing for sure, but I still believe that the subsequent positive support we were to receive [in Congress] from the Idaho delegation was, in part, tied to that conversation.[21]

The final GMP was published in November 2006. The plan formed around the idea that "Minidoka's unique resources are the thousands of diverse individual stories from people throughout the United

States who were forever changed by their experiences at Minidoka."
The stories would present a mosaic of perspectives "as to how this
stark chapter of American history relates to current events, civil and
Constitutional rights, and American ethnic issues."[22]

## Friends of Minidoka—2003

During the interlude between 2001 and 2006, Japanese Americans and
their allies organized and incorporated Friends of Minidoka (FOM) in
2003, to be an independent source of programmatic and other support
for the NPS at Minidoka. Two of the four founding board members
were Ron James of Twin Falls and Emily Hanako Momohara, then a
resident of Seattle and a member of the Seattle chapter of the JACL.
She had a profound understanding of the emotional complexities
among those who had been incarcerated at Minidoka, among them
her immigrant great-grandparents, American-born grandmother, and
great-aunts and -uncles. As she and James started up the FOM, she
wrote that their goal was to find:

> two Japanese American community leaders who would bring knowl-
> edge and trust to the organization. We asked Roger Shimomura
> and Dan Sakura to serve along with us as the initial incorporating
> board of directors in January 2003. Shimomura was incarcerated at
> Minidoka as a young child and is an internationally renowned art-
> ist and leader in the larger national Japanese American community.
> Sakura's...[family] was also incarcerated at Minidoka.[23]

"Luckily for us all," Momohara wrote, both accepted. In its second
year, when the FOM board enlarged its membership, Bob Sims also
agreed to serve.[24]

One of the FOM's early enterprises was to help the Seattle JACL
organize a July 2003 pilgrimage to Minidoka. When over 100 people
expressed interest, the organizers provided bus transportation from
Seattle to Minidoka. This emotional and successful event began to
break down the guarded attitudes that Momohara had observed among
former incarcerees toward the federal government. The sharing of
stories had a "gravitas of honor and urgency," Momohara wrote.[25] The

pilgrimages continued every year thereafter. Superintendent King felt that the creation of FOM increased the chances that this new park would thrive.

Another FOM initiative established an annual Minidoka Civil Liberties Symposium. Board member Jim Azumano had attended a civil liberties event in San Francisco and returned home very impressed. "I could see that [Japanese Americans] were making strides in finding new and innovative ways to educate all Californians as to the urgency of equal access for all Americans to the civil liberties they were entitled to," he said. He sought the opinion of Bob Sims: "Could *we* do this?" Sims made a few calls and said they could. "Besides being plugged into the academic world, Sims knew all manner of historians, attorneys, judges, artists, Minidoka incarcerees, JACL members, and Nikkei leaders who could contribute to serious discussions about...the inconsistent application of civil rights in our great land of freedom," wrote Azumano. Bob Sims organized and presided over the first program in 2006 and most of the subsequent programs until 2014.[26]

## NATIONAL HISTORIC SITE—2008

Superintendent King and the FOM board members seized or created other possibilities for developing Minidoka's educational mission. An opportunity materialized to acquire a homestead site adjacent to the National Monument, a parcel of about 137 acres known as the Herrmann Farm. This property contained the Minidoka fire station in its original location. It would be up to the U.S. Congress to approve a boundary change adding this acreage to the monument.

Further, the historic connection between the Minidoka camp and Bainbridge Island, Washington, resulted in a special NPS linkage. Residents of Bainbridge Island were the first Nikkei community forced to leave their homes during World War II. They were sent to Manzanar Relocation Center. After eleven months at Manzanar, most of the Bainbridge group asked and were permitted to join other Washington State Nikkei who had been sent to Minidoka. After the war, nearly half of the Bainbridge Islanders reestablished themselves on Bainbridge Island. In the decades that followed, a large number of civic and Nikkei organizations in the Seattle area collaborated to create the Bainbridge Island Japanese American Exclusion Memorial. Its motto and mission is *Nidoto Nai Yoni*: Let It Not Happen Again.

Congress in 2008 acted to designate the eight-acre Bainbridge Island site as a satellite unit of Minidoka and expanded the boundaries of the Minidoka monument to include the Herrmann Farm. This law gave Minidoka its new name: Minidoka National Historic Site. These actions repealed the former action of President Clinton under the Antiquities Act, providing Minidoka a more secure shelter under the bipartisan cloak of Congress.[27]

## The Honor Roll—2011

In 2009 Congress created the Japanese American Confinement Sites grant program, which invited educational and interpretive initiatives to support Japanese American confinement sites. This program gave the FOM board a chance to take care of some old business: reestablishing the honor roll near Minidoka's entry gate.

William Vaughn, an architect who had joined the FOM board in 2007, took the lead on the project. He had special personal reasons for being interested. During the war years, Vaughn's family operated a carrot seed farm near Hazleton, Idaho. It faced serious losses because of the general shortage of agricultural labor. Several Nisei at Minidoka agreed to work at the farm. In the end, the farm survived thanks to its Minidoka workers; in fact, the farm had one of its most productive years ever. The family never forgot them.[28] Vaughn felt he had a debt of honor to repay. Now, as an adult, he also understood the profound injustice of the incarceration.

Vaughn led the FOM board in co-sponsoring, along with the NPS and the Nisei Veterans of America, a successful grant request from the confinement sites program. He researched the original honor roll, concluded it was lost for good, designed the replica, and volunteered as project manager while it was constructed and installed.

On July 3, 2011, the day of the Annual Minidoka Pilgrimage, the new honor roll was dedicated. Bob Sims, by this time off the FOM board, was still a regular participant at the pilgrimages. As one who appreciated the power of a good story, he must have been well satisfied.

Sims's own path to that particular pilgrimage also made a good story. He had learned about the wartime cancellation of constitutional rights for Japanese Americans almost by accident. But after that, he took one deliberate step at a time. He accompanied the history of Minidoka as it unfolded from the old boxes at the Historic Society, from his research, from his deep connections with people, from his writing and slideshows, and from his service and leadership on boards and planning teams. With the institutionalization of an educational mission in the Minidoka National Historic Site, he might have thought of it as the "forever" substitute for the finite possibilities of what one professor could teach in his allotted lifetime.

## Notes

1. Robert Sims, "Symposium Presentation Notes, When No One Remembers—What is There?" June 19, 2014, Boise State University Special Collections and Archives, Mss. 356, Robert C. Sims Collection on Minidoka and Japanese Americans, digital file. (Hereafter cited as "Sims Collection.") Excerpt from Mark Strand's poem, "In the Afterlife," is from *Almost Invisible: Poems* (New York: Alfred A. Knopf, 2012), 38.
2. Robert Sims remarks in "Oral History Workshop," transcript of JACL Northwest Intermountain Regional Convention, November 23, 1973, Boise, Idaho. Sims Collection, Box 51, Folder 3, 1–3.
3. Sims Collection, "Symposium Presentation Notes," 4.
4. Sims Collection, "JACL Graduation Banquet" (lecture, Caldwell, Idaho, June 9, 1989). Sims Collection, Box 51, Folder 19, 3, 7.
5. Terry Zontec, "National Register of Historic Places Inventory, Nomination Form," February 12, 1979. Idaho State Historic Society Preservation Office.
6. Bessie M. Shrontz Roberts-Wright, *Hunt for Idaho: Evacuees 1942–1945 and Homesteaders 1947–1949 at Minidoka Prisoner of War Camp 1942–1945* (Idaho: self-published, 1994), 159.
7. Ibid., 177–79.
8. "Centennial Project Proposal for: Minidoka Relocation Center, prepared for Centennial Project Committee, 1987." Idaho State Historical Society Archives, AR-75, Box 44, file "Minidoka Relocation."
9. Marty Peterson, interview with editor, October 3, 2017.
10. Sims Collection, "Symposium Presentation Notes," 3.
11. Jeffrey F. Burton, Mary M. Farrell, Florence B. Lord, *Confinement and Ethnicity: An Overview of World War II Japanese American Relocation Sites* (Tucson, AZ: Western Archeological and Conservation Center, National Park Service, Department of the Interior, 1999). A reprint, with a new foreword, was published by

University of Washington Press, Seattle, in 2002. Available online at www.nps. gov/parkhistory/online_books/anthropology74/index.htm.

12. From William J. Clinton through the Office of the Press Secretary of The White House, Memorandum for the Secretary of the Interior, re "Preservation of Japanese American Internment Sites," November 9, 2000. Copy in Sims Collection, Box 57, Folder 6.

13. "An Interview with Neil King," in Teresa Tamura, *Minidoka: An American Concentration Camp* (Caldwell, Idaho: Caxton Press, 2013), 269–70.

14. Neil King, "Place2 6/1462," 1–2 (unpublished manuscript, July 26, 2–17).

15. Email from Maya Lemmon to Bob Sims, Dec. 18, 2000, Sims Collection, Box 57, Folder 6.

16. The Antiquities Act of 1906, (Pub.L. 59—209, 34 Stat. 225, 54 U.S.C. §§ 320301—320303).

17. Sally Jewell, Secretary of the Department of the Interior from April 2013 to January 2017, reminded Americans many times that the Department of the Interior "is in the forever business."

18. Email from Neil King to Bob Sims, January 18, 2001. Sims Collection, Box 57, Folder 6.

19. Neil King, "Place2 6/1462," 4 (unpublished manuscript, July 26, 2017).

20. Neil King, "Bob2," 1 (unpublished manuscript, July 26, 2017).

21. Neil King, "Beginning 4/937," 2–4 (unpublished manuscript, July 26, 2017).

22. National Park Service, Department of the Interior, *Minidoka Internment National Monument, General Management Plan* (Pacific West Region, Seattle: November 2006) 1.

23. Emily Hanako Momohara, "Friends of Minidoka," 2 (unpublished manuscript, October 20, 2017).

24. According to annual reports held by the Idaho Secretary of State, the FOM's board in February 2005 included Jim Azumano, Alan Momohara, Jerry Arai, Lisa Farrier, and May Nampa of Seattle; Emily Hanako Momohara of Lawrence, Kansas; Rev. Barbara Bellus and Saran Sakura of Portland; Dr. Robert Sims of Boise; and Steve Thorson and Maya Hata Lemmon of Twin Falls. Ron James, Roger Shimomura, and Dan Sakura had cycled off the board.

25. Momohara, 3.

26. Jim Azumano, interview with editor, October 27, 2017.

27. Public Law 110-229, Sec. 313 of May 8, 2008; and Public Law 113–171, of September 26, 2014.

28. Jim Azumano, interview with editor, October 2017.

13

# Creating the Minidoka
# National Historic Site:
# Twenty-Five Years plus Sixty Days

### Daniel Sakura

## EDITOR'S NOTE

*In 2000 Daniel Sakura was working in the White House as the chief of staff of President Bill Clinton's Council on Environmental Quality, a division of the Executive Office of the President, and as liaison to the Department of the Interior. As such, he was in a position to review and move proposals for historic and other commemoration in the National Park System—including Minidoka—toward Antiquities Act proclamations. Sakura currently serves as a senior advisor at the National Park Foundation in Washington, DC, and is a board member of Friends of Minidoka.—SS*

Most efforts to create a new unit of the National Park System (NPS) take years of hard work. But the Minidoka unit was created after a sixty-day process. How could that be?

To avoid creating new national park units that would put a financial strain on the system, Congress has required the NPS to conduct detailed studies to determine if a site meets the standards to become a national park unit. This "legislative path" frequently requires Congress to authorize the NPS first to study a site and then to pass additional legislation to designate it as a national park unit.

However, the Antiquities Act of 1906 provides an "administrative path" to create national monuments via presidential proclamation for federally owned sites that contain "objects of historic and scientific interest." While there is no formal study requirement, the proclamation and supporting documentation will describe the historic or scientific basis for the designation.

Following such a designation, Congress may later ratify such a monument as a national historic site. For Minidoka, Congress passed bipartisan legislation to do exactly this in 2008.[1] The act expanded the site's boundary to include additional lands adjacent to the Minidoka monument and the Eagledale ferry dock site on Bainbridge Island, Washington. This legislation ensured that a future president could not disestablish, transfer management of, or significantly reduce the boundary of the site via presidential proclamation or other administrative action.

All successful national park campaigns follow their own unique paths. But they invariably require strong local support, partnerships with national organizations, high levels of congressional or agency support—or some combination of these elements. Due to a confluence of many factors, Minidoka's "campaign" for designation took only two months. But consider what came together in those sixty days.

It started with a memo from President Clinton to the Department of the Interior (DOI) on November 9, 2000, inviting a campaign for Minidoka and ended with him signing the monument proclamation on January 17, 2011. Underpinning this fast designation were two forces: one was support in the White House for preserving the site; the other was the significant local support that had been generated and nurtured for years by the JACL, historian Bob Sims, and others. Local support had produced two important endorsements by the State of Idaho as to the historic significance of Minidoka to the state: its placement on the National Register of Historic Places in 1976, and its commemoration during Idaho's 1990 Centennial of Statehood.

Minidoka also benefitted from previous designations of war relocation sites at Manzanar (California) and at Rohwer (Arkansas). In 1992, when Congress created the Manzanar National Historic Site to preserve the site of the Manzanar Relocation Center, it also directed the NPS to conduct a Japanese American National Historic Landmark Theme Study. The purpose of the study was to "identify, evaluate and nominate as national historic landmarks those sites, buildings, and structures that best illustrate or commemorate the period in American history from 1941–1946 when Japanese Americans were ordered to be detained, relocated or excluded pursuant to Executive Order 9066, and other actions."

Such actions produced a ladder effect in which efforts to preserve one camp site built political support to designate additional sites.

Because of that study, the NPS conducted archeological surveys and background information on all such sites, including Minidoka. In 1999, the NPS published the results of these surveys in its report *Confinement and Ethnicity*. The report included an excellent history of Minidoka and its archeological resources, which included the National Register and Idaho Centennial commemorative plaques located at the site. The report documented remains such as the sentry station and waiting room. These were certainly "objects of historic interest," a key element for a presidential proclamation. This and other information also might help defend a president's proclamation should it be challenged in court.[2]

The personal history and background of President Clinton played a role in Minidoka's 2001 designation. In the early 1990s, Rosalie Gould, a citizen of Arkansas, worked successfully to designate the cemetery at the Rohwer War Relocation Center as a National Historic Landmark. At the time, Bill Clinton was governor of Arkansas. In 1993, not long after Clinton's election as president, DOI officials learned about the Rohwer effort. In effect, Rohwer became a rung in the ladder for future actions to preserve and interpret other camp sites. In late 1999, as the outgoing Clinton administration finalized its last budget request, officials at DOI and the White House Council on Environmental Quality assembled a package of initiatives for DOI's Fiscal Year 2001 budget request to Congress.

These initiatives included funding for the Manzanar Visitor Center, for publication and release of *Confinement and Ethnicity*, for the designation by the U.S. Forest Service of the Gordon Hirabayashi Recreation Site in Coronado National Forest near Tucson, and for the Bureau of Land Management to acquire former WRA camp lands from private landowners willing to sell. The success of these initiatives set the stage for Minidoka.

When the National Japanese American Memorial Foundation invited the president to a ceremony on November 9, 2000, dedicating the Japanese American National Memorial to Patriotism in Washington, DC, U.S. Attorney General Janet Reno agreed to speak. She announced that the president had sent a memo that day to DOI asking for recommendations on preserving and interpreting the various confinement sites—and to respond within sixty days.[3]

My role was to fly to Idaho, tour the Minidoka site, and seek input from stakeholders in southern Idaho such as the Jerome County Historical Society and Idaho Farm and Ranch Museum (IFARM), the South Central Idaho Tourism and Recreational Development Association, Steve Thorson, Maya Hata Lemmon, JACL, and the Bureau of Reclamation, which managed a portion of the site. All of them registered constructive comments, concerns, and suggestions. Bob Sims, who participated in the process, was also considered a stakeholder. He recommended enhancing interpretation at Minidoka to include a more substantial place to gather and a reconstructed barracks on the site.[4]

After the meetings with stakeholders and city and county elected officials, I concluded that public support and the supporting data would warrant a recommendation to use the Antiquities Act to designate the site as Minidoka Internment National Monument. It was clear that stakeholders had laid groundwork for the designation over a period as long as twenty-five years—ever since the 1976 listing on the National Register of Historic Places.

That's what it took: twenty-five years plus sixty days. Minidoka, in turn, was part of the momentum—or laddering—that produced later designations. Tule Lake became an NPS unit as part of the Valor in the Pacific National Monument in 2008. The Honouliuli site in Hawaii was preserved in 2015. They had in common local partners who worked in the communities near the camps—and often hundreds of miles away from the Japanese American communities who had been confined at the site.

As one whose family was forcibly moved and confined at Minidoka, I express my deepest appreciation for the work of Bob Sims and countless others who worked to preserve the camp sites as lasting historical and educational resources.

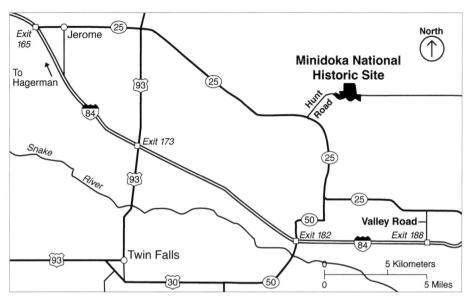

Minidoka National Historic Site location map. *National Park Service.*

## Notes

1. The congressional act creating the Minidoka National Historic Site was Public Law 110-229.
2. "Minidoka Relocation Center," chapter 9, *Confinement and Ethnicity: An Overview of World War II Japanese American Relocation Sites*, Jeffery F. Burton, Mary M. Farrell, Florence B. Lord, and Richard W. Lord, Western Archeological and Conservation Center, National Park Service (1999).
3. Rudi Williams, "National Japanese American Memorial to Patriotism Dedicated," *Department of Defense News*, November 15, 2000. Online at archive. defense.gov/news/ newsarticle.aspx?id=45581.
4. For a list of stakeholders and their recommendations, see www.nps.gov/ parkhistory/online_books/internment/reporta7.htm.

One of eight guard towers located around the perimeter of the camp. Armed military police were able to observe and control any unauthorized movements of Minidoka's incarcerees. *Courtesy of Oregon Nikkei Endowment, Bill Welch Collection, Johnson & Son photograph, 2006.61.04.*

# PART THREE

# THE LEGACY OF ROBERT C. SIMS

# 14

# Okage Sama De

## Hanako Wakatsuki

I knew from early childhood that my family went to "camp." I had four generations of family in camp, but I never understood what that meant. In third grade, I had to do a book report and chose a book that was written by a family member. It was my great aunt Jeanne Wakatsuki's coming-of-age book about camp, *Farewell to Manzanar*. This book report was easy for me because I already knew the story: how after the bombing of Pearl Harbor, the United States launched into a two-front war; how my family was put into camp for about three and a half years; and how we were never supposed to talk about it. But as a third grader, I did not understand the complexity of this history, or my family's story, or what "camp" really meant.

Growing up in Idaho, this topic never came up in my history classes. As a child not seeing this history told, I thought that it must have been an obscure event; I remained unaware of its impact on a large population of Americans well beyond my family. Therefore, I never learned about Minidoka or the Japanese American incarceration experience during my primary or secondary schooling.

When I attended college at Boise State University, I was taken under the wing of Dr. Robert Sims who found me because he recognized my last name from my great aunt's book. When I first spoke with him over the phone, he asked me if I knew about Minidoka; I lied and said, "Yes," because I knew that he was the former dean of my college and I did not want to sound "stupid." (We laughed about this later, when I confessed.) After the call, I quickly googled "Minidoka," and was shocked to find out that it was an incarceration site in Idaho. I felt betrayed by the Idaho school system where I had never learned that the state that I grew up in had the same type of prison camp where my great-great grandmother, great-grandparents, grandparents, aunts, and uncles had been incarcerated. I familiarized myself with this story again from a broader historical perspective. Since then, I have been involved with the preservation of Japanese American Confinement Sites across the United States.

Dr. Sims asked me to join the board of Friends of Minidoka when I was still an undergraduate student. He wanted me to work with the National Park Service to help preserve the Minidoka National Historic Site. I was able to get the board to fund projects and educational programs at the site. Through his guidance and mentorship, I learned how to become an advocate, a preservationist, and a public historian. He was always there to help or listen. We worked on several projects over the years to bring speakers for various Boise State programs. We once created a partnership with Boise State's Construction Management Department to build a replica guard tower that now stands at the front entrance of the Minidoka National Historic site.

Bob Sims, Hanako Wakatsuki, and Frank Kitamoto at the 2010 Minidoka Pilgrimage. *Courtesy of Emily Hanako Momohara.*

Dr. Sims encouraged me as my career progressed and perhaps was the single most important influence in my career trajectory. Without meeting him, I probably would not be in the field of Japanese American confinement history. I worked at the Tule Lake Unit of the World War II Valor in the Pacific National Monument, one of the ten prison camps, which later became a segregation center in northern California. I volunteer for the Manzanar National Historic Site on their public archaeology programs, and serve on the board of the Heart Mountain Wyoming Foundation that preserves the prison camp near Cody, Wyoming. I also serve on the board of the National Japanese American Memorial Foundation, which preserves the Japanese American Memorial to Patriotism During World War II in Washington, DC. I was able to come full circle connecting my family's incarceration history and my current profession. In 1942, the Department of the Interior managed the prison camps when they were operated by the War Relocation Authority, and I currently work for the National Park Service as the Chief of Interpretation and Education at the Minidoka National Historic Site, which is managed by the Department of Interior. Across generations, the wartime confinement of Japanese Americans is where my family, Dr. Sims, and I intersect.

I now realize many things: how the confinement began an insidious process of ripping away my family's dignity; how it also awakened a strength that my grandparents had to find within themselves during this unbelievable time; and how Dr. Sims had the courage and passion to devote his life's research to a topic that was not a particularly popular field at the time. The strength, courage, and passion of these people built the foundation on which I stand. I feel that part of Dr. Sims's legacy continues through me as I walk my path in public service and public history. I hope I can be half the advocate that he was. Working at the Minidoka National Historic Site allows me to honor my family and Dr. Sims, to remind the American public what happens when the country lets race prejudice, war hysteria, and the failure of political leadership to dictate our policies. We cannot let this happen again.

There is a Japanese saying that allows me to express my gratitude for those who came before me and whose honor, courage, and purpose have been my examples: *Okage sama de*—I am what I am because of you.

*Facts and views in this essay are the responsibility of the author and do not reflect the opinions or policies of the National Park Service.*

# 15

# The Story of Ise Inuzuka

## Jim Azumano

**B**ob knew the individual histories of many Minidoka families. He retained and propagated family trees in his mind, so when people would come up to him and introduce themselves at a symposium, he would know some of their relatives and mention them by name.

During those years of incarceration at Minidoka, many families lost the businesses and farms which had provided them income with which to pay property taxes. When they could not pay their annual assessments, the county tax collector could foreclose on the property. This was about to happen to my mother, Ise Inuzuka, and her sisters. The property was the Inuzuka's family home in Portland, Multnomah County, Oregon. Ise Inuzuka asked to meet with Harry L. Stafford, the director of the Minidoka camp. She asked him to plead on her behalf with Multnomah County. She told him that she would pay all of the back taxes after they were released from Minidoka and in a position to earn enough money to do so. Stafford duly noted the request but could make no guarantees; one of his staff made a note and logged the conversation.

Ise Inuzuka, age 23, chosen as Sweetheart of Minidoka for the St. Valentine's Day competition at Minidoka Relocation Center. *National Archives and Records Administration, 210-CMA-B-001.*

Many years later, Bob was examining Stafford's records. He noticed the staff note and made a copy of it for his research purposes.

While at Minidoka, Ise was proclaimed the "Sweetheart of Minidoka" for one of the camp's social events, an event covered in one of the camp newspapers, all of which Bob had read while doing his research. A little later, Ise married George I. Azumano on a pass into Twin Falls, also noted in the camp newspaper.

When the war ended, my aunts returned to Portland and found their home occupied by squatters who refused to leave. They went to the Multnomah County courthouse for help and met with a county commissioner who was delighted that they had returned. They said they intended to pay their taxes. He said, "I know you will. I've been waiting for you." Their property had not been foreclosed upon. For decades after that, my aunts could not understand why his greeting included, "I've been waiting for you," and puzzled over it.

I first met Bob when I joined the Friends of Minidoka board in 2004. He remembered Ise's name, the document he had copied, and the name of Ise's husband—Azumano. He gave me a copy of the document. With this "circumstantial" evidence, I realized that Mr. Stafford had telephoned Multnomah County and interceded for Ise Inuzuka and the family. The county officials removed the property from the foreclosure list (or declined to list it). The title was still confirmed to the Inuzuka family. This enabled the War Relocation Authority to confront the squatters and demand that they vacate the premises immediately. Which they did. I shared Bob's copy of the note with my mother's family, and the Inuzukas finally understood why the county commissioner said, "I've been waiting for you."

Although this story is a tiny sample from among the stories of the other 110,000 evacuees, it demonstrates the focus and dedication of Bob Sims on the minute details of how historic events impact individual families. Bob and I became friends, and I truly miss the warmth and personal dignity that Bob gave to each incarceree and their family members.

# 16

# The Robert C. Sims Collection on Minidoka and Japanese Americans, 1891–2014

Cheryl Oestreicher

Boise State University Albertson Library
Special Collections and Archives

History is about examining the past and connecting it to the present, and archival records serve to study history and preserve people's lives. When Robert C. Sims arrived at Boise State University in 1970 to teach history, he was among those young historians who expanded the kinds of questions asked of the past. No longer interested solely in elite decision makers in the realm of government, politics, and warfare, they explored the experiences of people and groups affected by those decisions. Sims observed that, while many of the histories about the forced relocation of Japanese Americans in World War II had been sound, they omitted the perspective of those who experienced relocation. In other words, "History is something that happens to people, and the actual participants in the events are the only ones who can adequately tell it."[1]

In fall 2016, the Boise State University Albertson Library Special Collections and Archives opened the "Robert C. Sims Collection on Minidoka and Japanese Americans, 1891–2014." His papers consist of sixty-six boxes and about two hundred books representing over four decades of research. Materials include reports, letters, photographs, articles, interviews, notes, speeches, presentations, correspondence, scholarship, maps, publications, the site's newspaper *The Minidoka Irrigator* and yearbook *Minidoka Interlude*, and other documents created by people relocated to or employed at Minidoka. These materials led to his examination of topics such as medical care, education, labor, art, postwar resettlement, redress, people's lives post-incarceration, and the impact of incarceration on community and family and how it disrupted basic cultural identities.

Researching and documenting the past was Sims's core work, but his passion was to share his discoveries. As an academic he published in scholarly journals but was more dedicated to bringing this topic to the general public. Through presentations and lectures spanning over forty years, he depicted a balanced view of events and people to audiences across Idaho and the northwest. More than anything, he wanted the public to become aware of this hidden history both to understand their heritage and to forestall similar unjust actions in the future.

Though Minidoka was his core interest, he also researched Japanese Americans and their Idaho experience prior to World War II. One of his earliest works was about the Japanese pioneers who settled in Idaho in the 1890s, how they made economic progress despite racial prejudice, and how their interests were similar to or different from those of the Japanese Americans forced to Minidoka. He collected family photographs, newspaper articles, reports, census records, and other documents that describe their lives and the expressions of racial prejudice against them. His analysis was published as *Japanese American Contributions to Idaho's Economic Development* in 1978, likely the first publication about this topic in Idaho.

Sims was an undisputed authority on Minidoka and Japanese history in Idaho. We are honored to have his collection at BSU and grateful to his family for the donation. The goal is that people will use this collection to learn, educate, write, or publish the as yet untold stories emerging from Minidoka and Idaho Japanese history. Dr. Sims started to tell the stories, and others must continue his legacy.

For a full description and detailed inventory, please consult the finding aid at archiveswest.orbiscascade.org/ark:/80444/xv13632, or contact Special Collections and Archives, Albertsons Library, Boise State University, 208-426-3958, archives@boisestate.edu.

## Note

1. Robert Sims "Oral History Workshop," JACL Northwest Intermountain Regional Convention, November 23, 1973, Boise, ID. Sims Collection, Box 51, Folder 2, 16.

# Acknowledgments

BETTY SIMS

This project has called for the skills, knowledge, and experience of many people. My earliest thanks go to Dr. Cheryl Oestreicher, director of Archives and Special Collections at Boise State University, and Susan M. Stacy, editor of this book. Cheryl and her competent staff, in processing Bob's sixty-six boxes of research and writing, noted that a selection of his writings might well form the basis of a book on Minidoka. Susan, after looking over his previously published papers and other works, agreed with Cheryl and agreed to serve as our editor for whatever project we might undertake. Our daughter Sarah Sims joined the discussion, and our shared convictions on the value and timeliness of Bob's work urged us forward.

Susan did the heavy lifting from beginning to end, starting with that review of Bob's archive, selecting items for republication, securing permissions, and working with the other contributors to this book. I had no idea how many times it was possible to "work over" an essay before it was both accurate and a reflection of the author's intent.

Our initial planning team grew to include two key individuals: Neil King, the first superintendent of Minidoka after it was designated as a national monument in 2001, and Hanako Wakatsuki, who had recently been appointed Chief of Interpretation and Education at the Minidoka National Historic Site. Together, we sharpened our focus and our mission.

Jim Azumano, Emily Hanako Momohara, and Dan Sakura—each a child of a parent who had been incarcerated at Minidoka—contributed their own personal experiences and allowed us to include them in the book. Each had worked with Bob in one way or another to support the development and educational mission at Minidoka. I thank them for their assistance. Incidentally, the trio of Bob, Neil, and Jim Azumano formed a special team of their own after 2001 when the National Park Service entered the picture. Each had something to learn about Minidoka from the other two and, as it turned out, became close friends

195

who laughed a lot amidst their work. I'm grateful for the richness they added to Bob's life and to this book.

The important task of selecting images to complement the narrative fell to Sarah, Hanako, and Mia Russell, the executive director of Friends of Minidoka. Teresa Tamura, author and photographer, graciously permitted the use of photos from her fine book *Minidoka: An American Concentration Camp*. I thank Boise State University's Communication and Marketing Department for permitting the use of a photo of Bob by photographer John Kelly.

It was enormously satisfying to have such a pool of talent and experience, and I am grateful to each of them.

Judy Austin, retired editor of *Idaho Yesterdays* and longtime friend and colleague of Bob's, suggested that we contact Washington State University Press because of its impressive reputation for "undeniably Northwest reads." I am so grateful for that suggestion. Beth DeWeese, then manuscript editor for the press, confirmed their interest, setting in motion a relationship that has been delightfully warm and productive. Beth's technical support, prompt responses to questions, encouragement, and, most of all, belief that our project had value not just to us, but to our region and its readers, kept us on track and in good spirits as we completed the work.

What would we do without mentors? Bob's included Robert Skotheim, a past president of Whitman and Occidental Colleges, and Robert's wife, Nadine. Dr. Roger Daniels, Charles Phelps Taft Professor Emeritus at the University of Cincinnati, whose speech at Boulder in 1968 awakened Bob to the facts of Japanese American incarceration during World War II, continued his interest in Bob's teaching and writing career. I thank each of you for your encouragement to Bob and me over the years.

My personal cheering section includes friends and family who have checked in over the years from Boise, Pocatello, San Diego, Long Beach, San Francisco, Arizona, Los Angeles, Seattle, Lostine, and Portland. Sarah in Boise was able to be on our project team, and our sons Todd and Barry and their families have been with us in spirit every inch of the way. Thanks to my siblings, as well as to Bob's family and friends in Oklahoma. Too many to list, but you know who you are; your continued interest and support have been essential.

I acknowledge my college roommate and longtime friend, Mary Tate, for her role in my cheering section as this project progressed. Mary was a Boise community leader, a voracious reader, quick-witted, Idaho history buff, and a fan of Bob's. She was pleased we were honoring his work in this way and each time we visited she asked about the status of "the book." Her health was failing in recent years, and she died in March 2019, but her steadfast interest and support are remembered.

I thank Robert Hirai, past president of the Boise Valley Japanese American Citizens League and now Honorary Consul of Japan in Idaho, for his assistance and friendship to Bob over the years, and, after Bob's death, to me. He has played an important role in Idaho in nurturing better understanding and friendships between cultures at the local, state, and international levels.

I am deeply grateful to two special organizations for financial grants made to Washington State University Press to help defray publishing expenses for this book: The Friends of Minidoka and the Boise Valley Chapter of the Japanese American Citizens League, and their leaders, Mia Russell and Katie Newman respectively. Their generous grants helped keep the price of the book as low as possible to promote sales, leading to greater exposure and educational impact, and ultimately serving the cause of social justice, which was Bob's original motivation and intent. It is fitting and satisfying to continue his life work with this publication.

Susan Stacy

For me, the first impulse is to thank the librarians and archivists of Boise State University who became a special part of this project: Cheryl Oestreicher, Jim Doran, Bethany Owens, Alex Meregaglia, and Gwen Hervochon. Cheryl provided our group with meeting and research rooms, computer and technical aid, her staff's time, and her own enthusiastic presence in our early planning stage. All historians should be so lucky to have a support crew like this one.

I am deeply grateful for Neil King's many contributions to this book. He rounded up contributors Emily Hanako Momohara and Jim Azumano, persuading them to write their personal stories of the Minidoka part of their lives, and providing many of his own stories.

They certainly enrich this book. They all gracefully endured the evolutions of editing, and their full accounts are now part of the Sims Collection at Boise State.

A special thank you to Dan Sakura, who also endured the evolutions of editing. His role at the Clinton White House during the "sixty days" leading to the president's Antiquity Act proclamation for Minidoka is part of this book. His story provides valuable schooling, a model perhaps, for others hoping to preserve important parts of the past.

My thanks to Judy Austin, with whom I share a devotion to Word-Perfect, and who shared her knowledge about versions more recent than mine. She helped our group understand the unique characteristics of academic press publishing. Part of that process included receiving comments from people who read our early manuscript. They are meant to remain anonymous, and I thank them for the obvious time they took to read carefully and comment candidly.

The book includes snapshots taken by Marty Peterson during Idaho's Centennial of Statehood. Those were valuable, as were our conversations about the celebration at Minidoka. Thank you, Marty. I thank Hanako Wakatsuki for sharing her understanding of the old government euphemisms; she raised my consciousness about why they should not be perpetuated in contemporary prose. Sarah Sims volunteered to gather illustrations, becoming an authority on the contents of Bob's photos and slides. Thank you, Sarah. Ken Swanson, an ace authority on military history in Idaho and well beyond, helped with the table on army organization in Europe in World War II, proving that a good historian is far better than a cloud. And to Teresa Tamura, for the generous gift of her photography and for her close reading of the manuscript, thank you.

Beth DeWeese: a warm voice on the phone, a master email writer, a sympathetic and patient editor, a reliable promise keeper. I wish you well in your retirement, Beth, counting myself lucky to have caught your WSU Press coattails before it was too late.

Any historian would be beyond lucky to have a client like Betty Sims. Thank you for your confidence in me and our work, your steady movement forward at all times, those cups of tea and friendship, and your direct approach to problem solving. I learned a lot from you.

APPENDIX A

# Remarks on Signing the Bill Providing Restitution for the Wartime Internment of Japanese American Civilians

### President Ronald Reagan
### August 10, 1988

The Members of Congress and distinguished guests, my fellow Americans, we gather here today to right a grave wrong. More than 40 years ago, shortly after the bombing of Pearl Harbor, 120,000 persons of Japanese ancestry living in the United States were forcibly removed from their homes and placed in makeshift internment camps. This action was taken without trial, without jury. It was based solely on race, for these 120,000 were Americans of Japanese descent.

Yes, the Nation was then at war, struggling for its survival, and it's not for us today to pass judgment upon those who may have made mistakes while engaged in that great struggle. Yet we must recognize that the internment of Japanese-Americans was just that: a mistake. For throughout the war, Japanese-Americans in the tens of thousands remained utterly loyal to the United States. Indeed, scores of Japanese-Americans volunteered for our Armed Forces, many stepping forward in the internment camps themselves. The 442d Regimental Combat Team, made up entirely of Japanese-Americans, served with immense distinction to defend this nation, their nation. Yet back at home, the soldiers' families were being denied the very freedom for which so many of the soldiers themselves were laying down their lives.

Congressman Norman Mineta, with us today, was 10 years old when his family was interned. In the Congressman's words: "My own family was sent first to Santa Anita Racetrack. We showered in the horse paddocks. Some families lived in converted stables, others in hastily thrown together barracks. We were then moved to Heart Mountain, Wyoming, where our entire family lived in one small room of a rude tar paper barrack." Like so many tens of thousands of others,

President Ronald Reagan signs the Civil Liberties Act of 1988, August 10, 1988, Washington, DC. *Densho, the Kinoshita Collection, encyclopedia.densho.org/sources/en-denshopd-p10-00006-1.*

the members of the Mineta family lived in those conditions not for a matter of weeks or months but for 3 long years.

The legislation that I am about to sign provides for a restitution payment to each of the 60,000 surviving Japanese-Americans of the 120,000 who were relocated or detained. Yet no payment can make up for those lost years. So, what is most important in this bill has less to do with property than with honor. For here we admit a wrong; here we reaffirm our commitment as a nation to equal justice under the law.

I'd like to note that the bill I'm about to sign also provides funds for members of the Aleut community who were evacuated from the Aleutian and Pribilof Islands after a Japanese attack in 1942. This action was taken for the Aleuts' own protection, but property was lost or damaged that has never been replaced.

And now in closing, I wonder whether you'd permit me one personal reminiscence, one prompted by an old newspaper report sent to me by Rose Ochi, a former internee. The clipping comes from the *Pacific Citizen* and is dated December 1945.

"Arriving by plane from Washington," the article begins, "General Joseph W. Stilwell pinned the Distinguished Service Cross on Mary Masuda in a simple ceremony on the porch of her small frame shack near Talbert, Orange County. She was one of the first Americans of Japanese ancestry to return from relocation centers to California's farmlands." "Vinegar Joe" Stilwell was there that day to honor Kazuo Masuda, Mary's brother. You see, while Mary and her parents were in an internment camp, Kazuo served as staff sergeant to the 442d Regimental Combat Team. In one action, Kazuo ordered his men back and advanced through heavy fire, hauling a mortar. For 12 hours, he engaged in a single-handed barrage of Nazi positions. Several weeks later at Cassino, Kazuo staged another lone advance. This time it cost him his life.

The newspaper clipping notes that her two surviving brothers were with Mary and her parents on the little porch that morning. These two brothers, like the heroic Kazuo, had served in the United States Army. After General Stilwell made the award, the motion picture actress Louise Allbritton, a Texas girl, told how a Texas battalion had been saved by the 442d. Other show business personalities paid tribute—Robert Young, Will Rogers, Jr. And one young actor said: "Blood that has soaked into the sands of a beach is all of one color. America stands unique in the world: the only country not founded on race but on a way, an ideal. Not in spite of but because of our polyglot background, we have had all the strength in the world. That is the American way." The name of that young actor—I hope I pronounce this right—was Ronald Reagan. And, yes, the ideal of liberty and justice for all—that is still the American way.

Thank you, and God bless you. And now let me sign H.R. 442, so fittingly named in honor of the 442d.

Thank you all again, and God bless you all. I think this is a fine day.

---

The President spoke at 2:33 p.m. in Room 450 of the Old Executive Office Building on August 10, 1988. H.R. 442, approved August 10, was assigned Public Law No. 100383.

Source: Ronald Reagan, Remarks on Signing the Bill Providing Restitution for the Wartime Internment of Japanese-American Civilians, Online by Gerhard Peters and John T. Woolley, The American Presidency Project, www.presidency.ucsb.edu/node/255076.

## APPENDIX B

# General References on
# Japanese Settlement in United States

### I. Population: Number of Persons of Japanese Ancestry in Mainland

| | | | |
|---|---|---|---|
| 1880 | 140 | 1940 | 126,826 |
| 1890 | 2,027 | 1950 | 141,687 |
| 1900 | 24,282 | 1960 | 260,113 |
| 1910 | 72,030 | 1970 | 370,071 |
| 1920 | 110,848 | 1980 | 476,596 |
| 1930 | 138,312 | 1990 | 600,076 |

Source: Sims Collection, "Japanese in Idaho, Document #2," Box 52, Folder 15.

### II. Significant Dates

1882 Chinese Exclusion Act. Prohibited all immigration of Chinese laborers.

1907 Gentlemen's Agreement. Ended immigration of Japanese laborers. Japan agreed to stop issuing passports to workers, severely restricting immigration into the United States.

1913 California Anti-Japanese Land Law. Prohibited Japanese leasing or owning land.

1921 Emergency Immigration Act. Effectively ended Japanese immigration.

1921 Idaho Anti-Miscegenation Law. Amended to include prohibition against Japanese marrying Caucasians.

1922 *Ozawa v. United States.* U.S. Supreme Court decision declaring Japanese immigrants ineligible for citizenship.

1923 Idaho Anti-Japanese Land Law. Prohibited Japanese leasing or owning land.

1924 National Origins Act (Immigration Act of 1924). Limited the number of immigrants allowed entry into the United States by establishing a national origins quota. It completely prohibited immigration from Asia. There was no quota for Japan.

1942 February 19. President Roosevelt signs Executive Order 9066, establishing the basis for removal of all persons of Japanese ancestry from the West Coast.

1943 January. Call for volunteers for an all-Japanese American military unit.

1944 February. Military draft for Japanese Americans.

1952 McCarran Walters Act. Eliminated racial barriers to immigration and naturalization. Issei eligible for citizenship.

1955 Idaho Anti-Japanese Land Law repealed.

1959  Idaho Anti-Miscegenation Law repealed.

2000  Twenty World War II Nisei veterans awarded Congressional Medal of Honor.

2010  Nisei Veterans of the 100th Battalion, the 442nd Regimental Combat Team, the Military Intelligence Service, the OSS, and the Counter Intelligence Corps awarded the Congressional Medal of Honor, highest civilian honor granted in the United States.

### III.  War Relocation Centers for Japanese Americans during World War II

Listed in order of their establishment, and showing closing dates and peak resident population.

| | | | |
|---|---|---|---|
| Manzanar | Manzanar,<br>Inyo County, CA | March 21, 1942–<br>November 21, 1945 | 10,046 |
| Poston | Poston,<br>Yuma County, AZ | May 8, 1942–<br>November 28, 1945 | 17,814 |
| Tule Lake | Newell,<br>Modoc County, CA | May 27, 1942–<br>March 20, 1946 | 18,789 |
| Gila River | Rivers,<br>Pinal County, AZ | July 20, 1942–<br>November 10, 1945 | 13,348 |
| Minidoka | Hunt,<br>Jerome County, ID | August 10, 1942–<br>October 28, 1945 | 9,397 |
| Heart Mountain | Heart Mountain,<br>Park County, WY | August 12, 1942–<br>November 10, 1945 | 10,767 |
| Granada | Amache,<br>Prowers County, CO | August 27, 1942–<br>October 31, 1945 | 7,318 |
| Topaz | Topaz,<br>Millard County, UT | September 11, 1942–<br>November 30, 1945 | 8,130 |
| Rohwer | McGehee,<br>Desha County, AR | September 18, 1942–<br>November 30, 1945 | 8,475 |
| Jerome | Denson,<br>Drew/Chicot Counties, AR | October 6, 1942–<br>June 30, 1944 | 8,487 |

Source: *WRA: A Story of Human Conservation* (Washington, DC: United States Department of the Interior, War Relocation Authority, 1946), 197.

## APPENDIX C

# War Relocation Authority
# Population Numbers

Literature, histories, and memoirs frequently refer to various population totals when writing about the forced removal of Nikkei from the West Coast. Authors may or may not provide specific explanations. Many writers use rounded numbers.

The following numbers are from an article by Roger Daniels, published in *Japanese Americans: From Relocation to Redress*, "The Forced Migrations of West Coast Japanese Americans: 1942–1946: A Quantitative Note." Daniels obtained these numbers from War Relocation Authority records.

### I. Movement of people into the camps, 1942–1946

| | |
|---:|---|
| 90,491 | from assembly centers |
| 17,491 | direct evacuation |
| 5,918 | born in camp |
| 1,735 | from Immigration and Naturalization (INS) internment camps |
| 1,579 | seasonal workers (furloughed from assembly centers to work crops, then moved to camps) |
| 1,275 | from penal and medical institutions |
| 1,118 | from Hawaii |
| 219 | voluntary residents (mostly non-Japanese spouses) |
| 120,313 | Total population ever under WRA control |

### II. Movement of people out of the camps, 1942–1946

| | |
|---:|---|
| 54,127 | returned to the West Coast |
| 52,798 | relocated to interior of United States |
| 4,724 | to Japan |
| 3,121 | to Immigration and Naturalization Service internment camps |
| 2,355 | armed forces |
| 1,862 | died |
| 1,322 | to institutions |
| 4 | unauthorized departures |
| 120,313 | |

# Glossary

## A. Generational Terms

Nikkei   Japanese emigrants and their descendants throughout the world

Issei   Immigrant generation of Japanese to the United States (first generation)

Nisei   Children of Issei (first American-born generation)

Kibei   Nisei children sent to Japan for part of their education and returned to United States

Sansei   Third generation

Yonsei   Fourth generation

## B. Other Terms

Alien Land Law—Laws enacted by certain western states that forbade Asian immigrants from purchasing, owning, or leasing land.

assembly center—A term used by the U.S. government to describe a temporary camp for incarcerating Japanese Americans and legal residents of Japanese ancestry during World War II. Assembly centers were generally situated on fairgrounds near or in cities along the West Coast and were surrounded by fences, watchtowers, and armed guards. These were holding facilities until the more permanent Relocation Centers were ready for the internees.

Civil Liberties Act of 1988—Act signed by President Ronald Reagan providing an apology and redress payments to all those incarcerated by the War Relocation Authority and other U.S. government agencies. The act also established a Civil Liberties Education Fund to support research and education programs relating to the incarceration.

Commission on Wartime Relocation and Internment of Civilians (CWRIC)— A congressional committee charged with studying the internment and incarceration of Japanese Americans and legal residents of Japanese ancestry during World War II. This commission made formal recommendations for appropriate remedies (1982).

concentration camp—A controversial term because of its association with the death camps used by Nazi Germany to kill Jewish people. Some writers use the term "American concentration camp" to refer to a place where people are imprisoned not because of any crimes they committed, but simply because of who they are. (See discussion of this issue by Robert C. Sims in chapter 11 of this book; see also *The Power of Words Handbook*, Japanese American Citizens League, 2003.)

evacuees—A word used by the War Relocation Authority to describe Japanese Americans and legal resident aliens of Japanese descent who were incarcerated during World War II.

evacuation—The act or state of withdrawing, departing, or vacating any place or area, especially a threatened area. During World War II, the U.S. government forcibly removed Japanese Americans and legal residents of Japanese ancestry from the West Coast and forbade their return until 1945. The government used the term "evacuation" for this process. In scholarly historical analysis, the term "evacuation" and its derivative "evacuee" are considered euphemisms for the government's treatment of Nikkei during World War II.

Exclusion Zone—A zone established by the Western Defense Command (U.S. Army) from which Nikkei were to be removed (excluded). This zone encompassed Military Areas #1 (western halves of Washington, Oregon, California, and southern half of Arizona) and Military Area #2 (the remainder of California).

Executive Order 9066—Signed by President Franklin Roosevelt on February 19, 1942, an act which authorized the U.S. Army to designate areas from which "any or all persons may be excluded."

incarceration—the forced confinement of Japanese and Japanese American people in War Relocation camps during World War II. In general, this term means "confinement or imprisonment," and in this volume it also connotes prison-like conditions for people who were treated as if guilty of sabotage, espionage or suspected of disloyalty. The term replaces the U.S. government's wartime euphemistic use of "internment" to describe the forced confinement of Japanese and Japanese American people. Individuals or groups so incarcerated are referred to as "incarcerees."

incarceree—an incarcerated person. See "incarceration."

internees—Persons who are interned, especially during wartime. This term has been used to define Japanese Americans and legal residents of Japanese ancestry who were interned and incarcerated during World War II. Legally, this term refers to the imprisonment of civilian enemy aliens during wartime.

internment camp—see "relocation center."

Japanese American Citizens League (JACL) – A civil rights organization established in 1923 to advocate for progress in combating prejudice, racism, and bigotry against Japanese Americans.

non-aliens—A term used during World War II by the U.S. government to refer to Nisei and Japanese Americans. This was a euphemism intended to obscure the fact that they were American citizens. See Bob Sims, chapter 11 of this book.

No-No boys—Young men sent from War Relocation Centers to prison for refusing the U.S. Army draft. The term referred to a pair of "No" answers when they responded to questionnaires intended to determine their loyalty.

Public Law 503—Law signed on March 21, 1942, which provided penalties for individuals who violated the exclusion orders.

racism—The belief that race accounts for differences in human character or ability; the belief that particular races are "superior" to others; discrimination or prejudice (pre-judgment) based on race.

redress—To remedy, rectify, or amend a wrong done. This described the process and remedy for the internment and incarceration of Nikkei during World War II.

relocation—The act or state of being established in a new place. This was the term preferred by the U.S. government referring to the act or state of forcibly removing Nikkei from the West Coast and incarcerating them in War Relocation Centers. Like "evacuation," this was considered a euphemism by critics of the policy. The term was also used during the period of closing the camps when the War Relocation Authority was encouraging Nikkei to move as soon as possible to new locations in the Midwest and East.

relocation center—The term used by the U.S. government to define the places administered by the War Relocation Authority to forcibly confine Japanese Americans and Issei during World War II. Like the term "assembly center," it was used by the government to give an impression to the general public that the forcibly moved Japanese and Japanese Americans were placed in pleasant facilities and settings. This was in contrast with the reality of crude and crowded barracks, desolate climates, barbed-wire fences, guard towers, and armed sentries with weapons turned toward those inside the fences.

resettlement—The War Relocation Authority used this term when referring to the movement of Nikkei from War Relocation Centers to areas outside the Exclusion Zone.

War Relocation Authority (WRA)—The U.S. government agency charged with administering the War Relocation Centers.

# Bibliography

The accumulation of histories, memoirs, biographies, films, government publications, fiction, anthologies, and image collections—both online and in print—about Minidoka, Japanese Americans, and concentration camps in American history continues to grow. Included here are sources referred to in this book, sources recommended by Robert Sims in his talks, and websites and other resources.

## SPECIAL RESOURCE

Robert C. Sims Collection on Minidoka and Japanese Americans, 1891–2014. Boise State University Albertsons Library Special Collections and Archives.

## BOOKS, ARTICLES, AND REPORTS

Armor, John, and Peter Wright. *Manzanar: Photographs by Ansel Adams, Commentary by John Hersey.* New York: Times Books, 1988.

Arrington, Leonard J. *The Price of Prejudice: The Japanese-American Relocation Center in Utah during World War II.* Logan, UT: Utah State University, 1962.

Asahina, Robert. *Just Americans: How Japanese Americans Won a War at Home and Abroad.* New York: Gotham Books, 2006.

Bosworth, Allan R. *America's Concentration Camps.* New York: Norton, 1967.

Burton, Jeffrey F., Mary M. Farrell, and Florence B. Lord. *Confinement and Ethnicity: An Overview of World War II Japanese American Relocation Sites.* Tucson, AZ: Western Archeological and Conservation Center, National Park Service, Department of the Interior, 1999. Reprint, Seattle: University of Washington Press, 2002.

Cole, Diana Morita. *Sideways: Memoir of a Misfit.* Nelson, BC: Diaspora Press, 2015.

Commission on Wartime Relocation and Internment of Civilians. *Personal Justice Denied.* Washington, DC: U.S. Government Printing Office, 1982; reprint, with a new foreword, Seattle: University of Washington Press, 1997.

———. *Personal Justice Denied, Part 2: Recommendations.* Washington, DC: U.S. Government Printing Office, June 1983. Reprinted with a new foreword in *Personal Justice Denied,* Seattle: University of Washington Press, 1997.

Conrat, Maisie and Richard Conrat. *Executive Order 9066.* Los Angeles: UCLA Asian American Studies Center, 1972.

Crost, Lyn. *Honor by Fire: Japanese Americans at War in Europe and the Pacific.* Novato, CA: Presidio Press, 1994.

Daniels, Roger. *Coming to America: A History of Immigration and Ethnicity in American Life.* New York: Harper Collins Publishers, 1990.

———. *Concentration Camps: North America. Japanese in the United States and Canada during World War II.* Malabar, FL: Robert E. Krieger Publishing, 1981.

———. *Concentration Camps USA: Japanese Americans and World War II.* New York: Holt, Rinehart and Winston, Inc., 1971.

———. *The Decision to Relocate the Japanese Americans.* Philadelphia: J. B. Lippincott Co., 1975.

———. *The Politics of Prejudice: The Anti-Japanese Movement in California and the Struggle for Japanese Exclusion.* University of California Publications in History, Vol. II. Berkeley and Los Angeles: University of California Press, 1962.

Daniels, Roger, Sandra C. Taylor, and Harry H. L. Kitano, eds. *Japanese Americans from Relocation to Redress*, 2nd ed. Seattle: University of Washington Press, 1991.

De Leon, Arnoldo. *Racial Frontiers: Africans, Chinese, and Mexicans in Western America, 1848–1890.* Albuquerque: University of New Mexico Press, 2002.

Duus, Masayo Umezaawa. *Unlikely Liberators: The Men of the 100th Battalion and 442nd.* Honolulu: University of Hawaii Press, 1983.

Fiset, Louis. *Imprisoned Apart: The World War II Correspondence of an Issei Couple.* Seattle: University of Washington Press, 1997.

Ford, Jamie. *Hotel on the Corner of Bitter and Sweet.* New York: Ballantine Books, 2009.

Fugita, Stephen S., and Marilyn Fernandez. *Altered Lives, Enduring Community: Japanese Americans Remember Their World War II Incarceration.* Seattle: University of Washington Press, 2004.

Funke, Teresa R. *The No-No Boys* (Home-Front Heroes Series). Fort Collins, CO: Bailiwick Press, 2008.

Gesensway, Deborah, and Mindy Roseman. *Beyond Words: Images From America's Concentration Camps.* Ithaca, NY: Cornell University Press, 1987.

Guterson, David. *Snow Falling on Cedars.* New York: Harcourt Brace, 1994.

Hall, David L. "Internment and Resistance: The Japanese American Experience in the Minidoka Relocation Center, 1942–1945." M.A. thesis, Washington State University, 1987.

Harrington, Joseph. *Yankee Samurai: The Secret Role of Nisei in America's Pacific Victory.* Detroit: Pettigrew Enterprises, 1979.

Harris, Catherine Embree. *Dusty Exile: Looking Back at Japanese Relocation during World War II.* Honolulu: Mutual Publishing, 1999. [Poston WRC, Arizona]

Harvey, Robert. *Amache: The Story of Japanese Internment in Colorado During World War II.* Dallas: Taylor Trade Publishing, 2003. [Amache WRC, Colorado]

Hayashi, Robert T. *Haunted by Waters: A Journey through Race and Place in the American West.* Iowa City: University of Iowa Press, 2007.

Higa, Karen. *The View From Within: Japanese American Art From the Internment, 1942-1945.* Los Angeles, CA: Japanese American National Museum, 1992.

Higashide, Seiichi. *Adios to Tears: The Memoir of a Japanese-Peruvian Interned in United States Concentration Camps.* Seattle: University of Washington Press, 1993, 2000.

Hill, Kimi Kodani, Ruth Asawa, et al. *Topaz Moon: Art of the Internment.* Berkeley, CA: Heyday Books, 2000.

Hirahara, Naomi, and Heather C. Lindquist. *Life After Manzanar.* Berkeley, CA: Heyday Books, 2018.

Hirasuna, Delphine, and Kit Hinrichs. *The Art of Gaman: Arts and Crafts from the Japanese American Internment Camps, 1942–1946.* Berkeley, CA: Ten Speed Press, 2005.

Hosokawa, Bill. *Nisei: The Quiet Americans.* New York: William Morrow, 1969.

Houston, Jeanne W., and James D. Houston. *Farewell to Manzanar.* Boston: Houghton, Mifflin Co., 1973.

Ikeda, Tsuguo, and Akio Yanagihara. *Minidoka Stories I and II.* N.p. 2003.

Inada, Lawson Fusao. *Only What We Could Carry: The Japanese American Internment Experience.* Berkeley, CA: Heyday Books, 2000.

Inouye, Richard K. "For Immediate Sale: Tokyo Bathhouse—How WWII Affected Alaska's Japanese Civilians." In *Alaska at War, 1941-1945.* Anchorage: Alaska at War Committee, 1995.

Irons, Peter. *Justice at War: The Story of the Japanese Internment.* New York: Oxford University Press, 1983.

Irons, Peter, ed. *Justice Delayed: The Record of the Japanese American Internment Cases.* Middletown, CT: Wesleyan University Press, 1989.

Kashima, Tetsuden. *Judgement without Trial: Japanese American Imprisonment during World War II.* Seattle: University of Washington Press, 2003.

Kitagawa, Daisuke. *Issei and Nisei: The Internment Years.* New York: The Seabury Press, 1967.

Kitano, Harry. *Japanese Americans: Evolution of a Sub-Culture.* Englewood Cliffs, NJ: Prentice-Hall, 1969.

———. *Race Relations.* Englewood Cliffs, NJ: Prentice-Hall, 1984.

Kleinkopf, Arthur. *Relocation Center Diary: 1942–1946.* Idaho and Pacific Northwest History Collection, Twin Falls Library.

Larson, T. A. *Wyoming's War Years.* Laramie: University of Wyoming, 1954.

Lew, William W. *Minidoka Revisited: The Paintings of Roger Shimomura.* Clemson, SC: Lee Gallery, Clemson University, 2005.

Mackey, Mike, ed. *Remembering Heart Mountain: Essays on Japanese American Internment in Wyoming.* Powell, WY: Western History Publications Book, 1998.

———. *Guilt by Association: Essays on Japanese Settlement, Internment, and Relocation in the Rocky Mountain West.* Powell, WY: Western History Publications, 2001.

Maeda, Laura. "Life at Minidoka." *The Pacific Historian* (Winter 1976), 20/4:7.

Maki, Mitchell T., Kaleigh Komatsu, and Kimberly Komatsu. *In America's Shadow.* Los Angeles: Thomas George Books, 2003. (Children's picture book, a project of the California Civil Liberties Public Education Program.)

Masuda, Minoru, Hana Masuda, Dianne Bridgman. *Letters from the 442nd: The World War II Correspondence of a Japanese American Medic.* Seattle: University of Washington Press, 2011.

Matsuoka, Jack. *Poston. Camp II, Block 211: Daily Life in an Internment Camp.* San Mateo, CA: Asian American Curriculum Project, Inc., 2003

McKay, Susan. *The Courage Our Stories Tell: The Daily Lives and Maternal Child Health Care of Japanese American Women at Heart Mountain.* Powell, WY: Western History Publications, 2002.

Mercier, Laurie, and Carole Simon-Smolinski, et al. *Idaho's Ethnic Heritage: Historical Overviews, Volume 1,* "Idaho's Japanese Americans," Boise: Idaho Centennial Commission, Ethnic Heritage Committee, March 1990.

*Minidoka Interlude, September 1942–October 1943.* Originally published Hunt, ID: Residents of Minidoka Relocation Center, 1943. Later versions [1989?, 1990, 1995] edited by Thomas Takeuchi. Fifth edition available from Friends of Minidoka, www.minidoka.org.

Moore, Brenda. *Serving Our Country, Japanese American Women in the Military During World War II.* New Brunswick, NJ: Rutgers University Press, 2003.

Muller, Eric L., ed. *Colors of Confinement: Rare Kodachrome Photographs of Japanese American Incarceration in World War II.* Chapel Hill: University of North Carolina Press, 2012.

Nakadate, Neil. *Looking After Minidoka: An American Memoir.* Bloomington: Indiana University Press, 2013.

Nakashima, George. *The Soul of a Tree: A Woodworker's Reflections.* New York: Kodansha USA, Inc., 1981, 2011.

Nakashima, Mara. *Nature, Form, and Spirit: The Life and Legacy of George Nakashima.* New York: Harry Abrams Publishers, 2003.

National JACL Power of Words II Committee. *Power of Words Handbook: A Guide to Language about Japanese Americans in World War II.* April 27, 2013. jacl.org/wordpress/wp-content/uploads/2015/08/Power-of-Words-Rev.-Term.-Handbook.pdf

Nelson, Douglas W. *Heart Mountain: The History of an American Concentration Camp.* Unpublished M.A. thesis, University of Wyoming, 1970. Also published by the State Historical Society of Wisconsin, Madison, 1976.

Ng, Wendy. *Japanese American Internment during World War II: A History and Reference Guide.* Westport, CT: Greenwood Press, 2002.

Obata, Chiura, Janice Tolhurst Driesbach, and Susan Landauer. *Obata's Yosemite: The Art and Letters of Chiura Obata from His Trip to the High Sierra in 1927.* Yosemite National Park, CA: Yosemite Association, 1993.

Oda, James. *Historic Struggles of Japanese Americans: Partisan Fighters from America's Concentration Camps.* North Hollywood, CA: N.p., 1980.

Okubo, Miné. *Citizen 13660.* Seattle: University of Washington Press, 1983, 2014. First published 1946 by Columbia University Press (New York).

Ostergard, Derek E., George Nakashima, and American Craft Museum. *George Nakashima, Full Circle.* New York: Weidenfeld & Nicolson, 1989.

Pak, Yoon K. *Wherever I Go, I Will Always Be a Loyal American: Schooling Seattle's Japanese Americans during World War II.* New York: RoutledgeFalmer, 2002.

Return to Topaz '93 Anthology Committee. *Return to Topaz '93: Recollections, Reflections, Remembrances.* Salt Lake City: Return to Topaz '93 Anthology Committee, 1993.

Robinson, Gerald H. *Elusive Truth: Four Photographers at Manzanar (Ansel Adams, Dorothea Lange, Clem Albers and Toyo Miyatake).* Nevada City, CA: Carl Mautz Publishing, 2002.

Robinson, Greg. *A Tragedy of Democracy: Japanese Confinement in North America.* New York: Columbia University Press, 2009.

———. *By Order of the President: FDR and the Internment of Japanese Americans.* Cambridge: Harvard University Press, 2001.

Robinson, Greg, and Elena Tajima Creef, eds., *Mine Okubo: Following Her Own Road.* Seattle: University of Washington Press, 2008.

Ross, Michael Elsohn, and Wendy Smith-Griswold. *Nature Art with Chiura Obata*. Minneapolis: Carolrhoda Books, 2000.

Sakoda, James M. "The Residue." In Yuji Ichioka, ed., *Views from Within: The Japanese American Evacuation and Resettlement Study*. Los Angeles: University of California Press, 1989.

Schrager, Adam. *The Principled Politician: The Ralph Carr Story*. Golden, CO: Fulcrum Publishing, 2008.

Shimomura, Roger. *Minidoka on My Mind: Recent Work by Roger Shimomura*. Seattle: Greg Kucera Gallery, 2007.

Shimomura, Roger, Ben Ahlvers, Karin M Higa, and Roger Daniels. *Shadows of Minidoka: Paintings and Collections of Roger Shimomura*. Lawrence, KS: Lawrence Arts Center, 2011.

Shrontz Roberts-Wright, Bessie M. *Hunt for Idaho: Evacuees 1942–1945 and Homesteaders 1947–1949 at Minidoka Prisoner of War Camp 1942–1945*. Self-published by the author, 1994.

Sims, Robert C. *Japanese American Contributions to Idaho's Economic Development*. Boise: Boise State University Center for Research, Grants, and Contracts, May 1977.

Sone, Monica. *Nisei Daughter*. Seattle: University of Washington Press, 1979. First published 1953 by Little Brown (Boston).

Smith, Page. *Democracy on Trial: The Japanese American Evacuation and Relocation in World War II*. New York: Simon & Schuster, 1995.

Stewart, Todd, Natasha Egan, and Karen J. Leong. *Placing Memory: A Photographic Exploration of Japanese American Internment*. Norman: University of Oklahoma, 2008.

Stone, Geoffrey R. *Perilous Times: Free Speech in Wartime from the Sedition Act of 1798 to the War on Terrorism*. New York: W. W. Norton & Co., 2004.

Strawn, Susan, "Gaman: Embroidered Mittens from the Minidoka Relocation Center," *PieceWork*, September/October 2017.

Takami, David A. *Divided Destiny: A History of Japanese Americans in Seattle*. Seattle: University of Washington Press, 1998.

Tamura, Linda. *Nisei Soldiers Break Their Silence: Coming Home to Hood River*. Seattle: University of Washington Press, 2012.

Tamura, Teresa. *Minidoka, An American Concentration Camp*. Caldwell, ID: Caxton Press, 2013.

Tanaka, Chester, et al. *Go For Broke: A Pictorial History of the Japanese American 100th Infantry Battalion and the 442d Regimental Combat Team*. Novato, CA: Presidio Press, 1982.

Thompson, Jeffrey. *Nisei Paradox*. Staged play reading. Boise, ID: 2017. See also Ronald E. Bush review, "The Nisei Paradox," www.id.uscourts.gov/Content_Fetcher/index.cfml/Summary_of_The_Nisei_Paradox_2794.pdf?Content_ID=2794.

Tremayne, Russell Mark, Todd Shallat, and Melissa R. Lavitt. *Surviving Minidoka: The Legacy of WWII Japanese Incarceration*. Boise, ID: Boise State University Publications Office, College of Social Sciences and Public Affairs, College of Idaho, 2013.

United States War Relocation Authority. *Final Accountability Roster of the Minidoka Relocation Center*. Records of the War Relocation Authority, National Archives and Records Service, General Services Administration, Washington, DC. University of Washington microfilm.

U.S. Department of the Interior, National Park Service. "History of the Internment and Incarceration of Nikkei at Minidoka Relocation Center." In *Minidoka Internment National Monument General Management Plan*, November 2006.

Ushida, Yoshiko. *Desert Exile: The Uprooting of a Japanese American Family*. Seattle: University of Washington Press, 1982.

Wakatsuki, Hanako, Mia Russell, and Carol Ash. *Images of America: Minidoka National Historic Site*. Charleston, SC: Arcadia Publishing, 2018.

Wegars, Priscilla. *As Rugged as the Terrain: CCC "Boys," Federal Convicts, and World War II Alien Internees Wrestle with a Mountain Wilderness*. Caldwell, ID: Caxton Press, 3013.

———. *Golden State Meets Gem State: Californians at Kooskia Internment Camp*. Moscow, ID: California Civil Liberties Public Education Fund, 2002.

———. *Imprisoned in Paradise: Japanese Internee Road Workers at the World War II Kooskia Internment Camp*. Moscow, ID: Asian American Comparative Collection, University of Idaho, 2010.

Weglyn, Michi. *Years of Infamy: The Untold Story of America's Concentration Camps*. New York: William Morrow and Co., 1976.

Yamada, Mitsuye. *"Camp Notes" and Other Poems*. Berkeley, CA: Shameless Hussy Press, 1976.

Yamada, Mitsuye. *"Camp Notes" and Other Writings*. New Brunswick, NJ: Rutgers University Press, 1998.

Yamaguchi, Precious. *Experiences of Japanese American Women During and After World War II: Living in Internment Camps and Rebuilding Life Afterwards*. Lanham, MD: Lexington Press, 2014.

Yasui, Minori. "Minidoka." In John Tateishi, ed., *And Justice For All: An Oral History of the Japanese American Detention Camps.* New York: Random House, 1984.

Yenne, Bill. *Rising Sons: The Japanese American GIs who fought for the United States in World War II.* New York: Thomas Dunne Books, 2007.

Zhu, Liping. *A Chinaman's Chance: The Chinese on the Rocky Mountain Mining Frontier.* Boulder: University Press of Colorado, 1997.

## WEBSITES AND ONLINE RESOURCES

Boise Public Library. Japanese-American Internment Camps in Idaho and the West, 1942–1945. Includes list of Boise Public Library holdings: magazine articles, websites, War Relocation Authority material, books, and videos. farrit.lili.org/?s=Japanese-American+Internment+camps.

Boise State University Archives and Special Collections Library. Robert C. Sims Collection on Minidoka and Japanese Americans, 1891–2014. Finding Aid: archiveswest.orbiscascade.org/ark:/80444/xv13632.

Densho: The Japanese American Legacy Project. Founded to collect personal testimonies and other documents of Japanese Americans incarcerated in internment camps during World War II, the Densho mission has been expanded to "educate, preserve, collaborate, and inspire action for equity." Resources include oral histories, documents, photographs, newspapers, and other primary source materials, as well as free social studies curricula and tools for elementary and secondary teachers. densho.org.

George and Frank C. Hirahara Photograph Collection, 1943–1945. Washington State University Libraries, Manuscripts, Archives, and Special Collections. Gift of Patti Hirahara. content.libraries.wsu.edu/digital/collection/hiraharag.

Hirahara Family Photo Collection. Anaheim Public Library Heritage Center. Collection of 2,000 photographs curated by Patti Hirahara, taken by George and Frank C. Hirahara while incarcerated at the Heart Mountain War Relocation Center 1943–45. www.anaheim.net/2626/Hirahara-Family-Photo-Collection.

University of Washington. Special Collections. *Children of Minidoka.* Includes photographs, student essays, articles from *Minidoka Irrigator*, other documents, and bibliography. www.lib.washington.edu/specialcollections/exhibits/harmony/minidoka.

Wing Luke Museum of the Asian Pacific American Experience. Seattle. www.wingluke.org.

# Contributors

**Jim Azumano** has served as city or county administrator in several jurisdictions in Oregon and Idaho. He was director of education for Northwest Food Processors, director of rural policy under Oregon Governor Ted Kulongoski, and a member of the board of Friends of Minidoka. A graduate of the University of Oregon, Jim is married and has four children, eight grandchildren, and seven great-grandchildren. Now retired on the Oregon coast, he advises local governments, fishes, and tools hard leather.

**Neil King** retired from the National Park Service in 2008 after 38 years. His concluding assignment was superintendent of Minidoka National Historic Site, Hagerman Fossil Beds National Monument, and liaison with City of Rocks National Preserve. He also worked at Mesa Verde National Park, Indiana Dunes National Seashore, and Craters of the Moon National Monument. He holds a BA degree in archaeology and fine arts. He lives in Idaho, where grandchildren, cooking, leather work, reading, and fishing are his primary interests.

**Emily Hanako Momohara** is an artist residing in Cincinnati. An associate professor of art at the Art Academy of Cincinnati, she heads the photography major. Exhibits of her work have appeared nationally and internationally, most notably at the 21c Museum and the Japanese American National Museum. She holds a BFA in photography and a BA in art history from the University of Washington and an MFA in expanded media from the University of Kansas. Her grandmother and great-grandparents were incarcerated at Minidoka during WWII. Momohara's work concerns themes of culture, mix-raced identity, immigration, and social justice and can be seen at ehmomohara.com.

**Cheryl Oestreicher** is the head of Special Collections and Archives and associate professor at Boise State University. She holds a PhD from Drew University and an MLIS from Dominican University. She previously worked at Auburn Avenue Research Library on African American Culture and History, where she processed civil rights collections, and at the University of Chicago, Drew University, and Princeton University. She is the author of *Reference and Access for Archives and Manuscripts*, forthcoming in 2020 by the Society of American Archivists.

**Daniel Sakura** is currently Senior Advisor for Lands and Special Projects at the National Park Foundation, responsible for programs to conserve lands for natural and historic sites. He has helped acquire or develop confinement sites other than Minidoka, among them Manzanar Visitor Center; the Herrmann Farm and Bainbridge Island additions to Minidoka, Topaz WRC, Valor in the Pacific National Monument at Tule Lake, and Honouliuli National Monument. His BA is from University of Chicago; his JD from Georgetown University Law Center. Dan lives with his family in Chevy Chase, Maryland.

**Betty Sims** and Bob Sims met while she working for the U.S. Army in Germany in 1960 as a recreational specialist. After the family moved to Idaho in 1970 she worked as a social worker, investigator/mediator with Idaho Human Rights Commission, and training manager for Micron Technology. She holds a BA from Whitman College, and an MA from the College of Idaho. Since retiring, she has taken classes through BSU's Osher Institute for Lifelong Learning, and over the years she has served in various capacities as a community volunteer.

**Sarah Sims** is the daughter of Bob and Betty Sims. She recalls traveling with her father to conferences and watching his Minidoka PowerPoint slide shows. She received a BFA from the Art Institute of Chicago. Sarah and her husband are raising three daughters in Boise. She works for the City of Boise as a library assistant.

**Susan M. Stacy** lives in Boise where she is a consulting historian. She was educated at Georgetown University, University of Pittsburgh, and Boise State University with degrees in foreign service, urban and regional planning, and history respectively. She has published histories of Idaho Power Company, Idaho National Laboratory, flood control on the Boise River, and others. Idaho topics continue to be her focus.

**Hanako Wakatsuki** is chief of interpretation and education at Minidoka National Historic Site. She co-authored two *Images of America* books: *Minidoka National Historic Site* and *Old Idaho Penitentiary*. As a public historian and preservationist she advises on projects concerned with Japanese American confinement sites during WWII. Her BA in history and BS in political science are from Boise State University; her MA in museum studies, from Johns Hopkins University. Her current focus is on educating the public about the Japanese American incarceration story. She serves on the White House Initiative on Asian American Pacific Islanders as Region 10 lead.

# Index

34th Division, 135
36th Division, Texas, 135; 141st Regiment, 136
100th Battalion, 18, 135, 139, 141
442nd Regimental Combat Team, 18, 82, 105, 134–36, 139–41; honors recognition, 139, 173. *See also* Acceptance; All-Japanese combat units
1399th Engineer Construction Battalion, 141
5307th Composite Unit, Provisional, 137–38

Acceptance of Nikkei due to: farm labor, 68–69, 123–24; military service, 127, 173; sports, 126. *See also* 442nd Regimental Combat Team
Adams County, ID, 26, 29
Adams, Lucy W., 86
Adler, Hans Günther, 160
Agricultural labor. *See* Labor
All-Japanese combat units, 18, 78, 94, 105, 127. *See* names of combat units
Amalgamated Sugar Company, 43, 46, 69, 124. *See also* Sugar beets; Malheur
*American and Japanese Relocation in World War II: Fact, Fiction, and Fallacy*, 156
American Dream, 19
American Federation of Labor (AFL) Building Services Union, 151
American Jewish Committee, 154
American Legion, 29, 118, 120
Americanism. *See* Schools
Americans for Historical Accuracy, 156–57
Amerman, Helen, 98. *See also* Schools
Anti-Chinese attitudes, 4, 5–6
Anti-Japanese laws: immigration, 6, 19, 105, 107, 139; land, 3–6, 19, 56–57, 105, 107, 114–15; miscegenation, 57, 105, 107; naturalization, 6, 19–20, 36, 56–57, 79, 105
Antiquities Act of 1906, 171–73, 179–80, 182
Armed guards, 24, 25, 26, 31, 42
Assembly centers, 16, 32, 41, 43, 68, 120, 104. *See* Puyallup, North Portland
Axis powers, 117
Azumano, George, 192
Azumano, Jim, 175

Bainbridge Island, WA, 175–76

Bainbridge Island Japanese American Exclusion Memorial, 176
Baker, Lillian, 156–57, 158
Bannock County, ID, 58
Baseball. *See* Nisei baseball
Beck, Dave, 151
Beet Growers Association. *See* Idaho Beet Growers Association
Biddle, Francis, 105
Bingham County, ID, 58
Black, Hugo, 154
Blackfoot, ID, 4
Bodner, John, 159
Boer War, 154
Boise City, ID, 9, 72, 103
Boise State University, 187–88, 193
Boise Valley, 57
Bonners Ferry, ID, 61
Bonneville County, ID, 58
Bosworth, Allen, 80
Bottolfson, Clarence A., 35–36
Boys State, 164
Bureau of Land Management, 181
Bureau of Reclamation, 73–74, 163, 165–68, 181–82
Burley, ID, 114
*Burley Herald*, 128
Burma Road, 137
Burroughs, Edgar Rice, 103

Caldwell, ID, 9, 50, 60, 66, 149. *See also* Labor camps
California Historical Society, 159
California State Historical Resources Commission, 155
California State Director of Parks and Recreation, 155
Camps, labor. *See* Labor camps
Canyon County, ID, 58
Carr, Ralph, 36n1
Carver, John, 26, 29
Cassia County, ID, 114
Caucasians, 48, 57, 63, 66–68, 71, 123
Centennial of (Idaho) Statehood, 167–68, 180

Chinese. *See* Anti-Chinese attitudes
Church, Frank, 110, 166
Citizenship for Issei. *See* Anti-Japanese laws
Civil Liberties Act of 1988. *See* Civil Rights Act of 1988
Civil Liberties Symposium (Minidoka), 163, 175
Civil rights, 24, 77, 111–12
Civil Rights Act of 1988, 109, 139, 199–201
Civil Service, 99
Clark, Chase: as Idaho governor, 10–14, 18, 23–36; opposition to Japanese labor, 39, 43, 63–66, 119–20; and failed leadership, 53, 61, 77; racism, 116, 119–20, 177; as federal judge, 18, 36, 77, 82
Clark, Thomas C., 29, 42
Clinton, President Bill, 110, 111, 139, 169–71, 173, 179–81
College of Idaho (Caldwell), 58
Colorado National Forest, 181
Colorado River War Relocation Center, 87
Commemoration, 159, 165–67; plaques, 155, 181
Commission on Wartime Relocation and Internment of Civilians. *See* U.S. Commission on Wartime Relocation and Internment of Civilians
Concentration camp: as euphemism, 110–11, 153–60; on commemorative plaques, 155, 160. *See also* Euphemisms
*Concentration Camps, USA*, 155, 165
Conference on Relocation and Redress, 113
*Confinement and Ethnicity*, 169, 181
Confinement sites grant program, 176
Congressional Gold Medal, 13
Constitution. *See also* Civil rights; U.S. Constitution
"Core value," 171–72, 173–74
*Corum nobis*, writ of, 108
Counter Intelligence Corps, 139
Craters of the Moon National Monument, ID, 173
Curfews on Nikkei laborers, 66, 123
Custer Battlefield National Monument, 168

Daniels, Roger, 28, 35–36, 113, 155, 165
Dayson, Diane H., 154
DeWitt, John L., 26, 29, 41, 62, 77
Discrimination, legal. *See* Anti-Japanese laws
Draft (military), 79, 81–83, 94, 134; perspectives on, 172

Eagledale ferry dock, Bainbridge Island, 180
Eden, ID, 114, 122
Education. *See* Hunt High School; Schools
Eisenhower, Milton, 30–31, 33–34, 42, 93, 107

Ellis Island Museum, NY, 153–54, 160
Emmett, ID, 140
Emmett High School, 140
Emmett National Guard Armory, 140
Ethnic Heritage Committee, Idaho Centennial, 167
Euphemisms, 23, 25, 153–60
Evans, John, 167
Exclusion zone, 9, 56. *See also* Military Area No. 1; Relocation, forced
Executive Order 9066, 9, 62, 104, 105, 106, 181
Executive Order 9102, 66

*Farewell to Manzanar*, 165, 187
Farm Security Administration, 42, 48, 69–70
Federal Bureau of Investigation (FBI), 60
Federal Employment Service, 44
Federated Christian Church, 99
Filer, ID, 123, 126
Filer High School, 45
First Security Banking Corporation, 61–62
Ford, Gerald, 107
Forced removal. *See* Removal
Four Rivers Cultural Center, OR, 170
"Free zone" Nikkei. *See* Nikkei, "Free Zone"
Freedom of Information Act, 141
Friends of Minidoka, 103, 111, 174–75, 176–77, 188, 192. *See also* Honor Roll
Fryer, E. Reeseman, 86
Furuyama, Eugene, 164

Gallup poll, 117
Geisel, Theodor (Dr. Seuss), 106
General Management Plan. *See* Minidoka General Management Plan
Gila River War Relocation Center, AZ, 87
Gold Star mothers. *See* Service flags
Gooding, ID, 118–19
Goodman, Louis E, 81–82
Gordon Hirabayashi Recreation Site, Coronado National Forest, AZ, 181
Gould, Rosalie, 181
Grange, 15. *See also* Idaho grange
Grangeville, ID, 14, 33
Grenada (Amache) War Relocation Center, CO, 87
Guard tower project, 188

Hagerman Fossil Beds National Monument, ID, 169
Hand, Learned, 110
Hanna, Paul, 87
Harmonaires, 45, 125–26

Harris, David A., 154
Hazelton, ID, 120, 176
Heart Mountain Wyoming Foundation, 189
Herrmann Farm (Minidoka), 175–76
Hilberg, Raul, 160
Hirabayashi, Gordon, 108–9, 181
Holocaust, 154, 156
Home front, 133–34
Homesteads for veterans, 129, 163
Honor board. *See* Honor roll
Honor roll, 134, 147–49, 166, 170, 176–77. *See also* Friends of Minidoka
Honouliuli National Historic Site, Hawaii, 182
Hood River, OR, 148
Hoover, J. Edgar, 105
Hosoda, Max and Itono, 140
Hosokawa, Robert, 90
Hunt camp. *See* Minidoka War Relocation Center
Hunt High School, 44, 49, 123, 125–26. *See also* Schools

Idaho Beet Growers Association, 13–14, 30
Idaho Centennial Commission, 110
*Idaho Daily Statesman* (Boise), 8, 11, 27, 29, 33
Idaho Falls, 4, 35, 48, 60
Idaho Farm Bureau, 118
Idaho Farm Labor Camp, Rupert, 49, 71
Idaho Farm and Ranch Museum, 182
*Idaho Farmer*, 57
Idaho Grange, 13, 15
Idaho Historical Museum, 153
Idaho House of Representatives, 115
Idaho Human Rights Education Center, 170
Idaho Nikkei, post-Pearl Harbor, 60–62
Idaho State Constitution, 20
Idaho State Historical Society, 133, 165
Idaho Statewide Inventory of Historic Places, 164–65
Idaho Sugar Company, 4. *See also* Sugar beets
Ikegama, Arita, 49
Imperial Japan, 23, 29, 122
Inouye, Daniel, 160
Inuzuka, Ise, 191–92
Irons, Peter, 108
Irrigation water (for Minidoka), 117, 118
Ishizuka, Karen, 154
Issei, and loyalty oaths, 78–80
Issei-Nisei generational identity, 93
"Issei Pioneers in Oregon" exhibit, 143

Jackson, Robert, 106
JACL Magic Valley chapter, 67, 115, 126
JACL National Council, 166

JACL Northwest Intermountain Region, 65, 164
JACL Pacific Northwest District Council, 166
JACL Pocatello-Blackfoot chapter, 3, 9, 11, 110, 164–68, 170, 171, 180, 182; and voluntary relocation program, 25, 28
JACL Seattle Chapter, 107, 174
James, Ron, 174
James, Thomas, 100
Jamieson, OR, 150
Japanese American Citizens Club of Southwest Idaho and Eastern Oregon, 9
Japanese American Citizens League (JACL), 7, 33, 59, 72, 164, 165; and 1942 Salt Lake City conference, 71–72; discourage voluntary relocatees to Idaho, 64–65; end of leadership in camps, 95; goals for Americanism, 93; observe field labor working conditions, 48–49, 69, 70. *See also* Masaoka; Okamura; Sakamoto; Yasuhara; names of JACL chapters
Japanese American Confinement sites, 169, 188
*Japanese American Contributions to Idaho's Economic Development*, 194
*Japanese-American Courier*, 115
Japanese American Memorial to Patriotism, 182, 189
Japanese American National Landmark Theme Study, 180
Japanese American National Museum, 153
*Japanese Americans: The Evolution of a Subculture*, 158–59
Japanese Association, 6–7
Japanese "Citizens Clubs," 7, 9
Japanese Farmers Association, 9
Japanese Hall (Ontario, OR), 59, 60
Japanese language, 68
Japanese settlement in Idaho, 3–8
Japanese settlement in Idaho pre-WWII, 3–9, 115–16, 164
Japanism, 93–94
Jerome, ID, 119
Jerome County, ID, 114, 170
Jerome County Historical Society, 170, 182
Jerome Relocation Center, AR, 138

Kasai, Mr., 48, 71
King, Neil, 169, 171–73, 175; on veterans, 173
Kitano, Harry, 158, 159
Kleinkopf, Arthur, 89–90
Kootenai County, ID, 11
Korematsu, Fred, 108
Kubota, Fujitaro, 170

Labor camp conditions, 46, 47–49, 69–70

Labor camp recruitment, 42–44
Labor camps: Caldwell, 50; Idaho Farm Labor Camp, 49; Nyssa, 47; Rupert, 123; Twin Falls Migratory Labor Camp, 44, 50, 120, 123, 125–26
Labor, Japanese Americans: closure of camps, 129; Minidoka as large supplier, 50, 68; and patriotism, 68, 71; as source of, 25, 33, 39–51, 68, 116, 123. *See also* Clark, Chase; Labor camps
Labor shortage in ID, 25, 116, 123
Labor unions, 15, 151
Legal discrimination against Japanese. *See* Anti-Japanese laws
Lemon, Maya Hata, 171, 182
Light, Jerome T., 85, 95, 97–99. *See also* Schools
Little Bighorn National Monument, 168
Loyalty (oaths, tests, questions), 77–83, 95, 105

Magic Valley chapter of JACL. *See* JACL, Magic Valley chapter
Magic Valley Region, 115, 117, 118, 120, 126, 129
Malheur County, OR, 9, 43, 55, 58, 59, 68, 120, 150
Malheur Dam, 59
Manzanar National Historic Site, 169, 180–81, 188, 189
Manzanar War Relocation Center, 87, 95, 155, 175
Masaoka, Mike (JACL), 48, 63, 65, 70, 72
Matsumoto, Roy, 138, 140
McCarran-Walter Act of 1952, 139
McClure, James, 168
Medal of Honor, 140
Merrill, Frank, 137
Mesa Orchards, Adams County, ID, 10, 26–27, 29
Mesa Verde National Park, 172
Migratory workers not from Idaho, 44–45
Military Area No. 1 (exclusion zone), 9–10, 41, 54, 56, 62, 157; map, 54
Military exclusion zone. *See* Military Area No. 1
Military Intelligence Service, 82, 139
"Military necessity," 23, 24, 60
*Minidoka*, novel, 103
Minidoka Civil Liberties Symposium, 163, 175
Minidoka Community Council, 99. *See also* Light, Jerome
Minidoka Education Section, 89
Minidoka General Management Plan, 111, 171–74
*Minidoka Interlude*, 193
*Minidoka Irrigator*, 39–40, 50, 67, 71, 127, 146, 193; at Boise State University, 193

Minidoka Mass Choir, 125–26
Minidoka National Historic Site, 163–67, 175–77, 180, 183, 188–89. *See also* Minidoka National Internment Monument; Friends of Minidoka; Vicinity map
Minidoka National Internment Monument, 110–11, 168–71, 179–82. *See also* Minidoka National Historic Site
Minidoka plat map, x
Minidoka Project Efficiency Rating Board, 35
Minidoka Reclamation Project, 114
Minidoka Victory Garden, 170
Minidoka vicinity map, 183
Minidoka War Relocation Center (Hunt camp): closure, 128–29; construction of, 119; evacuees to, 41, 46, 47, 53–54, 121; lead WRA camp for 1942 seasonal leave, 50, 68; living conditions, 3, 32, 15, 16, 18–19, 46–49, 104, 126, 157; neglect and preservation, 110–11, 165–66, 169–70. *See also* Minidoka National Historic Site; Minidoka National Internment Monument; Clark, Chase; Education; Labor; Loyalty oaths; Labor camps; Plat map; Population statistics; Schools
Momohara, Emily Hanako, 174
Monterey, CA, 10, 26
Montana, 69
Morrison-Knudsen Construction Company, 60–61, 117–18, 119
Mountain Home, ID, 4
Multnomah County, OR, 191–92
Myers, Dillon, 146

Nagaishi, Shigeo family, 145
Nakamura, William Kenzo, 139, 140
Nampa, ID, 4, 9, 10, 16, 46, 58, 53–54
National Japanese American Memorial Foundation, 182, 189
National Park Service, 111, 179–82, 188–89; and *Confinement and Ethnicity*, 169; and Friends of Minidoka, 174
National Park System, 163
National Register of Historic Places, 73, 110, 165–67, 180–82
Naturalization laws, 6, 36, 56–57, 79
Nazi death camps, 154, 160
New Deal, 86
Nikkei, "Free Zone," 53–74: defined, 54–55; differing perspectives, 54, 66–67, 74; discrimination and acceptance, 57–59, 68–69, 72; farm workers, 69–72; forced relocation and stresses, 54, 66–67, 122; post-war integration, 59–60;

urban-rural conflict, 41, 46, 47, 50, 70–71; voluntary relocatees, 55–60. *See also* Relocation
Nisei baseball, 59, 126
Nisei and loyalty oath, 77–83, 95, 105
Nisei soldiers, 133–41; and redress; 113; identity issues in schools and camps, 100. *See also* Education, Schools
Nisei Veterans of America, 176
Nisei veterans post-WWII, 139, 141
Nojima, Kim, 58
"Non-aliens," 153, 157–58
No-No Boys, 82–83
North Portland Assembly Center, OR, 41, 43, 50, 86, 143; and Malheur County, 68, 74
Northwest Nazarene College, 58
Nyssa labor camp, 47

Obama, Barack, 139
Ocasio-Cortez, Alexandria, 153
Okamura, Paul, 63–64
Ontario, OR, 8, 50, 60, 66, 73
Oral history, 164, 168, 171–74
Oregon Short Line Railroad, 4
Ozawa v. United States, 56, 79

Parma, 8
Patriotism, 49, 68, 71, 93–94, 158. *See also* All-Japanese combat units
Paul, Rodman, 159
Pearl Harbor, bombing of, 8, 67, 125, 187; and Chase Clark, 23, 25–27; fear of espionage, 60–61, 105; reactions of Japanese Americans, 8–9, 18; "Remember," 116, 122, 151; Twin Falls election, 67, 165–66
*Personal Justice Denied*, 23, 53, 113
Peterson, Martin, 168
Pilgrimage(s) to Minidoka, 140; in 1985, 167; in 2003, 174–75; in 2011, 176–77
Plat map, Minidoka, x
Pocatello, ID, 4, 58, 103
Pocatello-Blackfoot chapter of JACL. *See* JACL Pocatello-Blackfoot chapter
Pocatello Carpenters Union, 15
*Politics of Memory: The Journey of a Holocaust Historian*, 160
Population statistics: distribution of voluntary relocatees, 55–56; Japanese in Idaho, 4–5, 7–8, 28, 55, 58, 114; Nikkei in agriculture, 41; Nikkei in Idaho circa 1930, 58–59; Nikkei in Idaho circa 1950, 72; pre-war and post-war, 144
Portland, OR, evacuees, 16, 41, 46; post-war return, 147–48; and Inuzuka family, 191–92
Poston War Relocation Center, AZ, 72, 95, 99

Presidential Medal of Freedom, 139
Presidential Proclamation No. 4417, 107
Proclamation No. 7395, 171
Progressive education philosophy, 85–86
Public Proclamation No. 1, 62
Public Proclamation Nos. 1 and 2, 157
Public Proclamation No. 4, 30
Puyallup Assembly Center, WA, 14, 41, 43, 46, 53, 143

Questions 27 and 28, 78–81. *See also* Draft; Loyalty oaths

Racism, 3, 23–24; and war hysteria and political leadership, 53, 60, 109, 189; wartime propaganda, 106. *See* Clark, Chase, 23–36
Railroad construction, 56, 114
Reagan, Ronald, 109, 139, 199–201. *See also* Civil Rights Act of 1988
Redress, 73, 107–8, 199–201; JACL Redress Committee, 165
Relocation policy: and American constitutional ideals, 104, 106; forced, 9, 23, 30, 41, 94; lifting of exclusion policy, 128–29, 143–51; internment, causes of, 105, 107, 111; opposition to, 11, 104, 106–7; voluntary, 9–13, 25–32, 41, 55, 63, 66. *See also* Schools
Removal, forced. *See* Relocation
Reno, Janet, 182
Resettlement to Pacific Northwest, post-war, 72, 143–51
Robinson, Greg, 106
Roosevelt, Franklin D., 9, 86, 106
Ross, C. Ben, 8
Rowher (Cemetery) National Historic Landmark, AR, 80, 181
Rowher War Relocation Center, AR, 181
Rupert, ID, 49, 116, 123
*Rupert Irrigator*, 71
*Rupert Laborer* (Idaho Farm Labor Camp), 49, 76n48

Sakamoto, Jimmie, 93
Sakuma, Takeo, 127
Sakura, Dan, 169–70, 174, 179–82
Sakura, Mesa, and family, 79
Salt Lake City, UT: April 1942 conference, 12–13, 30–31, 35, 42, 113; Conference on Relocation and Redress, 113
Sato, Louie, 45
Seattle, WA, 16, 41, 46, 73, 109, 150–51
Seattle Council of Churches, 151
Seattle Evacuation Redress Committee, 107

Schools at Minidoka: Americanism, 92–94, 85–100, 126–27, 156; buildings, 87–89, 95; curriculum development ideals, 86–87, 92–93; enrollment, 89, 123; resettlement policy impacts, 96–97; teachers, 89–92, 96, 98. *See also* Light, Jerome
Segregation Program, 80–81
Selective Service Act, 8, 18, 79–82, 116, 127
Self-government at WRA camps, 93
Service flags, 127, 136–37, 170
Shimomura, Roger, 174
Shiosaki, Heroo (Hero), 167–68
Shiozawa, George, 165
Shitama, Kaz, 45. *See* Harmonaires
Simplot Company, 150
Sims, Robert C., 53: biographical information, xv–xx; co-founder, Minidoka Civil Liberties Symposium, 103; at dedication of Idaho Centennial project, 167–68; at dedication of Honor roll, 176–77; member of Friends of Minidoka board, 174–75, 176–77; and preservation of Minidoka site, 161–65, 168–71,172–73, 180–82; remembrances of, xii, 172–73, 180–82, 187–89, 191–92
Sims, Robert C., Collection on Minidoka and Japanese Americans, 193–94
Snake River Valley, 5, 31
Soldiers Home, Boise, 117
South Central Idaho Tourism and Recreation Development Association, 170, 182
Spanish-American War, 154
Spokane, WA, 55, 61, 63
Sports, 126
Sprague, Charles, 14, 43
Stafford, Harry L., 88, 192–91
Stallings, Richard, 168
Stanford University, 87
Stimson, Henry, 105, 134, 135
Storm, D.A., 26–27, 29. *See also* Mesa Orchards; Monterey
Stone, Geoffrey R., 109
Strand, Mark, 163
Sugar, 39
Sugar beet crop, 4, 32–33, 39–51; beet growers, 25; and Chase Clark, 23–36; and intimidation tactics by growers, 123–24; and labor shortage, 13–14, 30–33, 39, 41–42, 116–19; recruitment for labor, 13–15, 30–32; saving crop of, 42, 39, 46–47, 68–69, 123–24. *See also* Clark, Chase; Idaho Beet Growers Association; Schools; Labor; Labor camps; names of sugar beet companies

Sugar City, ID, 4
Sun Valley Stages, 122
Symms, Steve, 167–68

Tacoma, WA, 41
Tanaka, Jim, 50
Tarzan, 103
Terminology. *See* Euphemisms; Concentration camp
Texas "Lost Battalion," 136
Thorsen, Steve, 182
Tillman, A. J., 33
Tojo, Hideiki, 122
Trials, draft evasion, 81–83
Truman, Harry S., 82, 139
Tuition, 17
Tule Lake War Relocation Center, CA, 87, 155, 188–89; Segregation Program, 80–82, 95
Tucson, AZ, 181
Twin Falls, ID, 45, 62, 67, 103, 114, 116, 124–25, 165–66
Twin Falls Chamber of Commerce, 117, 118
Twin Falls High School, 45
Twin Falls Kiwanis Club, 67, 126
Twin Falls Migratory Labor Camp, 44, 50, 120, 123, 125–26; flags of six-star mothers, 127; post-1945 Nikkei residents, 129
*Twin Falls Times-News*, 119, 121

University of Idaho, 116
U.S. Army, 43; all-Japanese combat units, 78, 127, 134–35; and loyalty questionnaire, 78; announce relocation center at Minidoka, 113–14; organization structure, 135; language school and linguists, 137–38, 140
U.S. Army Nurse Corps, 78
U.S. Commission on Wartime Relocation and Internment of Civilians, 53, 60, 107–9, 110, 111, 113, 166–67
U.S. Constitution, 11, 27, 110; and constitutional rights, 11–12, 27–28; and No-No Boys, 82–83; during wartime, 103; and redress (First Amendment), 113; protection of, 109
U.S. Department of Interior, 168, 180
U.S. Employment Service, 14, 33
U.S. Supreme Court, 107, 154
Utah-Idaho Sugar Company, 33, 39–40. *See also* Sugar beets

Valor in the Pacific National Monument, 182, 188–89
Vaughn, William, 176

Veterans, 173. *See* Nisei soldiers; Nisei veterans post-WWII; Nisei and loyalty oath; Nisei Veterans of America
Veterans homestead lottery, 129, 163
Visalia, Rodney, 166
Voluntary relocation. *See* Nikkei, "Free Zone"; Relocation
Vosges forest, 136, 140

Wakatsuki, Hanako, 187–89
Wakatsuki Houston, Jeanne, 165, 187
Wake Island, 67, 118, 125
Wallgren, Mon, 150
War Department, 18
War hysteria, 9, 23, 53, 60–61, 104, 110. *See also* Racism
War Production Board, 117
War propaganda, 117. *See also* Geisel, Theodor
War Relocation Authority (WRA), 12, 42, 55, 66, 119, 128; and loyalty oath, 78–81; schools, 17–18, 85–86, 126–27; and Milton Eisenhower, 12–13; relocation, 30, 40–43, 66, 86; resettlement (out of camps), 78, 96, 128, 145, 163, 192. *See also* Eisenhower; Loyalty; Resettlement; Relocation; Schools
War Relocation Authority Western Regional Office, 86
War Relocation Board, 9
War Relocation Centers. *See* Euphemisms; Minidoka; names of centers
Wartime Civil Control Administration, 42, 51n3
Washington, DC, 182
Water rights, 32, 118–19
Weglyn, Michi, 165
Wells, Merle, 3, 165
Western Defense Command, 30, 41, 55, 62
Women's Army Corps, 134
Women's Army Auxiliary Corps, 78
World War II, 133–41. *See* All-Japanese combat units; Loyalty oaths; "Military necessity"; names of military units
Wyoming, 69

Xenophobia, 36

Yamaguchi family, 109
Yasuhara, Denny, 61
Yasui, Min, 108–9
*Years of Infamy*, 165
"Yellow Peril," 8, 105

Zontec, Terry, 165